Spreading Hate

Spreading Hate

The Global Rise of White Supremacist Terrorism

DANIEL BYMAN

UNIVERSITY PRESS

OXFORD
UNIVERSITY PRESS

Oxford University Press is a department of the University of Oxford. It furthers
the University's objective of excellence in research, scholarship, and education
by publishing worldwide. Oxford is a registered trade mark of Oxford University
Press in the UK and certain other countries.

Published in the United States of America by Oxford University Press
198 Madison Avenue, New York, NY 10016, United States of America.

CIP data is on file at the Library of Congress
ISBN 978-0-19-753761-9

DOI: 10.1093/oso/9780197537619.001.0001

1 3 5 7 9 8 6 4 2

Printed by LSC Communications, United States of America

Contents

Acknowledgments

Variations of a book like this have been on my mind since I began studying terrorism several decades ago. Even as the 9/11 attacks consumed my attention and that of many of my colleagues, the danger of white supremacist violence was clear. In the years that followed, violence from terrorist groups of all stripes would ebb and flow, but it was clear that, in many countries, white supremacists were often outpacing jihadists. Even more frightening, they were becoming a louder and more visible presence in politics and society, often exploiting jihadist violence, fears of immigrants, and other concerns to make inroads. In both Europe and the United States, white supremacists also interacted with, and echoed, the rhetoric and campaigns of major political figures, adding to their importance. It also became clear to me that, while many of the counterterrorism methods that were effective against jihadists could also be used against white supremacists, the differences were often profound and needed to be understood in order to better fight them. Hence this book.

I relied heavily on friends and colleagues as sounding boards for ideas, and their advice and encouragement helped me power through the often-frustrating process of researching and writing. My thanks to Jason Blazakis, Bruce Hoffman, Matt Levitt, Chris Meserole, Kenneth Pollack, Jeremy Shapiro, Brent Sterling, and Tamara Cofman Wittes for their many insights and ideas. I am not alone in my interests and concerns, of course, and other scholars, government officials, civil society members, and others have examined aspects of the white supremacist world and thought about how to combat them. Many generously agreed to spend time helping me understand different aspects of the movement, the role of social media companies, and the limits and possibilities of counterterrorism. My thanks to Daniel Benjamin, Kathleen Blee, Jean-Yves Camus, Maura Conway, Mike German, Beth Goldberg, Seamus Hughes, Daniel Kimmage, Kate Klonick, Jonathan Leman, Cassie Miller, Rafal Pankowski, Eric Rosand, Åsne Seierstad, Peter Simi, Megan Squire, and Benjamin Wittes. Some whom I interviewed in government, several community organizations, and the social media world asked not to be named. I am thankful to all these people for making me smarter on white supremacist groups and how to fight them—and for their own many contributions to understanding and opposing this scourge.

Particular thanks go to Heidi Beirich, J. M. Berger, David Cunningham, Daniel Koehler, Will McCants, Mark Pitcavage, Jacob Aasland Ravndal, and Erin Saltman for their comments on select chapters of this book.

Georgetown University and the Brookings Institution are excellent homes for scholars who seek to work on today's problems. I am grateful for their support as institutions and for the people there. Particular thanks go to Joel Hellman at Georgetown's School of Foreign Service; Keir Lieber, the director of Georgetown's Security Studies Program; Natan Sachs, who heads Brookings' Middle East Center; and John Allen, the president of Brookings.

This book benefited tremendously from the research assistance, editing, and ideas of many students and aspiring scholars. My thanks to Lilly Blumenthal, Shelby Butt, Lauren Finkenthal, Adam Kline, Emma McCaleb, Israa Saber, Becky Twaalfhoven, and Eric Woods for their help. Particular thanks go to Freddy Ludtke for his exceptional assistance.

An idea is not a manuscript, and a manuscript is not a book. At each stage in the process, I was guided by those wiser in the ways of publishing. My thanks go to David McBride and Holly Mitchell of Oxford University Press and my astute agent, Larry Weissman.

Although many people helped with this book, I am solely responsible for this book's contents and any mistakes. The U.S. government reviewed this book to prevent the disclosure of classified information, but nothing in these pages should be viewed as implying that the U.S. government authenticates my factual statements or endorses any of my findings. This book also draws on previously published work: "Counterterrorism and Modern White Supremacy," in *Studies in Conflict & Terrorism* (2021), and my coauthored piece with Mark Pitcavage, "Identifying and Exploiting the Weaknesses of the White Supremacist Movement" (Brookings, 2021).

Finally, I'd like to thank my family. Much of the drafting of this book occurred during the 2020–2021 plague months, so we had a chance to get even closer to one another. To our delight, and perhaps surprise, this closeness was one of the few joys in an otherwise grim year. I am grateful for their love, patience, and good humor.

Introduction

Spreading Hate

Brenton Tarrant was proud of his guns. Tarrant, who shot 51 Muslims at the Al Noor Mosque and Linwood Islamic Centre in Christchurch, New Zealand, in 2019, made sure to give his viewers close-ups of his weapons, which he had decked out in different emblems of white supremacy, in a video of his attack he broadcast on Facebook Live. As Tarrant intended, the various emblems represented the white power movement's past and where it is today.

At least two of Tarrant's rifles referred to 11-year-old Ebba Åkerlund, who died in 2017 when a rejected Muslim Uzbek asylum seeker hijacked a truck and drove it through a crowd in Stockholm, Sweden, killing her and four others. Tarrant linked this hijacking to a seemingly endless war of Christian civilization against the barbaric forces of Islam. Other weapons and cartridges bore the labels "Vienna 1683" and "Malta 1565"—referring to the failed Ottoman sieges in both locations—and "Acre 1189," a battle during the Crusades. Also proudly displayed were the names of several Serb leaders who fought the Ottomans; Charles Martel, who halted the spread of Islam in Europe by winning the Battle of Tours in 732; and David the Builder, the Georgian king who drove the Seljuk Turks out of Georgia after triumphing at the Battle of Didgori in 1121. Tarrant's weapons also displayed the Schwarze Sonne, or Black Sun, a symbol used by modern neo-Nazi groups and the Azov Battalion, which fights in Ukraine.

Tarrant, however, thought beyond Europe. The number 14 is emblazoned on one assault rifle, referring to the 14-word credo of white supremacists first put forward in the United States by David Lane, a white supremacist ideologue and member of the 1980s-era terrorist group The Order: "We must secure the existence of our people and a future for White children." The same rifle also says, "Here's [your] migration compact," referring to the UN agreement that attempted to coordinate an international response to migrant flows.[1]

In both the technology he used and his style, Tarrant revealed himself to be at the cutting edge of the white supremacist movement. Along with his video, Tarrant released a manifesto, "The Great Replacement," echoing a thesis, which originated in France, of a "white genocide," a fear common among white supremacists that whites are being deliberately obliterated through a mix of immigration, intermarriage, and other means. Tarrant praised then– U.S. president Donald Trump as a "symbol of white supremacy."

Yet, for all this mix of the esoteric historic and current events, Tarrant also littered his manifesto with in-jokes and references to internet memes. Much of it was simply "shitposting," throwing out a wide range of ideas to troll the broader public in the hope of provoking a reaction from a broader online audience, which would increase attention to his manifesto.[2] Indeed, at least part of Tarrant's goals seemed in keeping with white supremacist ideas of accelerationism: trying to worsen societal polarization, with the goal of hastening an inevitable race war that will allow whites, once again, to rule the land.

Tarrant's attack was another iteration of a deadly wave of white suprem- acist terrorism that exploits the internet and involves the use of individuals and networks, rather than well-organized groups, to strike at the movement's enemies. This wave really began in 2011, when Anders Behring Breivik warned "the civil war has started" as he proceeded, in the name of white power, to kill 77 people, mostly youths at a camp for a left-leaning political party, in two dramatic attacks in Norway in 2011.[3] Breivik's attacks horrified the world, and his soulless evil was well captured in the award-winning Netflix movie *22 July*. The killings, however, did not end with Breivik's arrest and trial. Breivik posted a deranged manifesto on the internet in which he decried the alleged misdeeds of Muslims, liberals, and others. This statement became a classic among his fellow white supremacists, as did his model of a lone warrior going in guns blazing while harnessing the power of the in- ternet to spread a hateful message. Later attacks in Germany, England, Texas, and other parts of the world far from Norway all followed Breivik's script. None of these mass shooters belonged to a clearly defined group, but all felt themselves to be part of a vast movement, even if it existed only in their own minds.

The transnational white supremacist movement, which is behind some of the world's most dangerous terrorist attacks, is innovative, widespread, and deeply enmeshed in the politics of the United States, Europe, and other parts of the world where migration, racial equity, and social and economic change are challenging traditional power structures. Indeed, successes in racial equality often generate a backlash among these extremists: Stormfront.org, America's most popular white nationalist website for many years, saw its biggest membership increase on November 5, 2008, the day after the United States elected its first Black president.[4] White power's ideas and deeds are global, with terrorists from one part of the world deliberately trying to inspire others far from home. By some measures, the danger is increasing in Australia, the United States, and Europe.[5] At the same time, the movement is often misunderstood, and its fissures and vulnerabilities ignored.

Racism and calls for white dominance, of course, are nothing new. A range of excellent works by historians, sociologists, anthropologists, and others have examined many aspects of these enduring and painful problems and how they have evolved over the years. Scholarly and legal activists like Michelle Alexander, Douglas Blackmon, and Bryan Stevenson are calling attention to how racism infuses economic development, punishment and incarceration, and other core political and social issues around the world.

Yet, for all the attention these issues have received, an understanding of their counterterrorism implications has lagged. Too often, counterterrorism thinking and policies are focused on Islamist groups like Al Qaeda or the Islamic State, while historical and current racist violence is examined under a different light. "If one of these guys was named Mohammad," a senior U.S. Homeland Security official once told me after a white supremacist attack, "the whole thing would be different." Whereas the terrorism label is often overused for everything Muslim-related, white power terrorists are more likely to be labeled "mentally ill," and those who champion parts of their ideology push back hard on using the "t-word" to describe any violent activities.[6] A 2017 study found that terrorism related to Muslims received almost five times as much media coverage as attacks by white supremacists and other non-Muslims.[7]

In addition, U.S. textbooks do not typically use the word "terrorism" in discussing the violence that killed thousands of the formerly enslaved and their white supporters to "redeem" the South from Reconstruction or the lynchings of African Americans to maintain white dominance in the years that followed. Yet, for many of the world's citizens, their stories cannot be told without understanding the role of violence. Ta-Nehisi Coates argues that "the plunder of black communities is not a bump along the road, but it is, in fact, the road itself that you can't have in America without enslavement, without Jim Crow, terrorism, everything that came after that."[8]

How has white power terrorism become so dangerous, and how can we fight it better?

To answer these questions, I draw on archives, interviews, and social media data to write an analytic history of the white power movement. This book explores how politics, technologies, and social forces are changing the white power movement of today and how counterterrorism services should adjust to fight white power violence more effectively.

Main Arguments

White supremacist violence is often played down, or even dismissed, as less important than jihadist violence and other forms of terrorism. Much of it kills few people—for example, beatings of minorities or firebombings of immigration facilities—and, thus, does not have the shock value of mass-casualty jihadist strikes, like 9/11 or the 2015 Paris attacks by ISIS. However, even bloodier events often do not receive the attention they deserve. In part, this is because their targets are often racial and religious minorities, immigrants, the LGBTQ+ community, or other marginalized groups. As a result, the attacks target "them," and Americans who do not fall into the targeted categories because they are in the white, straight, Christian majority can feel safe in their hearts, even if they oppose the violence in their minds.

This targeting of minority and marginalized communities, however, often makes white supremacist violence *more* consequential than jihadist violence. Jihadists are a tiny minority within the Muslim community, which itself is small in the West, and extremists have little public support in the West. Their attacks usually focus on changing Western foreign policy, for example by driving the United States out of the Middle East. In addition, their violence usually brings people together in shared outrage. White supremacists, in contrast, tap into deep historical roots of discrimination and prejudice, and their rhetoric and deeds are a violent echo of current cultural disputes. In addition, violence by a majority community is usually of more concern given its greater power and, by definition, greater potential numbers. As one expert told me, "there are a shitload of white people," and if only a fraction of a fraction respond, that is still a large number.[9] White supremacists do not want to change foreign policy toward a particular region but rather to warp democratic political institutions and democratic norms and shatter bonds among citizens—a far graver danger.

Indeed, in the last 15 years we have seen the danger the white supremacist movement poses again go beyond acts of violence, because it is interacting more, as it did during the civil rights era and before, with mainstream politics. In the United States, the election of the first Black president, Barack Obama—and the counterreaction to his presidency and subsequent election of Donald Trump—led to heightened sensitivity on racial issues and the mainstreaming of many once-marginalized viewpoints. In Europe, the recent surge in Muslim immigration has heightened sensitivity there to the presence of minorities. Homeland security and intelligence officials in the United States, Europe, and Australia warn that white supremacists pose the gravest terrorism threat today.[10]

This book argues that the nature of white supremacist violence and the power white supremacists exert are directly tied to the following five factors.

Ideas

The main targets of white supremacist violence have varied historically, and today there are numerous differences within the movement as to who is the primary enemy. Some of the bloodiest white supremacist attacks in the last decade—Breivik's attack in 2011, Dylann Roof's 2015 mass shooting at a Black church in Charleston, the 2018 Tree of Life synagogue shooting in Pittsburgh, Tarrant's killings in 2019, and Patrick Crusius's 2019 attack on "invaders" from Mexico at an El Paso Walmart—illustrate this variance, as do less dramatic attacks targeting and harassing the LGBTQ+ community and racially intermarried couples that make daily life fearful for many peaceful ordinary people. At times, white supremacists focus not on their enemy communities directly but on the government or the supposedly corrupt elites behind their enemies, for example the left-leaning political forces Breivik blamed for destroying Norway's purity. Conspiracy theories are a near-constant in the white supremacist ecosystem, often leading to odd reasons for the embrace of violence.

Who the primary enemy is varies with shooter, country, and time period. Jews, of course, have long been at the center of conspiracy theories, while Muslims went from a sideshow to center stage after the 9/11 attacks and then rose even higher on the enemies list with the rise of ISIS. Immigrants from nonwhite countries are also high on the haters' lists. The Black community in the United States has suffered constant abuses, while in Europe it is simply one among several minority communities white supremacists target. All white supremacists, though, would agree that whites are at risk of genocide, and they see themselves as defending their people.

Over time, as the movement has become more networked via the internet (and especially social media), white supremacists from around the world are sharing their fears, concerns, and hatreds. The white supremacist movement has long exceeded the borders of any particular country. Nazism, of course, did not originate in the United States, and in the 1970s, for instance, volunteers from the United States went to fight on behalf of the apartheid government in Rhodesia. The information revolution, however, has fundamentally altered the white supremacist movement. Ideas and strategies are now shared globally: Tarrant drew inspiration from Breivik, and Crusius from both of them. As Tarrant's homage to the slain Ebba Åkerlund indicates, jihadist violence in one country is used in others as proof of the danger immigrants pose. Social media and similar technologies enable constant dialogue within the movement, as well as organizational and operational coordination.

This networking and globalization of ideas also make it difficult to draw clear lines where the white supremacist movement begins and ends. In the United States, for example, white supremacists in recent years have often overlapped with antigovernment causes, with concerns about gun control and federal government overreach melding with fears that whites are being displaced.

Strategies

White supremacists have used numerous approaches—some successful, some disastrous failures—to achieve their goals. White supremacists have been most successful when they have tied themselves to the broader political establishment, as they were in the pre–civil rights era in the United States. They could count on law enforcement to look the other way or, at times, even help them, as they killed and intimidated Black people and other enemies to ensure their dominance.

Over time, however, mainstream politics turned against white supremacy, and new approaches arose. Some white supremacists favored small terrorist cells whose violence would supposedly lead to a mass uprising. Others sought to create whites-only territory, breaking off from the country as a whole. Popular approaches today involve trying to "accelerate" racial and other divisions, believing that polarization will lead to a race war in which whites will emerge triumphant. Around the world, we see white supremacists embracing "leaderless resistance," the idea that individuals and small groups, acting autonomously but united by a common mission, will overwhelm "The System" and foster its collapse. The good news is that most of these strategies are poorly thought through, and leaderless resistance has many weaknesses. The bad news is that even a foolish strategy can kill a lot of innocent people. The scariest news is that white supremacists in recent years have made inroads into broader popular discourse and politics, increasing their potential influence.

Technology

White supremacists exploit the technologies of their times, and these technologies, in turn, shape the nature of the movement. The accessibility of AR-15s and other semiautomatic weapons in the United States has contributed to the mystique of the lone shooter in America, while the difficulty involved in acquiring weapons in Europe has made the movement there less lethal than it would be otherwise, despite numerous attacks there.

Communications technology has had a particular impact in ways both advantageous and disadvantageous to the white supremacist. Television broadcasts of vicious attacks on civil rights marchers in the early 1960s led to a backlash against white supremacists, whose deeds better flourished when they were done in darkness with few beyond the local community seeing the carnage. The spread of the internet, particularly social media, on the other hand, has provided new and cheap ways for white supremacists to fundraise, coordinate their movement, and issue propaganda. Encrypted messaging apps allow some members to hinder law enforcement monitoring. At the same time, these new technologies have raised new vulnerabilities, allowing law enforcement to better identify and prevent violence. The rise of social media has also contributed to the further decentralization of the movement, increasing its spread but limiting its effectiveness.

Politics and Popular Support

White supremacy does not exist in a vacuum. When the political winds are favorable, white supremacist ideas are more likely to influence national political decisions on race, immigration, and similar issues. Many hateful ideas once relegated to the darker corners of the internet are now being discussed openly, increasing their legitimacy in the eyes of many believers. In such an environment, recruiting and fundraising become easier. Incendiary rhetoric makes the most extreme and susceptible individuals more likely to attack, believing they are championing a broader cause that has widespread backing. In addition, sympathetic politicians will oppose crackdowns on white supremacists and otherwise enable their activities, while intelligence and law enforcement professionals will move cautiously, afraid of getting ahead of their political superiors. Minority communities will live in greater fear, even if day-to-day violence is limited. Conversely, when political winds shift, white supremacists will be on the defensive. Their ideas are more likely to be rejected outright, and politicians will press law enforcement and intelligence services to aggressively investigate and disrupt their activities.

Politicians should draw a bright line with regard to violent white supremacy. Extremist ideas can overlap with more mainstream ones, but mainstream political and civil society leaders should constantly condemn and marginalize those who use violence or justify it, and they should work with law enforcement to this end.

Counterterrorism

Too often, the white supremacist danger is judged while omitting a key factor: counterterrorism. The FBI, European intelligence services, and local police on both sides of the Atlantic have at times conducted devastating campaigns against white supremacists, leading to the collapse of many Ku Klux Klan chapters, the disruption of various neo-Nazi groups in Europe and the United States, and the arrests of numerous bloody-minded individuals. Effective counterterrorism can turn white supremacists from a direct threat to the institutions of democracy and the daily lives of many citizens into a fragmented fringe movement that, while still capable of bloody attacks, is usually on the run, riven with infighting, and afraid to recruit and raise money openly.

Successful counterterrorism requires examining white supremacist violence through a terrorism lens. The terrorism label, with its emotional power and the resources that go with it, can help ensure that white supremacy returns to the margins of society and that violence is met with the force of law.

A Few Words on Concepts and Definitions

Following the use of the term proposed by historian Kathleen Belew, "white power" is a deadly social movement that mixes racism and anti-Semitism with hatred of migrants and liberals and seeks to overturn the existing order.[11] White supremacists aim to ensure that whites enjoy more status, privileges, and rights than nonwhites—they are "prowhite" in their own view—and they regard social inequality as natural.[12] Part of this conception is racial: Black people, the Latino population, and other non-Europeans are deemed genetically inferior. "Whiteness," in white supremacists' eyes, is usually mixed with Christianity: Jews and Muslims, even if fair-skinned, are not whites.

White supremacy has moved from a cause with a set of powerful groups like the Klan behind it to a diffuse social movement, which Ruud Koopmans defines as a system of "informal, shifting and often temporary coalitions of organizations, informal networks, subcultures, and individuals."[13] Such movements differ from normal politics in that, in Sidney Tarrow's words, they lack "regular access to institutions, act in the name of new or unaccepted claims and behave in ways that fundamentally challenge others."[14]

Indeed, it is common to speak of white supremacist groups or the broader movement as if they are unified, timeless, and largely identical in their beliefs. Although I argue that the movement shares many common conceptions, it has varied considerably over time: aspects of what motivated Klan groups in the 1960s appear in successor white supremacist organizations today, but, as I argue, the movement has changed considerably. Similarly, I look at groups and individuals around the world, but, of course, the political and historical contexts vary tremendously if one is talking about Europe, New Zealand, or the United States. Finally, the movement and groups are highly divided, and my analysis and counterterrorism recommendations stress how these fissures might be exploited. The white supremacist movement today blends aspects of the old Klan, neo-Nazis, Norse paganism, racist skinheads, the alt-right, and peculiar interpretations of Christianity. This book at times lumps these disparate elements together, but I also try to highlight the differences when they matter.

One can also champion ideas that, to some degree, white supremacists share without being a terrorist. An FBI study estimated that only a tiny fraction of white nationalists with extreme views had "a penchant for violence."[15] Politicians regularly arise outside mainstream parties—such as George Wallace and Pat Buchanan in the United States and Geert Wilders in the

Netherlands—to champion issues that overlap with the white supremacist agenda. In this book, I use overlapping, but not identical, terms such as "extremist," "militant," and "terrorist" to discuss the white supremacist movement. Following the usage of Jakob Aasland Ravndal, a white supremacist *extremist* endorses illegal violence to promote white supremacy: someone on Twitter, say, who tweets his support for a vigilante who beat up a Black person. A *militant* is one step further, an extremist who actually uses violence; to continue with the previous example, it would be the vigilante himself. A *terrorist* is a militant who uses violence in the name of creating a broader psychological effect: not just attacking a leftist or an immigrant out of anger or to oppose an enemy but deliberately trying to use the attack to create a psychological effect and send a broader message on behalf of the white supremacist movement.[16]

It is important to distinguish "right-wing terrorism" from white supremacist terrorism. The former is a broad term that includes a range of issues historically associated with the conservative side of the political spectrum; the specific issues vary historically and by country, and in the United States today, "right-wing terrorism" might refer to antiabortion sentiments, concern about gun control in the United States, opposition to immigration, and a desire to preserve state and local power at the expense of federal power. In Europe, "right-wing terrorism" might refer to a strong national identity, often linked to Christian religious heritage, anticommunism, and hostility to immigration. All these concerns can be valid political issues that have respectable organizations that lobby for them. These issues, however, at times involve terrorism when an adherent embraces violence and uses it to send a broader message.

It is also important to distinguish white supremacist groups from antigovernment extremism, although the two at times overlap. The latter is usually more about fears and conspiracies of government overreach (often involving seizing guns). Groups like the Oath Keepers, the Proud Boys, and the Three Percenters are not inherently white supremacists in their ideas, and much of the Boogaloo movement focuses on fomenting chaos and targeting the police, not racist ideas. As J. J. MacNab, an expert on antigovernment extremism, contends, "guns are [a] common denominator in most anti-government extreme groups. Racism is not."[17] However, in practice many anti-government groups blend their hostility to the government with racism and anti-Semitism is encouraged as individuals rise through the ranks.[18]

Outline of the Book

The chapters follow a loose chronological order, with some analytic themes examined in detail in particular sections. Chapter 1 examines the U.S. white power movement in the early twentieth century and follows it through its defeats in the civil rights era in the 1950s and 1960s. Even though tsarist Russia and of course Nazism are among the most important chapters in the long history of anti-Semitism, white supremacy, and hate in general, the lesson from various Ku Klux Klan groups in the United States is particularly instructive for the current situation. Klan groups had many enemies (Jews, Catholics, immigrants, and of course the Black community), whereas the tsarist and Nazi movements focused on Jews. Even more important, Russia and Nazi Germany are cases of state persecution, while the Klan groups were nonstate actors, like many groups today: their relationship to the state varied, and that story is important for understanding the white supremacist movement today.

In chapter 2 I trace the shift of white power ideology and supporters from their entrenchment in the state to their emergence as a revolutionary force from the 1970s through the 1990s. Smaller organizations, like The Order, which favored terrorism against the government as well as minority groups, replaced large movements, like the Klan, which had considered itself a supporter of the social order and an adjunct to the police.

Chapters 3 and 4 look at Europe. In chapter 3 I examine the emergence in Europe in the 1970s and 1980s of similar, often overlapping types of white supremacism, with a focus on white power rock and roll and how it shaped the world of white power youth, particularly the skinhead movement. Chapter 4 looks at the legacy of Anders Behring Breivik, the deadliest white power terrorist in Europe, and how the white power movement in Europe and worldwide has tried to emulate him.

Chapter 5 examines another legacy of another deadly attack—Brenton Tarrant's 2019 massacre of Muslims in New Zealand—and details the ways social media has both empowered the white supremacist movement and created new weaknesses within it. Chapter 6 details the different paths to victory white supremacist groups have pursued and the many problems they face in their efforts. Chapter 7 describes the orientation of the movement today, focusing on its strategies; the danger posed by radical individuals, as opposed to formal groups; and the many weaknesses of the movement as a whole. This chapter contends that the government reaction to the white supremacist movement determines much about its threat and its very nature. The final chapter assesses the vulnerabilities of the movement, the ways government action shapes it, and the many problems governments have in targeting its followers.

Although the chapters focus on different historical periods, different issues, and different parts of the world, they all address similar challenges that confront white supremacists and the governments that oppose them. They explore white supremacist ideas about the world and how and why these have changed. They also explore white power groups' relationships with politics and technology, both of which are often beyond the control of extremists and can offer white supremacists opportunities but are frequently vulnerabilities. The chapters also explain why white supremacists, in keeping with their evolving ideas and conditions, often change their strategies and tactics, which range from the grim and deadly to the absurd and incompetent. Finally, all the chapters explore the weaknesses of these groups and how more effective government and civil society efforts usually lead them to fail.

1

A White Man's World

In 1914, James Thomas Heflin of Alabama introduced a resolution in the U.S. Congress calling for designating the second Sunday in May Mother's Day.[1] Heflin's career, which spanned the first half of the twentieth century, would be a happy footnote to history if it had stopped there. However, he embodied white power's entrenchment in the very structure of American politics and society. Elected as the mayor of LaFayette, Alabama, he had made his mark as a young lawyer serving as a delegate to his state's 1901 constitutional convention, where he declared, "God Almighty intended the negro to be the servant of the white man."[2] The new constitution he helped author barred Black citizens from voting in Alabama. He further achieved celebrity status by defending convict leasing, a practice of convicting African Americans, often on false or malicious charges, and then selling them to factories, mines, or farmers—a practice Heflin called necessary to ensure Black people stayed in their proper place.[3]

From there, Heflin went on to serve in the U.S. Congress as a Democrat in a time when the "Solid South" loyally voted for the party that had opposed Black equality during Reconstruction. In addition to playing a leading role in establishing Mother's Day and trying to ban the sale of liquor at the new Union Station in Washington, DC, Heflin introduced a bill requiring that the city's streetcars be segregated. As Congress deliberated, Heflin acted. Riding on a streetcar, he demanded that a Black man, Lewis Lundy, leave, later claiming that Lundy was drinking in the presence of white women. Lundy refused, and Heflin threw him to the ground. Lundy tried to run, and Heflin pulled out his gun and fired several shots, hitting a tourist as well as Lundy; the wounded tourist then refused to ride to the hospital in the same ambulance as Lundy. Heflin was indicted on charges of assault, but the charges were soon dropped, and he later bragged that the shooting was the highlight of his career.[4]

After eight terms in the House, Heflin was appointed to Alabama's Senate seat after the death of John Bankhead, Sr., and then was elected formally in 1924, running on a platform of racism, Prohibition, and anti-Catholicism.

During this time, he joined the Ku Klux Klan (KKK), which, in the 1920s, became a dominant force in Alabama politics and in those of many other states,
reaching its peak influence nationwide in the 1924 elections. In the 1926
elections, the Klan was able to rally its supporters to vote, and Klan-backed
candidates won the governor, U.S. senator, and attorney general seats, as well
as numerous lower-level positions, overturning the patrician elite and giving
it near-total control of Alabama. (During the elections, the police aided Klan
organizations by chauffeuring their supporters to and from the polls.)[5] The
Klan's strong overall performance in Alabama produced a fresh wave of mob
violence targeting Jews, the Black community, and other enemies—what one
historian called "an epidemic even by Alabama's distinctive standards."[6]

True to his principles, Heflin abandoned the Democratic Party in 1928 because it nominated Al Smith, a Catholic, for the presidency. (Smith lost in a
landslide to Herbert Hoover, in part because of his Catholicism.) Alabama
Democrats, however, did not forget Heflin's betrayal and refused to nominate
him for the Senate in 1930. He ran as an independent and lost.

Heflin's career did not end after his time in the Senate. He was on the left
side of the political spectrum on labor rights and industrial regulation; in
today's terms, he would be considered more of a populist than a conservative
or liberal. After losing his Senate seat, he served in the Roosevelt administration in the Department of Justice and the Federal Housing Administration.[7]
His nephew, Howell Heflin, would represent Alabama in the Senate from
1979 to 1997.

Heflin's unabashed racism and prominent role in Alabama and national
politics were not outliers but a reflection of how white racial dominance was
cemented into the foundation of American politics during his era. Slavery
has been with America longer than America has been without it, coming to
Florida with the Spanish in 1528 and then to the British colonies in 1619.
When the Civil War put an end to slavery, terrorist violence by the original
Klan and similar groups overturned Reconstruction-era attempts to achieve
a modicum of political and social equality for the formerly enslaved. By the
end of the nineteenth century, when Heflin's political career began, institutionalized segregation in the form of Jim Crow laws was formalized in much
of the South.

In the decades that followed, leaders with racial attitudes like Heflin's
dominated the politics of the South. The social and political superiority of
Christian whites was assumed, and violence was a common, and acceptable, response when this status was challenged. Mobs and the Klan were

interwoven with the government itself: the whites in positions of power used law, politics, and violence, all working hand in hand, against racial justice. The story of how Klan groups lost much of their influence is important both for its lessons and for understanding how and why the movement adapted.

The Klan before Civil Rights

The Klan and similar white supremacist groups, like the Knights of the White Camelia, initially emerged during Reconstruction; they killed thousands in the aftermath of the Civil War and overturned Reconstruction-era attempts to promote Black political and economic equality.[8] In the years that followed, organized white supremacists, along with local mobs, lynched between 4,000 and 5,000 Black Americans.[9] After 1877, however, many southern white supremacists saw little need for organized extralegal groups like the Klan, as the overturning of Reconstruction meant that racism was now embedded in the power structure of southern society.

In 1915, inspired by the film *Birth of a Nation,* which glorified the Reconstruction-era Klan, enterprising white supremacists met on Stone Mountain in Georgia to refound the Klan, burning a cross there. (Cross burning, which was not a ritual of the Reconstruction-era Klan, derived from the book on which *Birth of a Nation* was based—one of many instances when white supremacists turned to fiction as a guide to action). As historian Linda Gordon details, many Klan leaders at this time discouraged violence (though they often winked at it in practice), and many members saw the Klan chapters primarily as social associations. However, the 1920s' Klan chapters embraced a far wider array of causes than their predecessors had, railing against Jews, Catholics, immigrants in general, and a broad set of elites, all supposedly bent on subverting the white Protestant nature of America. Many Protestant clergy members led local Klan groups. In addition, Klan speakers at this time promulgated a vast array of conspiracy theories. Klan membership surged, with several million members nationwide (including around 500,000 women). The Klan becamebecome more popular outside the South than within it, with chapters in every state. Indiana, Oregon and parts of Pennsylvania were among the areas that had large numbers of Klan members per capita.[10] The Klan's political influence was striking. At its peak, 16 senators, 11 governors, and perhaps 75 House members were Klan members.[11] In the years when it enjoyed influence, Klan organizations pushed through immigration restrictions, eugenics laws that forcibly steril-ized "defective" people (who Gordon notes were typically poor and/or people of color), and in general made bigotry more acceptable.

In many southern states Klan organizations continued to focus on targeting African Americans, but Klan leadership in Texas railed that "thousands of Mexicans, many of them communist, are waiting for a chance to cross the Rio Grande and glut the labor marts of the Southwest."[12] Local mobs killed dozens of Mexicans; the *New York Times* reported: "the killing of Mexicans without provocation is so common as to pass almost unnoticed."[13]

Outside racial relations, antiimmigrant and anti-Catholic sentiment also regularly flared up nationwide.[14] Even before the Civil War, the "Know-Nothing" Party had surged in the 1850s by portraying immigrants, especially Catholics, as a threat to the American way of life. A poster in the Boston area declared Catholics to be "vile imposters, liars, villains, and cowardly cutthroats." Respectable figures, for example a U.S. professor of zoology, warned about "racial replacement" due to immigration.[15] The Klan and other white supremacist organizations would echo this anti-Catholic sentiment. In Indiana, a Klan hotspot in the 1920s, Catholic immigrants were the top villain.

Jews were considered even more suspect. For much of U.S. history, local laws or social practices prevented Jews from living in certain neighborhoods, allowed exclusionary quotas at elite schools, and otherwise placed limits on Jewish inclusion. Anti-Semitism became more pronounced as immigration, including Jewish immigration, surged in the 1880s and for several decades that followed. Tropes ranged from narratives of Jews as financial cheats to arguments that Jews would never assimilate and would not be loyal to the United States. The "science" of eugenics also arose at this time, casting Jews as a duplicitous, money-grubbing, and unnatural race at odds with American values. Anti-Semitism grew more organized, however, after World War I, and the Russian Revolution of 1917 increased Americans' fears that Jews were the force behind international communism. Tsarist intelligence put forward the idea that a secret cabal of Jewish financiers and power brokers controlled world events, in a fabricated document that described a purported Jewish plan for global domination, the "Protocols of the Elders of Zion," which quickly spread around the world. In the 1920s, prominent Americans, for example Henry Ford, drew on this and other tropes to warn against Jewish domination in newspapers and other publications. Ford, like many anti-Semites, embraced a wide range of conspiracies. He even wrote "jazz is a

Jewish creation" (ignoring its Black origins) and predicted that it would corrupt America through its "abandoned sensuousness of sliding notes." This, in
turn, led him to promote square dancing as a wholesome alternative, which
is why many states still teach square dancing in schools as part of physical
education.[16]

Anti-Semitism grew even stronger in the 1930s, with around 100 anti-
Semitic organizations emerging (before then, there had been perhaps
five in all of U.S. history). Some Hitler-admiring Americans even formed
militias modeled after the Nazi Party's Brownshirts (Sturmabteilung), with
thousands of members. Hundreds of thousands sympathized with fascism.
Followers of Father Charles Coughlin, who had a radio show with millions
of listeners, formed the anti-Semitic Christian Front, and its members dese-
crated synagogues, assaulted Jews, and put yellow stars on Jewish businesses.
Jews were equated with communism and blamed for pushing America toward war. Anti-Semitism reached the very top of American politics: a congressman from Pennsylvania read portions of "The Protocols of the Elders
of Zion" into the Congressional Record. The cause, however, was not well
organized and contained many different strands; one analysis noted: "the
American far Right was a bewildering ferment of groups and ideological
tendencies."[17] With the United States' entry into World War II, open hatred
of Jews became less acceptable, as did support for fascism, though the ideas
remained in circulation.[18]

In the mid to late 1920s and 1930s, Klan organizations fell from their place
at the center of U.S. politics in many states, and in 1928, as already men-
tioned, the Democratic Party even nominated Al Smith. This fall was in part
due to the abuse of power and corruption—problems that would plague the
Klan's successors in the decades to come.[19] Klan chapters used local recruiters
("Kleagles"), many of whom were Protestant ministers, to identify and win
over new members; each was given a percentage of the $10 initiation fee
each recruit paid. Klan groups also sold robes, flags, swords, and other para-
phernalia. Those at the very top got rich and lived lavish lifestyles.[20] In 1925,
David Curtiss "Steve" Stephenson, the grand dragon of the powerful Indiana
chapter, who was also influential in nearby states, was tried and convicted for
kidnapping, raping, and murdering a young white woman. Critics seized on
this and on instances of leader corruption, and many supporters became dis-
illusioned, while the Klan's reputation as a whole was tarnished. In addition,
with the passage of severe limits on immigration, the political salience of that
issue fell, and with it, a major source of grievance.

Even in its diminished state after the 1920s, the Klan was very much part of the established order and saw itself as a friend, not an opponent, of the forces of law and order. Klan organizations, especially in the American south, still had many ties with local sheriffs and police. Klan leader Samuel Roper, who orchestrated at least one lynching, later became head of the Georgia Bureau of Investigation even as he was a Klan member. While a police officer, he was an "exalted cyclops," a senior rank in the Klan, and he led the Georgia Klan on his retirement, becoming its imperial wizard in 1949.[21] An official history of Georgia's police department describes its union as "Klan-dominated."[22]

In a way, the Klan's decline was a sign of the victory of its ideas: you do not need an organization to defend white power when it is so entrenched in the system itself. Immigration was now limited, and Jews remained suspect and excluded from many institutions. The Klan was not necessary to ensure control of African Americans—state and local governments did that on their own, along with a healthy dose of societal norms and prejudices.

The Klan in the Civil Rights Era

Klan organizations rose again in the late 1950s and 1960s. The Klan at this time was less focused on fighting Catholicism, and antiimmigrant nativism also played little role in its rise. Race, in particular the challenges posed by the 1954 *Brown v. Board of Education* Supreme Court ruling and subsequent civil rights drives, animated white supremacists during this era.

After *Brown*, Klan membership quickly climbed again in response to the "threat" of integration, as the civil rights movement, and opposition to it, consumed the South in the early 1960s. The Klan drew on members who feared school integration and workplace competition from African Americans. School integration, they claimed, would create a "mongrel race": race mixing in the classroom would soon lead to intermarriage. They also stressed that, unlike politicians, they were willing to act: "Be a Man—Join the Klan" was a bestselling bumper sticker.[23] To be clear, the Klan was never truly popular: at its peak during this phase, in 1965, it enjoyed only 18 percent approval in the South, with most of those surveyed expressing vehement opposition because of the groups' violence.[24] Important organizations like the Baptist State Convention, which represented over 3,000 churches, condemned "the bigotry, prejudice, intolerance, and ill will" of the Klan.[25] However, it was often strong enough to intimidate those who opposed it, and when it fought segregation, it often had the approval of many white southerners. This approval, whether open or tacit, was enough to give Klan groups tremendous freedom to operate.

As with so many terrorist groups, Klan members saw themselves as on the defensive, claiming they were opposing Black violence and would stop it "if we have to kill every nigger in America!"[26] Conspiracy theories were rampant, with Jews and communists (often the same thing, according to white supremacists) under the bed and supposedly orchestrating the civil rights struggle. Many Klan members believed there was a Jewish-communist conspiracy to "mongrelize" the white race through intermarriage with Black people.[27] One neo-Nazi published a forged speech given at a supposed Emergency Council of European Rabbis that, he claimed, explained the Jewish plan to start World War III.[28] Less dramatic dangers included the threats of fluoridated water and the American Red Cross with its sneaky internationalist agenda. One Klan speaker even argued that U.S. involvement in Vietnam was a communist conspiracy, as white women would get "so hard up that they would marry and have intercourse with niggers."[29]

As before, Klan organizations in each state were independent of one another, with the exception of the United Klans, which had a regional structure and aspired to have a national one, with semiautonomous state "realms" under the Alabama-based "Imperial" headquarters. An FBI report from 1964 noted that there were 14 distinct major Klan organizations.[30] Each local chapter, or "klavern," had an exalted cyclops as its leader, replete with numerous office holders, ranging from "klabees" (treasurers) to "kludds" (chaplains). At the state level, this organization was duplicated, with each officer having the title "grand" before his name to signify the individual's importance.[31] Most states had multiple Klan organizations: in Georgia after *Brown*, U.S. Klans, for several years the largest Klan organization, competed with at least seven other Klan organizations; even though the U.S. Klans chapter in Georgia was the largest of them until the early 1960s, it did not control the overall movement.[32] The FBI report noted that "groups are wracked by rivalry and jealousy of each other's leadership and jurisdiction."[33] The common KKK brand, coupled with decentralization, meant that KKK members would be tarred with the brush of other Klan organizations when they conducted attacks that were unpopular or otherwise hurt the cause as a whole.

The rise and subsequent collapse of the Klan in North Carolina is illustrative of the movement as a whole. The Alabama-based United Klans of America, which succeeded U.S. Klans as the largest Klan organization in the early 1960s (with 20,000 active members in 17 states, and far more supporters), issued the *Fiery Cross*, the main Klan newspaper, and was led at the national level by Robert Marvin Shelton—described by the FBI as being slight with blond hair, somber, and "humorless."[34] In his excellent history *Klansville, U.S.A.*, sociologist David Cunningham describes the rise of the North Carolina chapter of the United Klans of America, the largest and most successful state chapter in the United States during the 1960s, under the leadership of J. Robert "Bob" Jones, a Navy veteran and awning salesman. In 1963, after its first rallies, the Klan expanded to 13 klaverns and just over 500 members in North Carolina alone. By early 1966, the FBI estimated that United Klans of America had 200 klaverns there and up to 12,000 active members. Jones sought to build a large movement that would serve as a political machine to advance white supremacy. It was strongest in areas where Black people were present in large numbers but were not the numerically dominant community. In general, Klan members reflected white society in North Carolina. To recruit, they used rallies and newspapers, but they also relied heavily on personal networks. Some of the core members came from families with a long history of KKK membership. Members themselves were well armed, and they often spent time at klavern meetings admiring one another's guns.[35]

The movement also had a strong financial base on which to build its activities. Members paid a $10 initiation fee to join and $2 monthly thereafter, plus a charge for robes ($10 for cotton but $15 if you wanted to impress your neighbors with satin), all of which went into the Klan coffers. As one critical member noted, leaders like Jones enjoyed a "first class, rib eye steaks, Cadillacs" lifestyle.[36] This overstated what was often the reality. One of Jones's henchmen recalled that he lived in a "old raggeddy house" and otherwise had a modest life.[37]

As this envy of Jones suggests, the Klan suffered from divisions between its leaders and members. Both opposed the civil rights movement, but the leaders like Jones stressed that it was masterminded by "international Communist banking led by Zionist Jews."[38] Black people, in the eyes of some leaders, were deemed too stupid to be behind the wide-ranging and increasingly effective civil rights movement. As one FBI agent put it, "they thought they were fighting Communism in their own stupid way."[39] The rank and file, in contrast, were far more obsessed with the Black community and the perceived dangers of school integration, rape, and civil rights in general.

Further, even in good times, Klan membership could be risky. Some members feared rejection by the many whites who disapproved of the Klan, which led some upper-class North Carolinians to avoid open association, in a state where many elites rejected the absolutist stance taken by leaders in states like Alabama and Mississippi. Factory workers and others feared that open membership might cost them their jobs (explaining, perhaps, why there were disproportionate numbers of small businessmen in the Klan).[40]

Despite these many problems, Klan violence was endemic for much of the civil rights era. Violence often occurred in tandem with the pace of integration: it increased after *Brown* and then spiked again during high-profile civil rights protests from 1963 to 1966, with hundreds of lynchings and arson attacks, as well as bombings of religious facilities and shootings.[41]

In general, Klan violence was a near-constant during times of tension, often not making the news. It ranged from attacks on synagogues to bombings of Black churches and the homes of local civil rights leaders, as well as beatings. Between 1956 and 1963, the Klan used dynamite 138 times. Some of the violence was perpetrated on the orders of Klan leaders, but much of it was simply individuals or local klaverns acting on their own.[42] As an internal FBI report noted, "the Klan naturally attracts men who are prone to violence."[43]

One of the worst attacks was in 1963, when a splinter group of the United Klans of America bombed the 16th Street Baptist Church in Birmingham, killing four children. The bombers believed the larger Klan group was too restrained. The FBI quickly determined the likely suspects, but the Department of Justice was slow to prosecute. The first federal charges would not be brought until 1977, and two of the bombers would not be convicted until 2001 and 2002.

The most common type of violence was flogging. Klan members took the offending individual, whose crime might be supporting civil rights or otherwise seeking equality, to a lonely wooded area where they stripped and beat their victim severely, with a warning to desist or leave the area.[44] Cross burnings, of course, were another constant form of intimidation—to convince an elected leader to vote the right way, to warn a store owner off integrating a lunch counter, and so on. In January 1964, area Klan chapters burned more than 150 crosses in five Louisiana parishes; in April 1964, 64 of Mississippi's 82 counties had a cross burning.[45]

Murders and bombings too were common as well. From 1954 to 1968, white supremacists murdered 41 people linked to the civil rights struggle.[46]

Aside from actual violence, area Klan members also harassed their foes with threatening phone calls, targeting local heads of the NAACP and others.[47]

The Klan was able to carry out so many attacks because, according to one history, it enjoyed a "general immunity from arrest, prosecution, and conviction."[48] Indeed, the Klan even saw itself as an informal arm of law enforcement. The police managed violence during the day, and at night the Klan would ride.[49] In many areas, the most important law enforcement official was the sheriff, who was popularly elected and whose deputies depended on him for their jobs. Sheriffs and other local officials often favored the Klan, or at least feared its opposition, inhibiting justice at the most local, and thus the most important, level.[50] In a 1964 assessment, the FBI noted that, in some areas, local law enforcement "is often tolerant of Klan activity" and pointed to numerous states where Klan members had infiltrated law enforcement or officers had joined Klan chapters.[51]

When a small group of Freedom Riders took a bus deep into the South to integrate bus stations, for their own protection they informed the Department of Justice and the FBI. The federal agencies, however, duly relayed this to local law enforcement, and the locals passed the information to the KKK. When the riders arrived in Birmingham, Alabama, Public Safety Commissioner "Bull" Connor promised the local KKK 15 minutes without interference, and they then beat the riders viciously with clubs and pipes.[52] The federal government's providing of this information suggests complicity, as the FBI must have been aware of what would happen to the civil rights workers.

The Klan also praised the FBI because of its role in fighting communism, which many Klan members saw as the hidden hand behind the civil rights struggle. The American Nazi Party went one step further, seeing the struggle against communism as another front in the struggle against Jews. Its long-time leader, George Lincoln Rockwell, admired the FBI's storied and racist director, J. Edgar Hoover, and declared in 1962: "ONLY the FBI [stands] between America (and therefore the World)—and Communist total victory! ... Heil Hoover!"[53]

In most states, Klan organizations coexisted with ostensibly peaceful political groups—often calling themselves "Citizens' Councils"—who opposed integration, and the Klan's strength was often linked to whether the local community had other options for fighting integration. Indeed, part of why the Klan was so large in North Carolina was that most of the political establishment cooperated with integration, albeit reluctantly, creating an opening for an avowedly segregationist movement.[54] In Mississippi and Alabama, in contrast, much of the political establishment opposed integration, giving segregationists an establishment alternative to the Klan, and as a result it was smaller there than in North Carolina. George Wallace, running for governor of Alabama in 1958, experienced this dynamic firsthand as he lost the election when his opponent played to the Klan. Wallace learned his lesson for subsequent elections and won in 1962, saying of his victory: "I started off talking about schools and highways and prisons and taxes, and I couldn't make them listen. Then I began talking about niggers—and they stomped the floor."[55] Indeed, Wallace's most famous declaration—"I say Segregation Now! Segregation Tomorrow! Segregation Forever!"—was a variant of the Klan motto that the Klan would ride "yesterday, today, forever," as long as white men lived.[56]

At this time, neo-Nazi groups played, at best, a minor role. The American Nazi Party was small, and the few Nazis had tense relationships with most Klan organizations. Part of this was generational, as Nazism was particularly unpopular after World War II and Klansmen considered themselves patriots. As Gorrell Pierce, a KKK grand dragon, noted, "you take a man who fought in the Second World War, it's hard for him to sit down in a room full of swastikas."[57] In Alabama, some of the Birmingham church bombers were associated with the neo-Nazi National States' Rights Party. The local Alabama Klan chapter expelled them, seeing the neo-Nazi linkage as unpatriotic.[58]

Although the Klan during the civil rights era did not enjoy majority approval in any state, it did command the support of a significant minority, as its opposition to integration made its violence and broader agenda attractive. The North Carolina Klan peaked in 1965; hundreds of thousands of North Carolinians attended Klan rallies that year.[59] The Klan also played an important role in state elections, endorsing a range of candidates whom it believed shared its agenda. Yet only a few years later, the Klan was a shell of its earlier self, devastated by infighting, a collapse in public support, and a tough federal counterterrorism campaign.

The Fall of the Klan

The Klan's violence proved its undoing. Attacks on the Freedom Riders, the murder of four girls in the Birmingham church bombing, and other attacks grabbed national attention, increasing pressure on the president to act. The most visible violence was often not directly linked to the Klan. In Alabama, for example, "Bull" Connor's use of dogs and firehoses against young civil rights marchers in 1963 was a government response, not that of the Klan. As President John Kennedy commented acidly, Wallace "has done a lot for civil rights this year."[60] Other major acts of violence, like the killing of Mississippi NAACP leader Medgar Evers, were committed by individuals with possible, but murky, links to local Klan groups.[61]

Nevertheless, the name of the Klan became shorthand for violence against the civil rights movement. During "Freedom Summer" in Mississippi in 1964, the White Knights of the Ku Klux Klan—a more violent rival of the United Klans of America—worked with their local sheriff's office and murdered civil rights workers James Chaney, Andrew Goodman, and Michael Schwerner in the so-called Mississippi Burning case.[62] Goodman and Schwerner were white Jews, and one of the ringleaders eventually convicted later declared: "those boys were Communists who went to a Communist training school."[63] Rather than oppose the government, the White Knights worked with, and bolstered, segregationist state and local officials. President Lyndon Johnson warned members to "get out of the Klan now and return to decent society before it is too late."[64]

More consequentially, after the attacks on civil rights workers, Johnson—and later, Attorney General Robert Kennedy—pushed J. Edgar Hoover to investigate the Klan. The FBI was already monitoring some Klan elements as part of its broader surveillance of the civil rights movement, but now the Klan became a target, leading the FBI to open its first state headquarters ever in Mississippi, with the number of FBI agents there surging from 15 to 150.[65] The killing of another civil rights volunteer, Viola Liuzzo—a mother of five from Detroit whom Klan members murdered in a drive-by shooting as she was driving marchers from Montgomery back to Selma—made Johnson even more irate.[66] The combination of politics, laws, and enforcement would move forward and crush the Klan.

The political impact of Klan violence was also devastating. The violence discredited the more "peaceful" antiintegration voices, associating them with extreme violence and helping Johnson to push through the Civil Rights Act of 1964. This act, the most significant civil rights act since Reconstruction almost 100 years earlier, banned segregated public accommodations, made it easier to move civil rights cases to federal court, and prohibited some forms of employment discrimination, among other major changes. Continued violence enabled Johnson to push through the even more ambitious Voting

Rights Act in 1965, which prohibited racial discrimination in voting. Violence also alienated more moderate members of the white establishment in the South, particularly the business community. In Mississippi, the business community feared boycotts, the loss of new industries, a cutoff of federal funding, and other financial losses that could result if the state persisted in rejecting civil rights.[67] Even many who shared the Klan's racist goals preferred to adhere to the laws and sought other ways to discriminate, such as instituting vouchers for whites-only private schools or subtler restrictions that inhibited, rather than barred, Black voting. Klan violence became an impediment to white dominance for these more pragmatic leaders.[68]

Television had a profound impact on the political reaction to violence. For decades, even the most brutal Klan violence remained abstract to many Americans outside the South and therefore could be ignored. Vivid television images, however, engaged the whole nation and made racist violence a political issue far from Mississippi, Alabama, and other hotspots. This, in turn, forced Johnson to act and set off a chain of events that led to the broad crackdown. As racial violence grabbed headlines nationwide, the House Un-American Activities Committee began to hold hearings and was often fed damaging information by the FBI.[69] The hearings highlighted reports of corruption within Klan organizations, creating the damaging (and largely false) impression that Klan leaders were simply running a scam on their members. These hearings further tarnished the Klan's image.[70]

Klan leaders like North Carolina's Bob Jones tried to walk a careful line with violence. Although he sought to use it to intimidate civil rights activists and other enemies, Jones recognized that a blanket endorsement of violence would lead local klaverns to go off on their own, often responding to a personal or local grievance rather than the concerns of the movement as a whole. If they did so, the statewide Klan would suffer any blowback and would have to defend the klavern in court, sapping the organization of always-scarce money. As a result, Jones opposed or canceled some proposed attacks. For example, Klan members planned to blockade the small town of Plymouth during civil rights unrest there. According to the plan, members with machine guns and other weapons would isolate the town while other KKK members would storm the Black neighborhood to "clean house." Jones feared the public backlash that would result from such a massacre and called it off at the last minute; many of his most committed members grew angry at his refusal to act, and rival leaders accused him of passivity.[71]

Legal support proved a particularly vexing problem for the Klan. Not providing legal support for members accused of violence or other crimes would be seen as a betrayal, costing the group membership and prestige. At the same time, the promise of organizational support made local Klan members more reckless. As one local Klan officer put it, legal defense funds "give people the feeling of 'I don't give a damn. I'll go out and shoot a nigger—' since I've got a bondsman and can get out right away and a good attorney." He then lamented: "we have some people who are not the brightest people in the world."[72]

The FBI Campaign

Because of its hostility to, and monitoring of, civil rights leaders like Martin Luther King, Jr., the FBI is often portrayed as supporting white supremacy, an image reinforced by instances of FBI agents simply observing and taking notes when white supremacists beat civil rights workers. In the context of the civil rights movement, this perception of hostility was true; the FBI's efforts against the Klan also helped it justify its overall efforts to spy on antiwar and pro–civil rights Americans, among others. In addition, almost all Klansmen supported the Vietnam War and many were considered pillars of their local (white) communities; their support for segregation, if peaceful, was also not an FBI concern. The FBI focused on trying to control and shape the activities of white hate groups, turning them away from violence but allowing them to continue as hate groups, ideally with an anticommunist focus.[73] The FBI's campaign against the Klan and other white power groups, once started, proved devastating, leading to the collapse of many important groups and the diminishment of even more.

Under Hoover, the FBI prioritized stability and addressing the communist threat, even seeing the civil rights movement as potentially subversive. Hoover repeatedly asserted that civil rights leaders and movement members were under communist influence. The FBI even smeared Viola Gregg Liuzzo, the Detroit mother of five murdered by Klan members. The FBI had had an informant in the shooter's car; to deflect attention from its indirect culpability, the Bureau claimed that Liuzzo had "needle marks in her arm where she had been taking dope" and "was sitting very, very close to that Negro in the car; that it has the appearance of a necking party."[74]

As absurd and harmful as his harassment of the civil rights movement was, Hoover also loathed the KKK, calling it "sadistic, vicious white trash." As noted, after the Liuzzo killing and other high-profile acts of violence, the Johnson administration, too, pushed the FBI to act. In 1964, the FBI initiated COINTELPRO-White Hate Groups, under the same covert action umbrella program it used against communist, civil rights, and left-wing organizations, which discarded due process and employed numerous dirty tricks against white power groups. Covert action allowed the FBI to act without oversight by Department of Justice lawyers, who would often require informants to testify and thus blow their cover.[75] Under the program, the FBI tried to "expose, disrupt, and otherwise neutralize" seventeen Klan and six other hate groups, including the United Klans of America (the largest group for most of this period, which, at its height, had 30,000 active members and far more supporters), the White Knights of the KKK of Mississippi, and the American Nazi Party.[76] A decade later, the deputy director of the FBI testified that FBI informants represented 6 percent or more of the Klan's total membership.[77]

These informants were often used to try to steer klaverns away from violence. They would speak against murder, cross burnings, and other forms of violence and instead would champion anticommunism and other stances the FBI favored. To advance the positions of informants and weaken those of hardliners, the FBI worked with local police to arrest or discredit hardliner leaders so Bureau-controlled informants would control the senior ranks of a group.[78]

The FBI also tried to foster infighting.[79] It constantly looked for dirt on Klan leaders' personal lives to discredit them.[80] The FBI planted fake information about informants in the Klan to discredit some figures and sent anonymous letters to Klan members to let them know they would be outed if they continued, ripping away the screen of anonymity.[81] The Bureau gave information to journalists hoping to expose the Klan and identified members to employers, leading to some losing their jobs. The FBI printed thousands of cartoons and sent hundreds of fake letters to portray the KKK leaders as corrupt and, ironically, as informants.[82] Corruption was a particularly potent allegation, as the Klan rank and file were sensitive to the idea that elites of all kinds, including their own leaders, were giving them the short end of the stick.[83] The FBI also directed informants to have sex with the wives of other members to foster dissension and planted rumors that this was taking place when it was not.[84] An FBI letter to one Klan grand dragon's wife said that he had "taken the flesh of another unto himself."[85] Similarly, the FBI sent a fake letter on United Klans of America stationery to the wife of the leader of the National States' Rights Party claiming that the leader was having an affair. The Bureau hoped that the recipients of such letters would become so focused on the problems in their marriages that they would limit "time spent in plots and plans."[86] The FBI also used COINTELPRO against other white supremacist groups, such as the American Nazi Party and the National States' Rights Party.[87] One Klan member recalls one leader, who turned out to be an FBI asset, talking up "all the wrong things Bob Jones is doing. He's embezzling money from the Klan fund, he's a drunkard, he chases women."[88]

All of this exacerbated factionalism, leading to the decline of several Klan chapters and at least one Klan-on-Klan killing. The United Florida KKK collapsed after a series of FBI-aided exposés and local crackdowns. Grand dragons fell in quick succession in Mississippi, Alabama, and other states, and the Louisiana Klan split into three factions, with membership falling in all of the organizations. The FBI even recruited the head of the Indiana Klan, which, by 1972, had the largest Klan membership of any northern state, as an informant. The Bureau estimated that total Klan membership was around 14,000 in 1964, and it fell to 4,300 by 1971 and then below 2,000 by 1974.[89] United Klans of America leader Shelton later admitted: "the FBI's counter-intelligence program hit us in membership and weakened us for about ten years."[90] The FBI, however, did not promote factionalism when the groups were not violent, believing that it would have less control over small splinters, some of which might use terrorism. Indeed, the FBI tried to preserve the less violent groups as an alternative attraction to members from the more violent groups it was trying to splinter.[91]

At the same time, the Klan's secrecy began to work against it. The organizations could not refute allegations of corruption without being more open, but that would lead to greater FBI penetration and public scrutiny. Jones, for example, refused to disclose the North Carolina Klan's financial details or have anyone other than his wife handle accounting.[92] In addition, as in the 1920s, corruption was a real problem, as some Klan leaders pocketed money given as dues or to support those arrested.[93] It was therefore easy for the FBI to claim that groups like these were really just stealing money from members.

COINTELPRO's abuses against civil rights organizations eventually spurred Congress to make it illegal for the FBI to use undercover operatives as agents provocateurs or to incite violence—a rule, many have contended, the FBI broke or at least skirted in the years that followed.[94]

The FBI also changed local policing, a less dramatic but high-impact shift that made states less complicit with Klan violence. Initially, the FBI simply passed on information it gained to local police because, in theory, they were the ones embedded in the community and empowered by state law. The FBI did so, however, even when it knew these police were sympathetic to the Klan or were even Klan members themselves—a common occurrence given that, in the testimony of former attorney general Nicholas Katzenbach, local police "were infiltrated by the very persons who were responsible for much of the violence."[95] As the FBI shifted to focus on the Klan, law enforcement officers themselves became a target for investigation. In Mississippi, the FBI helped the governor identify and dismiss KKK members from the state highway patrol, which was often responsible for protecting civil rights demonstrators.[96]

When there was the political will to do so, local policing devastated the Klan in several states or even prevented chapters from getting off the ground altogether. In Florida, the governor recognized that some local sheriffs and other law enforcement officials might be sympathetic to, or even members of, the Klan. In response, he centralized policing under a state-level Sheriff's Bureau and State Highway Patrol, which surveilled and tried to disrupt KKK events. As one detective recalled, "we'll pull a little traffic safety check—inspection stickers, driver's licenses, everything."[97] A state-level Klan leader suspected of Klan involvement was put under constant surveillance and then pulled over for "careless driving."[98] Police found a gun in his car, and he was arrested for having an illegal firearm. At another rally, attendees were cited for having faulty tag lights on their cars. Civil rights groups had long learned to cope with such constant police harassment, but Klan organizations were not prepared for local authorities to turn against them.[99]

Initially, North Carolina's police were ineffectual, with some officers supportive of the Klan. The Wilmington police chief and six of his deputies were Klan members, as were many other local law enforcement officers. Although the police did develop informants and gather information on Klan activity, their goal was to stop violence, not to disrupt the organization as a whole. North Carolina police focused on stopping the most egregious violence but allowed Klan groups to hold rallies, burn crosses, and otherwise rile up their members and try to intimidate African Americans and other foes.[100] In the eyes of the police, such actions did not really hurt anyone. Indeed, police were far more likely to disrupt civil rights rallies, seeing them as a source of disorder and potential violence, even where the white supremacists were the source of actual violence.[101]

Over time, however, policing shifted, and North Carolina began to police more the way Florida did. North Carolina political leaders saw Klan activity as an embarrassment, and federal pressure was an additional spur to action. Police stopped Bob Jones for speeding and used the charge to take away his driver's license, even though he could have gotten away with a fine. A few months later, they charged him with perjury in his 1951 divorce trial, where he had misrepresented the date he and his wife had separated. Police blocked Klan rallies and otherwise harassed participants. "Every time we turn around," Jones claimed with frustration, "we get arrested."[102]

Now, when the FBI passed information to the police, the cumulative effect could be devastating. In Miami, the United Klans of America building had several code violations related to their meetings. The FBI pushed local authorities to close the building to the Klan as a result—a small setback but a type of harassment that would make it far harder for local Klan chapters to organize.[103]

However, even when fighting the Klan, local police and state officials, along with the FBI, often focused primarily on controlling the group and only trying to stop the worst forms of violence, though the specifics of enforcement often varied considerably. Civil rights leaders complained of cross burnings, brick throwing, beatings, efforts to force Black drivers off the road, and other dangerous behavior, but some FBI agents would dismiss these as "pranks."[104] One leading FBI special agent who developed numerous Klan informants dismissed violent acts like cross burnings as something that "wouldn't hurt anyone."[105] Klan members, like many FBI officials and local police of the time, saw themselves as highly patriotic and vehemently anti-communist and their political opponents as questionable on both of these counts. As a result, the FBI and law enforcement had less enthusiasm for cracking down on KKK members, particularly the less violent sorts, than for various left-wing extremist causes of the time, for example the Black Panthers.

Policing cannot be divorced from public opinion. As criticism of overt white supremacy grew, it became harder for the police in North Carolina to openly embrace the KKK or even ignore its activities.[106] North Carolina leaders also feared the state would lose its appeal for northern businesses if national criticism continued.

Informants at both high and low levels of the KKK proved particularly important. All in all, the FBI developed hundreds of informants, penetrating the vast majority of North Carolina's klaverns.[107] This pattern was mirrored throughout the South, with the FBI developing around 2,000 informants in groups like the United Klans.[108] George Dorsett, North Carolina's "imperial kludd" (chief chaplain and senior leader), was secretly an FBI informant. After the death of one senior leader in a car accident, Dorsett told reporters that rival KKK leaders had killed him by unscrewing the steering column on his car, fostering dissension. The FBI even convinced Dorsett to form a rival group, the Confederate Knights of the KKK, and provided it with resources to challenge Jones.[109]

The Klan groups' own weak leadership and the dubious quality of many members also weighed heavily against them. The FBI noted that "Klan leaders are ambitious, opportunistic, unscrupulous, ruthless men who are constantly sparring for power."[110] Many, the FBI claimed, were alcoholic or mentally ill.[111] One Klan leader married a 14-year-old girl, dismaying some supporters who bought the Klan's rhetoric that it was dedicated to upholding high moral standards.[112] Nor did the Klan recruit the very best. A House in-vestigation found that many leaders were high school dropouts, some had received less than honorable discharges from the military, and others had fathered children with several mothers.[113] An FBI report claimed that Klan members as a whole are mostly "individuals of mediocre background" and of "limited education."[114] Shelton himself warned members that the Klan's biggest problems were "liquor, guns, and loose tongues."[115] This problem be-came a vicious circle for the Klan: as it began to hemorrhage members due to government pressure and, as recruits who had the respect of the community dropped out, recruiters became less diligent in their standards. Because the North Carolina Klan was large and many of its members were known, Jones, for instance, found that every foolish thing a Klan member did would be laid at the doorstep of the entire group, even if it was not approved.[116]

As law enforcement pressure on the Klan grew, it stepped up operational security and otherwise tried to maintain distance between its leaders and public activities and its darker, private face. Shelton, who led the United Klans of America, repeatedly claimed in interviews that it would expel indi-viduals who used violence, but FBI reports from private meetings indicate that talk of violence was constant, often carried out by small subgroups of the larger organization, with the bulk of members knowing little or nothing of any bloody deeds.[117] A typical meeting was similar "to a Moose meeting," as one member put it, where nothing is discussed openly that would in-criminate members.[118] The Klan in North Carolina publicly opposed spe-cific acts of violence, but it was a two-tiered organization: a small number of "white card members" were given secret instructions to use violence without the broader movement being told.[119] These members were often longtime Klansmen, trusted due to their years in the movement. Some also possessed special skills, like bomb-making.[120] In Mississippi, one imperial wizard stressed secrecy and discipline, and significant acts of violence, such as murder or firebombing, required his explicit approval (though local klaverns could perform whippings or cross burnings on their own initiative). United Klan members in one chapter in Mississippi drew the names of victims from a hat to ensure that no one knew for certain who was responsible for violence against any particular target.[121]

Eddie Dawson, a self-described "hothead" who was in prison during much of World War II due to discipline problems while in the army and who later developed a drinking problem, joined the North Carolina chapter of the United Klans of America around 1964, angered by the civil rights movement's efforts to integrate lunch counters in Tennessee. He worked closely with Bob Jones, often serving as a bodyguard, and was a white card member, or a member of the "Inner Circle," as he described it.[122]

Dawson's account of his activities, which involved intimidation and violence, is instructive both for their scope and for the problems he encountered. In Dawson's area of operations, the area Klan had penetrated the local sheriff's office, the highway patrol, and other government agencies and used the information it gained this way to intimidate the Black community. For example, a Klan member's wife worked in the local federal housing office and would tip off the Klan if a Black family was planning to buy in a white section. Dawson and his mates would also act on behalf of nearby chapters who were worried that their own cars and people would be recognized and reported to the FBI and police, because outsiders could act with impunity. Responding to efforts to integrate neighborhoods, interracial dating, or similar infractions, the Klan would then post a threatening sign to warn a family off, "drop a cross," shoot out windows, and "just go out to terrorize neighborhoods," as Dawson put it. He claims that they never meant to kill anyone, but "I'm not going to say that we never wounded nobody." Dawson's crew, however, at times attacked Black families they saw as disrespectful or otherwise acted without leadership approval, and the organization would be asked to pay for their bond and lawyers, which it could not easily afford. Federal trials proved particularly expensive, and it was "always money, money, money." Nonetheless, Jones opposed hiring a full-time lawyer for the North Carolina organization.[123]

This question of responsibility and money had no easy answer. However, Dawson recalled getting angry with Jones when he refused to use state Klan money to help him and other more local figures for lawyers when they used unauthorized violence. Dawson complained that the Klan was not there for him and he and his wife could not meet their house and car payments. In the end, the FBI was able to turn Dawson into an asset, agreeing to reduce his prison sentence if he infiltrated a different Klan group on the Bureau's behalf.[124]

A Change in the Courts

For most of U.S. history, violence against the Black community often went unpunished even in the rare cases when individuals were charged in a court of law. Klan leaders repeatedly escaped justice when local juries refused to convict. Even in one case where local Klan figures were convicted of violence, the judge suspended their sentences because they were "unduly provoked" by "unhygienic" outside agitators of "low morality."[125]

The federal courts, which had upheld racist laws and refused to convict Klansmen, became weapons against white supremacists as the civil rights movement progressed. In 1961, federal courts enjoined the Klan from interfering with interstate commerce—in this case attacking Freedom Riders who took buses from state to state—and demanded that Montgomery, Alabama, officials protect the riders.[126] In 1965, a federal judge denounced the Original Knights of the Ku Klux Klan for "interfering with the civil rights of the Negro citizens" and enjoined them from interfering with the rights of Black residents of Washington Parish, Louisiana, to vote, use public facilities, and otherwise exercise their rights. He denounced the Klan as "ignorant bullies, callous of the harm they know they are doing and lacking in sufficient understanding to comprehend the chasm between their own twisted Konstitution and the noble charter of liberties under law that is the American Constitution." In the decision, the judge declared that interfering with civil rights "is inherent in the nature of the klan. This is its ineradicable evil."[127] The courts, which had once shielded white supremacists, slowly became their enemy.

In 1966, the Supreme Court ruled in *United States v. Guest* that the murder of Lieutenant Colonel Lemuel Penn by Georgia Klan members while he was traveling home from Washington, DC, violated his constitutional rights as a U.S. citizen to engage in interstate travel, and thus federal charges could be leveled (state-level charges of murder had failed; an all-white jury had acquitted Penn's killers). Department of Justice lawyers committed to civil rights led the prosecution of Klan violence, not locals, who might be subject to political pressure or have ties to the extremists. In addition, the juries were more integrated and were drawn from regional rather than local pools, again reducing the likelihood of ties to the murderers and their ability to intimidate witnesses. At least some of the murderers of Liuzzo, Schwerner, and other civil rights workers initially escaped justice in state courts but eventually went to federal prison for civil rights violations. Samuel Bowers, who headed the White Knights of the KKK in Mississippi during its reign of terror, was eventually convicted on federal conspiracy charges, for which he served six years in jail; he was not convicted on murder charges in Mississippi until 1998.[128]

A Steady Decline

Just as the Klan had surged in response to integration, it quickly fell. In Mississippi, the two main groups, the White Knights and the United Klans, each had around 6,000 members at their peak in 1964. By 1967, the two groups combined numbered just over 1,000.[129] Changing political attitudes and social mores explain much of this fall, but also vital were vigorous campaigns against various Klan groups by the FBI and, in many areas, state governments.

The Klan's legal defense burden grew as arrests for cross burnings and other once-ignored offenses and citations became common. The financial strain also increased due to the cost of lawyers and as charges of contempt of court (and of not testifying before the House Un-American Activities Committee) led to fines. At the same time, the Klan's membership was falling, creating an unsustainable burden. The organization's failure, due to insufficient funds, to defend all of its members in court shook members' confidence and led to defections.[130] The Internal Revenue Service, prodded by the FBI, audited Klan leaders, adding to their financial woes.[131] Jones, Shelton, and several other leaders received short federal prison sentences for contempt. This furthered the disarray, as the organization lacked leadership at a critical time, and rivalries grew.

Some Klan organizations shrank in size or simply disbanded. Others further decentralized. Often the "white card" members, or others chosen by the leadership to use violence secretly, became more autonomous and simply struck out on their own. They might kill a Black man but not claim the murder for the KKK. The local community, both Black and white, would suspect who did it, creating fear without as much exposure for the Klan. In North Carolina, the more open side of the Klan also tried to portray itself as defending whites rather than stopping integration. Its members would travel to areas with civil rights demonstrations, claiming they were protecting the community from violence—a defensive claim white supremacists also embraced in the years to come.[132]

Black voters began to triumph at the ballot box, transforming the political landscape and leading to more government pressure against Klan organizations as Black voters and elected officials began to make their presence felt. In Mississippi, for example, Black registration has skyrocketed from 6 percent in the 1960s to over 80 percent today.[133] State and local politicians now courted the Black vote in many areas where in the past they had played to white supremacists. African American civil rights leader Andrew Young, when he was serving as a congressman from Georgia, noted: "when not many black people could vote, the politicians used to talk about 'the niggers—.' When we got 10 to 15 percent voting, they called us 'nigras.' When we got up to 25 percent, they learned how to say 'Nee-gro.' Now that we have 60 to 70 percent registered and voting, they say how happy they are to see 'so many black brothers and sisters here tonight.' "[134]

The Legal Battle Continues

Klan organizations suffered a devastating series of blows from civil lawsuits brought by the NAACP and the Southern Poverty Law Center (SPLC) in addition to those brought by the government. These lawsuits, like the government campaign, would shape the white supremacist movement in the United States in the postbellum era.

In 1980, three Klansmen in Chattanooga, Tennessee, drove down a street, firing shotguns at Black women in their path. Riots ensued after these Klansmen successfully claimed that they had not intended to commit murder and two of the three were not convicted while the third was only convicted of assault, serving just six months in jail and paying a $50 fine.[135] The local NAACP branch, working with the Center for Constitutional Rights, brought a federal class action lawsuit against the area Klan on behalf of the

Chattanooga Black community. The lawyers showed that the Klansmen were part of a broader conspiracy. The victims were awarded damages of $535,000, and the judge issued an injunction against the Klan from engaging in violence in Chattanooga.[136]

In 1981 in Alabama, area Klansmen lynched Michael Donald, a young Black man who happened to be in the wrong place shortly after a jury announced that it could not reach a verdict regarding a Black man accused of murdering a white policeman. Two Klan members, Henry Hays and 17-year-old James (Tiger) Knowles, brutally beat and then lynched Donald. Henry's father, Bennie Jack Hays—who as titan of the United Klans was the number-two Klan official in Alabama—declared the body "a pretty sight" as he looked at it. "Gonna look good for the Klan," he said. Earlier, the elder Hays had told Klan members: "if a black man can get away with killing a white man, we ought to be able to get away with killing a black man."[137]

In the past, the Klan as a whole had often been able to avoid responsibility for even the worst outrages of its members, claiming that its leaders had not ordered the violence and even that they would expel those who used it. The SPLC used "agency theory" to argue for vicarious liability—that the Klan should be liable for crimes its members committed in its name—just as if an employee of a corporation carried out the business of an organization as a whole.[138] Part of the genius of the SPLC's approach was to use civil courts, not criminal ones, to go after the Klan. Civil courts require a lower standard to establish guilt. Some states do not require a unanimous jury, and defendants do not always get access to counsel.[139] In the Donald lynching case, Knowles, contrite and in tears, admitted responsibility, called on the jury to "decide a judgment against me and everyone else involved," and pointed the finger at senior leaders in the Klan, helping to prove a broader conspiracy to deny Donald his civil rights. Knowles's testimony also enabled the SPLC to argue that the murder was part of the overall "corporate policy" of the Klan.[140] In 1987, the jury awarded $7 million in damages to Donald's mother.[141]

The verdict devastated the United Klans of America and its leader, Robert Shelton. Criminal trials had failed to stop the Klan, but bankruptcy via the courts at least helped put them out of business. By 1974, they could not regularly print their newsletter, The Fiery Cross, due to financial issues.[142] "The Klan, at this point, is washed up," said Klan member Henry Hays, commenting from death row.[143] In 1997, he became the first person executed in Alabama for white-on-Black crime since 1913. Shelton later lamented,

"The Klan is my belief, my religion. But it won't work anymore. The Klan is gone. Forever."[144]

Other lawsuits also forced the KKK to close down paramilitary camps in Texas, Alabama, and North Carolina. The trial model was to use anti-KKK conspiracy laws dating back from the Reconstruction era to combat white supremacists, with great care taken with jury selection and expert witnesses.[145] Similar SPLC cases devastated other Klan organizations and right-wing groups, and the SPLC emerged as a top enemy of white suprema-cist groups.[146]

The legal campaign against white supremacist groups hurt their finances and ensured that leaders and foot soldiers suffered for their crimes. Though it did not destroy them completely, this campaign marked a dramatic change: no longer would large, top-down organizations be able to use vio-lence covertly while maintaining a public existence. Both the government and powerful civil society organizations hunted them. The shift also reflected a change in popular sentiment. Although local juries at times allowed vio-lent white supremacists to go free, over time, courts increasingly became an enemy of the white supremacist cause.

The white supremacist world would adapt, though the adaptations left it weaker than it was before the civil rights era. Organizations decentralized, and smaller, covert movements came to dominate the white supremacist cause. Networks, rather than formal groups, rose, and new tactics emerged to reflect this lack of organization. The smaller groups, less connected to main-stream society and with less to lose, were often more radical and more vio-lent than their larger and more conservative predecessors. The constant legal action created a sense of victimization—no longer were white men on top. Many of the grievances—Black equality, a Jewish conspiracy, anger at leftists, and so on—endured, but the government, in their eyes, went from an institu-tion that protected white interests to one that opposed it.[147] Not surprisingly, the government itself also became an enemy.

2

Becoming Revolutionaries

The 1988 Fort Smith, Arkansas, trial of 14 white supremacists featured a who's who of the movement, including white power luminaries such as Louis Beam, Richard Butler, and David Lane. Charged with seditious conspiracy—essentially trying to violently overthrow the U.S. government—and conspiracy to murder a federal judge and an FBI agent, among other charges, the men represented a hodgepodge of important hate groups of the time: The Order; The Covenant, the Sword, and the Arm of the Lord (CSA); Aryan Nations; and various KKK organizations. These groups did not just hate Black people; several were dedicated to overthrowing the U.S. government, which they declared to be the "Zionist Occupation Government (ZOG). Those on trial had bombed the house of a priest, a Black police officer, and Alan Berg, a provocative Jewish talk radio host; and The Order had committed a spree of robberies. Prosecutors claimed that the men coordinated this and other violence, benefited from the robberies, and plotted even more crimes.[1]

The trial cast light on the previously murky world of post-civil rights era white supremacists and showed how they were increasingly networked, with group labels mattering less than individual connections. From the early 1970s through the late 1990s, the movement was in transition, with some activists leaving Klan chapters while smaller, often more radical, organizations and individuals came to the fore.

The defendants were unapologetic about their goals. Even before the trial began, Beam—a former grand dragon of the Texas Klan who would become one of the most influential white supremacists of his time—had told prosecutors he would kill international bankers and leading politicians, "most of them white—just like you." When pressed whether he would commit murder to eliminate these supposed threats, he declared, "Murder? It's not called murder when you kill an enemy."[2] Similarly, Robert E. Miles—a former Michigan KKK leader who became the head of the Aryan Nations Church—boasted that the trial would be a stage: "that's the temple of the devil and we're fighting for our race and our god."[3] Lane, not to be outdone, told the court: "I do not recognize a government whose single aim is to exterminate my race. . . . I have given all that I have and all that I am to awake the people from their sleep of death."[4]

Government prosecutors lost the case.[5] One of the key government witnesses, former CSA leader Jim Ellison, seemed to lack credibility: the fact that he had claimed to be the anointed "King of the Ozarks" with the gift of prophecy and had declared one CSA member "spiritually dead," in order to marry his wife, discredited his testimony.[6] The judge threw out much of the evidence, including incriminating computer disks, letters, and photographs. The material had come from an arrest in Mexico, and the FBI had not followed chain of evidence custody procedures properly; it had failed to ask Mexican authorities to obtain a warrant before seizing the materials.[7] Two of the defendants even developed romantic pen-pal relationships with the jurors, resulting in a marriage after the trial ended. ("I never knew when I was filling out the jury questionnaire that my life was going to change the way it has," one noted.)[8] Another juror later told a newspaper he supported white supremacy, and a third said there was nothing wrong with the killing of Berg.[9] Many jurors simply had trouble seeing past the absurdity of what the defendants sought to do; even though the law itself was about intending to overthrow the government, the implausibility of the plots made it hard for some jurors to convict.[10] Beam exulted: "ZOG has suffered a terrible defeat here today."[11] The government even returned seized weapons, including anti-tank guns, to the defendants.

Yet this white power victory proved short-lived. Lane and other members of The Order had already been convicted of a range of crimes in earlier trials, and a lawsuit by the SPLC on behalf of his group's victims would drive figures like Butler to bankruptcy. The government had also proven it was able to flip several prominent white supremacists, swaying them to testify against their fellow believers and creating deep fissures in the broader movement as a result.

The defendants at the Fort Smith trial marked a new form of white power terrorism—one that is with us today in many ways. Klan groups and similar organizations opposed to civil rights had seen themselves as bulwarks of the status quo. In their eyes, they were patriots preserving a system, guarding it against communists, Jews, and especially Black activism, while enforcing social order. Their heavy presence in law enforcement, politics, and other pillars of U.S. society reflected and reinforced this self-image. When political opinion shifted and the government and civil society turned on white supremacists, though, the state was no longer their friend, and politics had become a dead end. By the early 1970s, traditional white power groups were disbanded, penetrated, or demoralized. They needed a new approach if they were to put themselves back on top.

A Changing America

The civil rights movement changed America in the 1960s and 1970s, but it was not the only transformation that affected white male dominance. Greater equality for women, the sexual revolution, and other social changes shook society. Economically, factories were closing, and the steady economic progress white working-class men had made in the post–World War II era was ending.

With the benefit of hindsight, it is easy to overstate the changes; those who lived them saw them as uneven and slow at best. Society as a whole was only slowly emerging from its avowedly racist past. As late as 1970, the United States had over 10,000 "sundown" towns, where Black men and women could not live and were not allowed at night: "Nigger, Don't Let the Sun Go Down On You" was a typical sign in such communities.[12] Women's rights made progress, but it was slow, and LGBTQ+ rights moved even more slowly— leading scholars of the time described American attitudes toward gender and racial equality as "schizophrenic."[13] A new conservativism, which would culminate in Ronald Reagan's presidential win in 1980, was also brewing, in opposition to welfare, abortion, women's rights, and much of the progressive agenda. White supremacists were reacting both to changes the left pushed and to an evolving American right wing.

In addition to these society-wide changes, the federal campaign against Klan chapters and like-minded groups turned them against the U.S. government. In 1971, Robert Shelton, who led the United Klans of America, lamented that the FBI was "no longer the respected and honorable arm of justice that it once appeared to be." The *Fiery Cross* lambasted not only Jews and Black people but also the FBI's unfair targeting and supposed neglect of the threat of the Black Panther Party (when, in fact, the FBI mounted an aggressive covert action campaign against the group).[14] A year later, William Pierce—an American Nazi Party official who would play a transformative role for the movement as a whole and would find himself under regular monitoring by the Bureau—declared the federal government to be a "corrupt, unnatural and degenerate monstrosity."[15] The national media, whose sympathy toward civil rights had frustrated many segregationists, also became increasingly suspect as part of a broader conspiracy: the "Jewsmedia."[16]

Similarly, the movement shifted from focusing on mass political action (as the American Nazi Party had attempted to do in the past) and vigilantism (like that which KKK organizations carried out) to terrorism, executed by small groups or individuals. A successor to the American Nazi Party, the National Socialist Liberation Front, published a poster in the early 1970s that proclaimed "The Future Belongs to the few of us willing to get our hands dirty. Political Terror." The subtitle continued: "It's the only thing they understand."[17] The National Socialist Liberation Front sputtered out, but the concept—that you should still act, even without mass public support—endured, and a range of groups embraced it. Editorials in the *Fiery Cross* began to push the idea of action by an "elite minority," a necessary shift given the collapse of mass action.[18]

Historian Kathleen Belew details how the Vietnam War was a particular source of anger. The white supremacist movement had always drawn on veterans: its Reconstruction-era iteration drew on former Confederate soldiers and leaders; in the 1920s, key figures had fought in the Spanish-American War and World War I; and the civil rights–era Klan movement drew on World War II veterans. Vietnam, however, was a divisive war. Class distinctions shaped who fought, with college students and others with more wealth and higher social positions able to avoid the draft or, if they were drafted, avoid combat in Vietnam. Support for the war fractured too: images of dope-smoking, Che Guevara–loving hippies burning their draft cards appeared in the media, while so-called true patriots favored continuing the fight. These divisions and perceptions spilled over into the white supremacist world. The movement's avowed patriotism and embrace of gun rights—in contrast to the left's antimilitarism—made it easier for white supremacists to attract recruits in the U.S. military and to buy or steal weapons, explosives, and other military materiel. In addition, the presence of many veterans in the movement increased its paramilitary tendencies and capabilities.[19]

The myth had spread that soldiers were "denied permission to win," as President Reagan put it, and the shabby treatment many veterans received on their return further embittered some veterans with white supremacist leanings. Writing in 1982, Beam, a decorated veteran himself, contended: "America's political leaders, bankers, church ministers, newsmen, sports stars and hippies called us 'baby killers,' and threw chicken blood on some of us when we returned home."[20] He stated he would gladly machine-gun everyone who had sent them to war and then mistreated them when they returned. "Over here, if you kill the enemy, you go to jail. Over there in Vietnam, if you killed the enemy, they give you a medal. I couldn't see the difference."[21] These threats were not mere abstractions. When China's leader Deng Xiaoping visited Houston in 1979 as part of a U.S. tour, Beam tried to spray him with red paint in a hotel lobby, only to be foiled when a Secret Service member punched him.[22]

Beam's own journey illustrates the changing nature of the white supremacist movement. After returning from Vietnam in 1968, Beam joined Robert Shelton's United Klans of America. In 1976, Beam joined David Duke's Knights of the Ku Klux Klan, becoming its Texas leader. He provided paramilitary training to members, tried to recruit soldiers at nearby Fort Hood, and would also create and lead a Klan-sponsored local Texas militia he called the Texas Emergency Reserve.[23] Unlike many Klan leaders of the past, Beam focused on networking with, and organizing, leaders and groups within the broader white supremacist movement rather than on his own individual chapter.[24]

One of Beam's initial targets in the post–civil rights era—and one that would further seal the Klan's demise from its previous position as America's leading white supremacist organization—was Vietnamese refugees to the United States who became shrimpers and fishers along the Gulf of Mexico. The harassment he helped perpetrate involved more traditional Klan figures, but it took advantage of new grievances, notably the Vietnam War and the role of immigrants. The Klan entered the fray in 1979 after a dispute between a white crabber and a Vietnamese fisherman led to the shooting and death of the crabber in Seadrift, Texas. Even before the shooting, the local white community had resented the competition the Vietnamese posed and looked disapprovingly on their distinct customs and ways. They also resented the aid the refugees were receiving from the government and the Catholic Church. Area Klan members also feared, somewhat absurdly, that North Vietnamese communists were infiltrating the local Vietnamese community.[25] White supremacists also claimed, somewhat contradictorily (never a problem for this community), that the Vietnamese had smuggled gold out of Vietnam yet were living on massive welfare payments. They spread rumors that the Vietnamese were disease-ridden rapists. One local veteran and shrimper claimed: "Uncle Sam has broken his promise to the Vietnam veterans and kept his promise to the Vietnamese."[26]

Beam vowed to "fight fight fight" and see "blood blood blood."[27] White supremacists firebombed refugees' boats and mobile homes, beat shrimpers, and shot one in the leg. Low-level harassment was nearly constant as well. In 1981, armed Klansmen in robes rode past Vietnamese fishermen on a shrimp boat sporting a cannon and a Vietnamese fisherman figure hung in effigy. A local KKK member even showed up armed and in full Klan regalia when the refugees were giving depositions, making sure they saw him taking pictures of them.[28]

In a shift from the past, white supremacists also embraced military training camps. Drawing on a Texas Veterans Land Board grant, Beam created Camp Puller (named after the legendary Marine Chesty Puller) in an attempt to turn local KKK members into soldiers. In addition to establishing more camps in Arkansas, Colorado, Florida, Mississippi, West Virginia, and other states, he even tried to design an elite special operations force within the KKK. Overall, Camp Puller trained 500 men and even had a program for high-school-age "Explorer Scouts" to learn how to fire weapons, strangle enemies, and hijack airplanes. Locals often did not protest facilities like Camp Puller, fearing reprisals from the violent men there.[29]

As with attacks on civil rights workers, open intimidation and violence failed. Backed by the SPLC and the federal government, the Vietnamese fishers won a court injunction against the area Klan, and it was forbidden from paramilitary training.[30] Thirty years later, the Vietnamese community in Texas is thriving.[31]

The movement interacted uneasily with the conservative politics of the time, both adapting its themes and rejecting what the movement felt was the spinelessness and complacency of the broader conservative movement. White supremacists shared concerns President Reagan raised that the consolidation of communism in Nicaragua or other parts of Central America would lead hundreds of thousands of refugees to flee for America, a local version of the Vietnamese refugee crisis.[32] At the same time, however, Reagan's avowed antiracism and efforts to reach out to new immigrants horrified the white supremacists. "The old ways have failed miserably. . . . Out with the conservatives and in with the radicals," wrote Beam.[33] Indeed, the popular conservative president's rejection of their ideas led many white supremacists to accept that it was the system, not particular politicians, that was the problem.

In part to take advantage of this broader societal anger, some white supremacist leaders sought to change the image of white supremacy from the

white-robed Klansman into something more respectable—the "Klean Klan."
David Duke, for example, talked about moving from "cow pastures" to "hotel
meeting rooms."[34] Duke wore a suit and tie and claimed (falsely) that he did
not hate Jews and Black people but rather was simply "prowhite," even calling
one of his organizations the National Association for the Advancement of
White People. Duke also favored political action over violence. In a move
that would have horrified a previous generation of Klansmen, Duke also
dropped his Klan's ban on Catholics to broaden its appeal.

New and Old Ideas Mingle

As the Klan members' actions against the Vietnamese fishers suggest, the
end of the civil rights era brought other concerns to the fore. Some of the
new ideas can be linked to Nazism, but others involved a mix of different
influences. Networks and ideas cross-pollinated, producing an array of violent groups and individuals.

Klan organizations had kept their distance from Nazi ideas and symbols,
and by 1967 George Lincoln Rockwell, the founder of the American Nazi
Party, recognized that the open embrace of Nazi Germany hurt his cause. He
changed the party's name to the National Socialist White People's Party and
created a "White Power" salute to replace "Sieg Heil."[35] Although Rockwell's
party had only a few hundred members, it was an incubator, with key figures
like James Mason (who joined the Nazi youth wing at 14 and later authored
Siege, a series of influential essays) in its ranks. As Rockwell was changing
the party, however, a disgruntled Nazi whom Rockwell had expelled from
the party assassinated him, leaving the movement leaderless. Rockwell had
stressed mass politics as the key to victory, but his more action-oriented
followers would reject this emphasis and instead focus on violence.[36]

In 1978, William Pierce, a neo-Nazi who wrote under the pseudonym
Andrew McDonald, published *The Turner Diaries*, a fictional work that
would inspire white supremacists around the world after originally being
serialized in the neo-Nazi newspaper *Attack!*[37] Pierce was a physicist who,
fearing a communist takeover of America, had joined the extreme and conspiratorial John Birch Society, which had claimed that President Dwight
Eisenhower—among many others—was a secret communist agent. Pierce
then joined the American Nazi Party and led a splinter cell after Rockwell

died. In 1974, he founded the National Alliance, which, until Pierce's death in 2002, was America's leading neo-Nazi organization.

The Turner Diaries, which had sold over 500,000 copies by 2000 and would later be downloaded countless times, portrayed a dystopic world. The federal government has seized citizens' guns, leaving whites prey to their race enemies. Jews devour Christian children in secret rituals and enslave white women; Black men are constantly raping and killing; and liberals, feminists, and other white enemies tolerate or even encourage these abuses. A heroic secret society of warriors—"The Order"—fights back, with the protagonist, Earl Turner, among them.[38] The Order conducts terrorist attacks against race enemies and the federal government, including an attack on FBI headquarters with a homemade truck bomb. Working along with an overt political movement that seeks to abolish the dollar and keep women subservient, The Order eventually defeats "The System" and perpetrates a genocide against race enemies, uses nuclear weapons to obliterate China and Russia, and exterminates Black people in Africa, allowing white Afrikaners to take over the continent. Although Pierce was a neo-Nazi, *The Turner Diaries* is not tied to any particular ideological current, allowing a wide array of white supremacists to embrace these ideas and this model for action.[39] Describing Pierce's influence, Mark Potok, who worked at the SPLC, noted, "William Pierce doesn't build bombs. He builds bombers."[40]

A sequel novel, *Hunter,* told the story of Oscar Yeager, an assassin for the white supremacist cause. The novel is loosely modeled after the crimes of Joseph Paul Franklin, a white supremacist killer suspected of trying to start a race war by shooting 17 people between 1977 and 1980. He largely acted alone but had many acquaintances in the broader white supremacist movement and was a member of a Klan chapter and a neo-Nazi group.[41] Franklin was born James Vaughn, but, before he began his killing spree, he changed his name to Joseph Paul Franklin to honor the Nazi leader Paul Joseph Goebbels and Benjamin Franklin, tying himself and Nazism to one of America's founding fathers.

In addition to authoring *The Turner Diaries* and *Hunter,* Pierce had another success in using "art" to win converts. He pushed white power music and, for a while, owned Resistance Records, a leading white power label, in the early 2000s. Music, in Pierce's mind, had aided the left in the 1960s and 1970s, and Jews were "stealing our youth away using MTV." To counter this, Pierce pushed his own brand, often distributing it for free. T. J. Leyden, a former white power activist, remembered: "our motto was: 'You do not want the weekend patriot, you want his son.' "[42]

In addition to *The Turner Diaries*, the bizarre teachings of Christian Identity became an important intellectual influence within the white supremacist world by the 1980s. An offshoot of an obscure nineteenth-century British ideological movement notable for its extreme anti-Semitism, Christian Identity claims that Anglo-Saxons, not Jews, are the true "chosen people" referenced in the Bible. Jews are supposedly descended from Satan, while Black people and other nonwhites are "mud people." Christian Identity theology teaches that there is currently (or will soon be) a race war between whites and nonwhites, with Jews often the manipulators of Black criminals and other minorities. Christian Identity, like many variants of the white supremacist movement, embraced a range of conspiracy theories and sought to "wake up" ordinary Americans.[43] By 1996, Christian Identity churches and political organizations had thousands of adherents in the United States.[44]

Many Christian Identity congregations rejected violence, but violent individuals and organizations like Aryan Nations, the CSA, and White Aryan Resistance (WAR) emerged from Christian Identity, including many of those who went on trial at Fort Smith. These groups were often more extreme than the civil rights–era Klan, seeing Jews and the Black community as an existential threat that was perpetuating a creeping genocide against whites.

David Lane, who became an important ideologue, was one such extreme member. Lane was a lifetime racist and Hitler admirer. Like Pierce, he at first joined the John Birch Society, attracted to its extreme anticommunism. He then organized a Colorado chapter of the Knights of the Ku Klux Klan, David Duke's organization, but was expelled for distributing neo-Nazi literature. Lane also lost his job as a realtor because he refused to sell homes in white neighborhoods to Black buyers.[45] Over time, Lane became convinced that the Jews were the true enemy behind every evil plaguing America, and he even argued that Jews had controlled the founding fathers and that America had become "the most vile political entity on Earth."[46] He turned to Christian Identity and would later go one step further and turn to Odinism, believing that Christianity had robbed whites of their purity and vigor. Lane also joined Tom Metzger's WAR. Many white supremacists find their credo embodied in Lane's "14 words," which he penned in prison: "we must secure the existence of our people and a future for white children." Some groups add a fifteenth word, inserting "Christian" between "white" and "children."

Aryan Nations, founded as the political arm of the Church of Jesus Christ–Christian, proved a particularly important incubator. The church's leader, Richard Butler, admired Hitler, had a long history of fascist and extreme anti-communist activity, and sought a whites-only "national racial state" in the Pacific Northwest. Butler also convened the "Aryan World Congress" at his compound in Hayden Lake, Idaho. This annual meeting saw a range of white supremacists of different stripes there—hundreds by the mid-1980s (along with a few FBI informants).[47] Tom Metzger, the leader of WAR, attended, as did Beam, who would embrace Christian Identity and become prominent in Aryan Nations, and Don Black, another KKK grand wizard. Militia figures such as James Wickstrom and John Trochmann also attended. Lane settled there for several months as well, becoming "propaganda minister" for the Aryan Nations.[48] The congress was a talk shop where a range of white supremacists shared ideas, and it offered paramilitary training. Jim Ellison, the leader of the CSA, who later became a government witness, claimed that in 1983 white supremacists at Hayden Lake agreed to step up violence to topple the government and create an all-white state in the Northwest.[49] (The Aryan Nations should not be confused with the Aryan Brotherhood, a white supremacist prison gang.)

Embodying the mix of different strands were members of The Order (which also called itself the Silent Brotherhood), the ultraviolent white supremacist group that took its name from the fictional white resistance group in The Turner Diaries. The Order emerged as an important terrorist group and committed a spree of attacks in 1984 and 1985. Its leader, Robert Mathews, had, like many others, begun as an extreme anticommunist and then had later moved to the neo-Nazi National Alliance and then Aryan Nations but decided that the movement needed a small, action-focused arm. The charismatic Mathews presented the idea of creating such an arm at the Aryan Nations Congress in 1983. The group he formed had members from WAR, Aryan Nations, and other Christian Identity and white supremacist believers but consisted only of a few dozen individuals, with a few dozen more linked to the group indirectly. With a portrait of Hitler looking on, The Order's founding members swore an oath to save the white race "from the Jew and bring total victory to the Aryan race"—over the infant of a new recruit, a living embodiment of the white race they claimed to protect.[50] The Order spanned multiple states, allowing the group to operate widely and to enjoy safe houses in different parts of the country.[51]

In 1984, members of The Order assassinated Jewish radio host Alan Berg and bombed a synagogue in Boise. In addition to ridiculing white supremacists in general, the outspoken Berg had mocked Lane in particular when Lane had called in to Berg's radio show. After publicly airing his racist beliefs, Lane had lost his job selling advertisements.[52] The Order also bombed a pornographic theater in Seattle and the house of William Wassmuth, a Roman Catholic priest in Idaho who was a vocal opponent of the neo-Nazis.[53] Mathews especially wanted to kill Morris Dees, the head of the SPLC.[54] The Order also carried out a spree of robberies, including an armored car heist that netted $3.6 million, and used the stolen money to help other white power organizations as part of an effort to foment a race war—the same method the fictional group in *The Turner Diaries* employed. The members of The Order sought to awaken whites to the danger of the Zionist Occupational Government. For all the violence of The Order, Mathews told the members to avoid minor conflicts with racial minorities, seeing such conflicts as distractions that would bring law enforcement attention prematurely. Instead, the goal was to overthrow the government, and murders were to be saved for important figures such as Dees.[55]

After the murder of Berg, the FBI began a full-scale investigation into The Order. The Bureau tapped phones and tracked phone calls, vehicles, and travel patterns. The FBI also tapped into Aryan Nations' computer bulletin board, finding an array of death threats there.[56]

The FBI eventually penetrated the group with an informant and arrested most of its other members. After a failed arrest and a shootout with authorities from which Mathews escaped, The Order's leader holed up in a house on Whidbey Island on Washington's Puget Sound along with six of his confederates. Federal agents besieged the house and, after a two-day standoff with several exchanges of fire, dropped white phosphorous illumination flares onto the house, which set off a fire in which Mathews died.[57]

Other members of The Order were arrested, and some informed on their fellows, resulting in even more arrests.[58] In 1985, Lane, along with nine other surviving members of The Order, was convicted of conspiracy and racketeering, and Lane and several other group members were later convicted of killing Berg. Lane died in prison in 2007.

In a sign of the growing internationalization of movement figures, white supremacists around the world, many of whom had not been alive when Lane was operationally active, mourned his death. There were demonstrations in his honor in the United Kingdom, Germany, Russia, and Ukraine, as well as five American cities.[59] The Order itself also inspired spinoff groups, some composed of members with links to the original organization, that committed several murders and bombings before their members were caught and jailed.[60] For many future white supremacists, the fact that The Order acted rather than just talked was inspiring.

Although these groups' memberships were overwhelmingly male, women featured prominently in their visions for a white supremacist future. Lane and others portrayed white women as holy but delicate, needing protection so they could propagate the race—a quite different depiction from the misogynistic, epithet-spewing approach of many white supremacists today. As such, The Order recommended that no member should "raise their sword against ZOG, until he planted his seed in the belly of a woman."[61] Lane himself seemed like an unlikely leader in this area. One journalist described him as "a pitiful, lonely, sexually frustrated figure at neo-Nazi meetings."[62] While in prison, Lane lamented that "not one unmarried, attractive woman" ever visited him, while, he claimed, incarcerated Black Panthers enjoyed the attentions of thousands of white women.[63]

The movement also began to think more globally. Anticommunism and racism melded for many in the movement, and these were causes they championed internationally as well as at home. Before white supremacists gave up control of Rhodesia and ended the civil war there in 1980, when the country was renamed Zimbabwe, over 2,000 Americans, including some neo-Nazis, traveled there to fight.[64] White supremacists also plotted to topple the government of the island of Dominica.[65] As historian Belew contends, "after 1983, the nation in white nationalism was not the United States, but rather a transnational 'Aryan nation' that hoped to unite white people around the world in a violent conquest of people of color."[66]

Convergence with the Militia Movement

The increasingly antigovernment nature of the white supremacist movement led it to mix and overlap with antigovernment militias by the 1990s. Lane, Pierce, and other important white supremacist figures came out of the John Birch Society, with its deep-rooted paranoia about communist infiltration. Government support of civil rights and crackdowns on the Klan and radical white supremacist groups like The Order made the government a true enemy for white supremacists. In addition, revelations about COINTELPRO, other

FBI wiretapping and monitoring, and the Bureau's use of informants made it seem, with some justification, that the government was disrupting their constitutionally protected rights.[67] Critically, this white supremacist shift against the government also overlapped with a massive shift in the militia movement itself.

The end of the Cold War ended the long-feared communist threat, but over time, hostility toward the federal government replaced the danger of communism in the eyes of militia members. As Beam wrote, "communism now represents a threat to no one in the United States, while federal tyranny represents a threat to *everyone.*"[68] The government did not help matters. Its responses to two standoffs—Ruby Ridge and Waco—were so bungled that they fed conspiracy theories and left key agencies shy about confronting domestic groups. Militia movements surged in the 1990s.

In 1992, U.S. Marshals Service deputies sought to arrest Randy Weaver, who had refused to appear in court on a firearms charge. Weaver and his wife, Vicki—who had built a cabin together in northern Idaho, near the Canadian border, in an area known as Ruby Ridge—saw the world as corrupt and believed its end was nigh. Weaver claimed that he was not a "hateful racist," but he openly favored racial separation and embraced the ZOG conspiracy and various Christian Identity beliefs. Another dystopian novel, *Late Great Planet Earth,* which portrayed a world of true Christians fighting Jews and immigrants, shaped the Weavers' worldview.[69] A former Green Beret, Weaver was known to be wellarmed and had declared that he would not surrender to authorities. Adding fuel to the situation, a neighbor with a grudge over a land deal alleged that Weaver was threatening to kill the president and other public figures. There were also reports that Weaver was a member of Aryan Nations. Those reports appear to have been false, though Weaver did attend several meetings, had ties to members of the CSA, and had attended the World Aryan Congress in 1986.[70]

Weaver sold an informant from the Bureau of Alcohol, Tobacco, and Firearms (ATF) two sawed-off shotguns that were shorter than the legal limit, and the ATF tried to use this crime as leverage to turn Weaver into an informant against Aryan Nations. He refused. The ATF then filed charges against him not only for the gun violation but also claiming he was a bank robber, a false charge. He was arrested away from his home, released on bail, and told to appear in court.[71] Confusion about the date ensued, and he did not appear in court, leading the ATF to pass the case to the Marshals Service. The Marshals Service assumed the level of danger was high. A Department of Justice memo later noted that law enforcement personnel assumed that the former Green Beret "would shoot on sight" and had even booby-trapped his property, both exaggerated assumptions that inflated Weaver's perceived threat.[72] Sensationalist "journalist" Geraldo Rivera flew a helicopter over the property, and media reporting indicated that Weaver had fired at it—another false report that, nevertheless, was taken as fact.[73]

The sequencing is disputed, but it appears that when members of the Marshals Service reconnoitered Weaver's property, the family dog, Striker, detected them. They shot Striker to silence him, leading to a shootout that killed Weaver's 14-year-old son and a marshal, who was shot by Kevin Harris, a family friend of the Weavers. It is not clear who started the shooting, and both sides claimed self-defense. At this point, the FBI took over and besieged the Weaver home. Around 300 white power activists flocked to Weaver's home in Ruby Ridge in protest.[74]

The FBI rules of engagement at Ruby Ridge were exceptionally aggressive, allowing deadly force to be used without warning on any adult male seen with a weapon unless children would be endangered. The senior FBI hostage negotiator at Ruby Ridge said that it was the harshest set of rules he had seen in more than 300 standoffs, surpassing the standard approach, which only allowed agents to use deadly force in self-defense. When Weaver left his cabin to go to his dead son's body, a sniper shot him, wounding him in the arm. The sniper fired again as Weaver ran, wounding Harris and killing Vicki Weaver, who was standing behind the cabin door when Harris entered as she held her baby in her arms.[75]

Weaver would eventually be acquitted of almost all charges except for violating bail conditions and missing a court date.[76] The government also later admitted that it had falsified evidence related to the case. Harris, Weaver, and Weaver's family won settlements from the government totaling almost $3.5 million.[77] Subsequent government hearings and internal investigations blasted both the FBI and the Marshals Service for how they handled the siege, and an FBI official went to prison for destroying evidence and then lying about it to investigators.[78] The deaths of innocents, the lies, and the sense of federal overreach galvanized the white power movement even as it made federal agents far more cautious.

Similar government bungling led to a bloody end to a siege in Waco, Texas, a year later in 1993. There, a millenarian community led by David Koresh was preparing for the apocalypse in their compound. The cult was believed also to have a history of violence against its own members, and Koresh declared that he was assembling an "Army for God" to prepare for the end days. He also took multiple brides, some reportedly as young as 12, and began to accumulate weapons. The Davidians were also active gun traders and were well known in local militia circles as a result. False reports also circulated, including claims that Koresh operated a methamphetamine lab.[79]

Again, federal agents from the ATF and FBI laid siege, and again it ended in disaster. Koresh learned of the raid in advance. (A reporter who had been tipped off asked for directions to the compound from a mail carrier, who happened to be Koresh's brother-in-law.) As the raid commenced, ATF agents reportedly discharged their weapons, though who fired first remains unclear. In any event, there was a firefight with deaths on both sides. The ATF agents withdrew, and a siege commenced. Again, the FBI took over, and pressure grew to resolve the situation with force, with the FBI citing Koresh's physical and sexual abuse of children as its key justification for action and arguing that Koresh would never surrender peacefully. Fearing the Davidians' formidable arsenal, the government assembled a massive force, including tanks, armored personnel carriers, and almost 1,000 soldiers, police, and other law enforcement officials. When government forces finally stormed the compound, fires—probably set by Koresh's followers—raged and engulfed much of the compound. In total, four ATF special agents died along with over 80 Davidians, including pregnant women and 21 children.[80]

For the militia movement, the role of the ATF and the prominence the government gave to the Davidians' weapons caches was proof that the government was planning to disarm America. (Later conspiracy believers would claim that Hillary Clinton was responsible for the decision to storm Waco.) The same sniper who had accidentally killed Vicki Weaver was also at Waco, heightening conspiracy theories.[81]

Although Koresh's followers were multiracial, the white supremacist movement portrayed the victims as whites and presented the siege as another attempt by the federal government to suppress whites who just wanted to live their lives in freedom.[82] Other conspiracy theories flourished, aided by government lies and secrecy in attempts to cover up mistakes. A government investigation found that the FBI had failed to disclose important documents and information to the courts and Congress and some FBI officials had obstructed a special counsel investigation.[83] Texas state authorities quickly bulldozed the compound, claiming that this would prevent accidents in the various pits and ruined buildings, but the Davidians' lawyer argued that it had prevented the gathering of forensic evidence.[84] In nearby Austin, Waco also made a deep impression on a high school student, Alex Jones, who would become one of America's leading conspiracy theorists.[85] Waco and Ruby Ridge became rallying cries. As extremism expert J. M. Berger points out, "you don't need an actual injustice to fuel an extremist movement, but it helps."[86]

Despite the government's many mistakes, most Americans initially supported the actions of the FBI and other government agencies. However, as reports of bungling grew and investigations commenced, approval of the FBI's handling of the Waco standoff dropped from 70 percent, when the events occurred in early 1993, to 38 percent in October 1999.[87] The FBI and other government agencies became far more cautious and more likely to try to end standoffs with antigovernment groups peacefully.[88] The result was a difficult middle ground. As the SPLC wrote, "what [law enforcement] learned from Waco was that a heavy-handed approach risks a major loss of life. Yet, allowing the antigovernment movement to flout the law at gunpoint is surely not the answer."[89]

Increasing their impact, Ruby Ridge and Waco occurred against a background of broader change. The election of Bill Clinton, the Los Angeles riots, successful gun control legislation, and even NAFTA (the North American Free Trade Agreement) created a sense of fear and vulnerability among white supremacists. They worried that NAFTA meant more immigrants would come to America, the riots showed that minorities would use violence, and gun control robbed citizens of the means to stop the violence.[90] Globalization added to white supremacists' grievances, and in conservative politics criticisms of immigration became more prominent. After the 1994 signing of NAFTA, the number of Mexicans entering the United States almost doubled, and migration from other Central American countries surged.[91] Pat Buchanan ran insurgent campaigns for the Republican presidential nomination in 1992 and 1996, calling for cutting immigration. Although he lost to George H. W. Bush in 1992, Buchanan won over 20 percent of the primary vote, a huge slice against a sitting president. In addition to opposing immigration, Buchanan condemned other liberal values that white supremacists also opposed. At the 1992 Republican Convention, he claimed that a Clinton presidency would mean "abortion on demand . . . homosexual rights . . . [and] women in combat units." He also condemned immigrants: "they've got no right to break our laws and break into our country and go on welfare, and some of them commit crimes."[92]

Many militias' focus was not white supremacy but what they saw as government overreach, particularly with regard to gun control. However, in practice, this was often bound up with the issue of race. Part of ZOG's goal, after all, was to use government power to disarm upstanding citizens so they could be controlled and oppressed. Race mixing was part of this danger, in the eyes of many.[93] Symbols from the past also emerged in new contexts; the Confederate flag began to appear at "patriotic" rallies in northern cities like Detroit.[94]

Despite being incredibly well armed, the militia movement was less violent than might be expected. Many of its members were waiting for the federal government to bring the fight to them by attempting to seize their guns and handing over the country to the United Nations—a wait that may never end.[95] In addition, militia rallies did not generate the large opposing crowds that white supremacist rallies generated, reducing concerns for public safety. Frequently, however, militia members refused to leave property that the government foreclosed on or to give themselves up to criminal charges, claiming that the government was illegitimate. The resulting standoffs often led to violence.[96]

Conspiracy theories were (and remain) rampant among the militia movement, and these steadily merged with white supremacist paranoia. Many of these theories involved government gun seizures, but they also included claims that Federal Emergency Management Agency camps built for disaster relief were really internment camps for white Americans, that tens of thousands of UN troops were training on U.S. military bases, and so on.[97] White supremacists integrated these into their fear of ZOG, claiming that it wanted to admit immigrants to dilute the white population, use welfare to encourage Black people to have more children, support interracial marriage and abortion as demographic weapons, and otherwise constantly plot to put whites down.[98] The lack of evidence for most of these theories is taken as further proof: ZOG is able to suppress evidence of its power, except from the cognoscenti.[99] Former FBI agent Michael German contends that this conspiracy worldview constantly shapes white supremacists' interpretations of events and that they often lash out against an injustice or government aggression that is more perceived than real.[100]

Oklahoma City

The mix of antigovernment ideology and white supremacy culminated on April 19, 1995, the second anniversary of the Waco assault that had led to so many innocents being killed. In an attack ripped from the pages of *The Turner Diaries,* ex-soldier Timothy McVeigh parked a truck filled with homemade explosives alongside the Alfred P. Murrah Federal Building in Oklahoma City. The bomb blew off the front of the building, destroyed nearby cars, and damaged other buildings, killing 168 people, including 19 children. Terry Nichols, an army buddy of McVeigh, had helped build the bomb, and a third man, Michael Fortier, was also aware of the plot.[101] Oklahoma City was the worst terrorist attack in U.S. history at that point and remains the second worst after 9/11.

The government killings at Ruby Ridge had enraged McVeigh, a gun-lover who had just left the military and was living with his parents in exurban Buffalo when the fiasco occurred. During his time in the military, McVeigh had made derogatory remarks about Black soldiers and otherwise showed scorn for them.[102] Waco infuriated McVeigh, and he traveled there as the siege was unfolding.[103] McVeigh himself sought to inspire the masses, waking them up through his bloody attack, and would go to his death believing that he had succeeded.[104] Citizen militias are necessary in order that "all you tyrannical motherfuckers will swing in the wind one day," he said.[105]

In preparing for the attack, McVeigh mixed deadly skill with stunning incompetence. The homemade bomb he built out of fertilizer and other materials was as powerful as over two tons of TNT.[106] He used the same basic bomb design as the one described in great detail in *The Turner Diaries.* After the bombing, however, he drove away in a car with no license plate, which led a state trooper to pull him over for driving without a tag. He was carrying an unlicensed handgun as well. As if to make himself especially suspicious, he wore a T-shirt that declared on its front: "Thus, always, to tyrants"—the words of John Wilkes Booth after shooting Lincoln—and on its back Thomas Jefferson's pronouncement that "the tree of liberty must be refreshed from time to time with the blood of patriots and tyrants."[107]

Although McVeigh's bombing was often depicted as a man acting with only a small group of confederates, the broader network on which he drew was large. After leaving the military, he regularly went to gun shows popular with militia movement members to hawk *The Turner Diaries* and was also tapped into broader antigovernment and white supremacist networks, spending time with members of the Christian Identity movement.[108] He may have learned how to make his bomb at a popular gun show at Knob Creek in Kentucky. He listened to right-wing militia and nationalistic radio broadcasts and read their literature.[109] When he committed the bombing, he brought with him photocopied pages of *The Turner Diaries* that described attacks by the novel's white supremacist group The Order, one of which included the quote: "the real value of all our attacks today lies in the psychological impact, not in the immediate casualties." Another quote read: "they learned today that not one of them is beyond our reach."[110]

Shortly before McVeigh acted, an undercover informant provided very specific warnings from nearby Elohim City, a rural Oklahoma City community where many Christian Identity members lived and where members of CSA had plotted to blow up the Murrah building in 1983.[111] The informant reported that federal buildings in Oklahoma and Texas were being targeted for an attack that would occur on the second anniversary of the Waco bombing, but federal officials failed to act.[112] McVeigh also repeatedly phoned the National Alliance several times, though it remains unclear why he did so, and it appears he just listened to a recorded message.[113]

After the debacle of the Fort Smith seditious conspiracy trial, the Department of Justice decided to focus on individual prosecutions, not on broad group-level conspiracies.[114] Indeed, McVeigh's lawyers tried to show a broader conspiracy to deflect attention from him, leading the Department of Justice to avoid pushing any hint of a conspiracy.[115]

Why They Failed

White supremacists had a bloody track record from the end of the civil rights era through the 1990s, but they failed to ignite a revolution, expand their ranks significantly, or make any political progress. Three of the groups that dominated the movement before 9/11—Aryan Nations, Pierce's neo-Nazi National Alliance, and the World Church of the Creator—all quickly collapsed in the years that followed, often due to government pressure or the inability to transition to a new leader when one died or was arrested.

As it did against Klan organizations, the SPLC supported lawsuits against white supremacists. In 1998, Victoria Keenan, a Native American, and her son Jason were returning from a wedding in Idaho. Jason had accidentally dropped his wallet outside the Aryan Nations compound, and the Keenans stopped to retrieve it. As they drove away, a car backfired or a similar noise occurred that led the jumpy compound guards to assume they were under attack. The guards followed the Keenans' car, shooting out a tire and forcing the car into a ditch. The guards then threatened them at gunpoint.[116] With the help of the SPLC, the Keenans sued. The result was a judgment for over $6 million, effectively bankrupting the group and allowing the Keenans to take the Idaho compound and other assets. In 1990, the SPLC won judgments against WAR leaders Tom Metzger and his son John for the skinhead killing of an Ethiopian student in Oregon; the $12.5 million jury award bankrupted the group.[117]

Under legal and financial pressure, various groups splintered and splintered again—a desirable result, from the government's point of view, but one that made the movement even less coherent.[118] Even respected and strong personalities like Pierce and Butler could not unite the movement. When Pierce died in 2002, the National Alliance suffered leadership disputes and was poorly managed. It had 1,500 members in 2000 but, a decade later, had only a few dozen.[119] When Butler died in 2004, Aryan Nations also declined quickly. Over time, it and many other once-strong groups became more collections of like-minded individuals rather than formal groups.

In addition to arrests and organizational collapse, the groups failed on a strategic level. The beguiling script of *The Turner Diaries* proved a fantasy, not a blueprint. Even the most active group, The Order, failed to inspire the broader public to rise up. Timothy McVeigh's mass murder repelled, rather than inspired, the broader public. Less prominent violence by skinheads, Klansmen, and other racists made life miserable for their victims, but they did not stop the march of multiculturalism and gender equality or the flow of immigrants to the United States.

The Limits of the Government Response

The U.S. government, however, had its problems too. One was a post–Fort Smith reluctance to treat the white supremacist movement as a broader conspiracy, focusing instead on individual convictions. Fort Smith showed that many Americans had difficulty believing that self-professed patriots organized into small groups would, or could, overthrow the U.S. government. Although an individual-focused approach was easier legally, it created several problems. First, the reach of the government was limited as a result: cases like Oklahoma City, which indirectly involved dozens of people, only saw a few convicted. Second, this approach focused on the bombers and shooters to the neglect of groups as a whole. For many groups, it is the people who provide training, raise money, recruit, and otherwise sustain the organization who are the most important—not the person who pulls the trigger. The government's approach made it harder to disrupt the broader network.

After Ruby Ridge and then Waco, the government was also politically scarred when it came to antigovernment militias. At times, the resulting caution was positive. When the FBI engaged in a standoff with the Montana Freemen in 1996, it ended with successful negotiations that led the Freemen to surrender after 81 days.[120] However, government's reluctance to act decisively, for fear of a repeat of Waco or Roby Ridge, often allowed antigovernment groups to intimidate local communities and escape justice.

The FBI's counterintelligence efforts also had mixed results. The FBI proved skilled at infiltrating white supremacist groups and fostering suspicion in their ranks, depressing recruitment and hindering operations. However, terrorism expert J. M. Berger details the way the FBI used informants and undercover officers against the movement in the 1990s in Operation Patriot Conspiracy—PATCON. In this operation, undercover FBI agents posed as members of the Veterans Aryan Movement, a fictional group, and targeted real militia organizations. The investigations produced no significant criminal convictions, but when the operation's existence was inevitably leaked, the broader movement unsurprisingly saw this as part of a government conspiracy and blamed any problems on agents provocateurs. This led the movement to become even more inclined to believe conspiracies and further question the government's legitimacy. Oklahoma City, in their eyes, had been a government plot designed to discredit patriots and allow the seizure of guns.[121]

Finally, the effort against white supremacist groups often neglected politics. With even conservative leaders like Reagan condemning white supremacy and rejecting figures like Duke, this seemed a safe move. Yet many of the issues involving white supremacists moved toward the political mainstream. In the 1990s, congressional leaders often condemned the FBI, even alleging conspiracies, after the fiascos of Ruby Ridge and Waco. Some even claimed that militia members' fear of the federal government was legitimate and that the attacks were part of a Clinton administration conspiracy to prove the need for bans on assault weapons.[122]

Yet, despite these problems, counterterrorism officials could legitimately feel in the years after Oklahoma City that the white supremacist terrorist threat was contained. During President George W. Bush's eight years in office, white supremacists killed fewer than 20 people, according to data from the New America Foundation, mostly in one-off attacks that barely made the newspapers.[123]

Indeed, the next massive white supremacist attack occurred not in the United States but in Europe.

3

"Mein Kampf to a 4/4 Beat"

Ian Stuart Donaldson, the god of white power rock, embodied a European version of the antisystem shift occurring among white supremacists in America. A longtime white supremacist and Hitler admirer, Donaldson and his band, Skrewdriver, would later be referred to as the "godfathers" of white power music—a genre that would have a profound impact on the white power movement, especially its younger members. Even today, Skrewdriver songs written in the 1980s remain popular downloads in the white power community, and Donaldson himself is a hero to many.

Donaldson's legacy is interwoven with that of the skinheads, who embraced a working-class, white nationalist identity and proved exceptionally violent. Skinheads spread from the United Kingdom to the world as part of a generational change for the white power community. Although the specifics varied by country, from the 1980s to the 2000s, skinheads were responsible for much of the world's white supremacist violence.

The skinheads adopted a distinctive style, setting them apart from the mainstream. A black bomber jacket, steel-toed boots, and bleached jeans or combat pants complemented the necessary shaved head and provided a sharp contrast to the leftist, supposedly sissy, hippie culture of long hair and tie-dyes. Specific grievances and points of pride might be embodied by tattoos or jacket patches. Over time, the dress code became more threatening, with taller boots, military surplus jackets, and other touches. In part because of their distinctive dress code, skinheads saw themselves as a specific community rejected by the mainstream but bound to each other; "hated but proud" was one motto.

Europe does not have America's legacy of slavery to shape attitudes toward race, and there is no counterpart to the Klan. At the same time, European countries are not proud nations of immigrants (whatever the more conflicted realities on the ground may be in the United States), and they too have legacies of fascism, imperialism, and anti-Semitism that have conditioned attitudes toward white supremacist groups and their supporters. Furthermore, for much of the post–World War II era, many European states had strong communist or socialist parties, and the threat of communism, both internal and external, was far more real. For most of the postwar era, "right-wing" terrorism in Europe had only a limited overlap with white supremacy. Though many in the movement had little love for Jews or foreign migrants, they focused primarily on what they saw as an anticommunist mission, opposing left-wing street movements and socialist governments in Europe, as well as trying to preserve imperial legacies, as in France.[1]

In the 1970s and 1980s, just as American white supremacists were turning away from large and organized local groups and becoming part of more radical organizations and antisystem networks, so, too, a new generation of white supremacists was emerging in Europe—a generation not dominated by the shadow of World War II. In the United Kingdom, the National Front arose in the late 1960s, and its political party gained 15,000 members and received 250,000 votes in municipal elections. It attracted some open neo-Nazis as well as disgruntled conservatives and people who rejected Britain's move away from its empire.[2] A primary National Front demand was an end to nonwhite immigration and the expulsion of nonwhite immigrants from the United Kingdom; this demand had echoes in broader society. Enoch Powell, a conservative member of Parliament who had served as minister of health, warned of a race war if immigration was not controlled. He contended that white citizens "found themselves made strangers in their own country," with "their wives unable to obtain hospital beds in childbirth, their children unable to obtain school places, their homes and neighborhoods changed beyond recognition, their plans and prospects for the future defeated."[3] An economic depression in 1973 hit the working class hard, exacerbating hostility toward immigrants, many of whom were South Asian and African in origin. As Kristen Dyck points out, immigrants were blamed simultaneously for working too hard and taking jobs from "real" Brits and, at the same time, for being lazy freeloaders who came to the country to exploit the welfare system.[4]

Ironically, British skinheads initially modeled themselves after Jamaican immigrants, who in turn modeled themselves after antiauthority "rude boys" from the Kingston ghettos.[5] Punk rock, emerging in the 1970s, often defined itself in opposition to leftist, melodic, hippie bands like the Grateful Dead. One punk variant popular among skinheads was the "Oi!" variant, named after the common cockney greeting. Most bands were apolitical, and many skinheads rejected racism, but a strong strand emerged that embraced both.[6] One of the most famous punk bands, the Sex Pistols, released "Belsen Was a

Gas" in 1978, with the song calculated to outrage mainstream opinion.[7] The
Sex Pistols' Sid Vicious wore a swastika to further their shock value (though
the Sex Pistols, despite their desire to foster outrage, had a degree of sophistication that was rare in the genre and did not support racist skinheads and
neo-Nazism).[8] By 1980, skinheads were giving the "Sieg Heil" salute at Oi!
concerts.[9]

White supremacist political groups played an important role in shaping
the skinhead movement, using music as a lure and entry point, especially for
young people.[10] In 1977, the National Front established the Young National
Front, and the British Movement, an openly Nazi group, also established a
youth wing, emphasizing the need for street combat.

Donaldson himself began as an ordinary rock-and-roller. Skrewdriver's
1977 debut album, "All Skrewed Up," had both punk and rock-and-roll
influences and even included a cover of Pete Townshend's "Won't Get Fooled
Again." Donaldson, however, saw the emerging punk scene as too leftist and
became increasingly involved with the National Front. Its supporters flocked
to Skrewdriver concerts. Donaldson's refusal to denounce the National Front,
and racist skinheads in general, led mainstream concert halls and recording
labels to shun Skrewdriver. The original group broke up over the question of
how much to associate with white supremacy, but Donaldson re-formed it
(and would do so repeatedly), becoming more and more engaged with the
British far right.[11]

To mock the leftist "Rock against Racism" effort, Donaldson and the
National Front created a series of concerts they labeled "Rock against
Communism" in 1979, which sponsored concerts and sold skinhead albums
that mainstream labels would not issue. The group's concerts became known
for fights and riots that broke out between fans and local Black people or
Asians. Soon, Skrewdriver gigs mimicked Nazi rallies. As Donaldson sang
and preached from the stage, hundreds of skinheads shouted "Sieg Heil."[12]
Donaldson himself gave the Hitler salute in 1982 and in 1984 he released the
album "Hail to the New Dawn," with songs that were openly racist, for example "Free My Land."[13]

Donaldson's music railed against a range of foes. "For my race and nation,
Race and nation, Race and nation, Race and nation" was the chorus to the
Skrewdriver song titled, predictably, "Race and Nation." Another set of lyrics
declared: "Refugee, you're not fooling me / Refugee, you just want a jobs mo-
nopoly," with a chorus raging: "Get out of my country / Get out, we don't want
you around / Get out, is what the people shout / Get out, get out of my sight /

Get out, parasite." The song concluded by calling for politicians to "send the bastards back / If they don't fucking like it, they'll be in body bags."[14] Some Skrewdriver songs, like "European Battle Song" and "Europe Awake," also emphasized white unity and how it crossed borders.[15]

For the National Front, music sales were vital both for recruiting new members and for helping to keep it afloat financially. Donaldson also helped expand the reach of white power music beyond the United Kingdom, signing a contract with Rock-O-Rama, a German label, to export National Front–backed bands into Germany. The British influence on the German scene was profound. German white power music celebrated the skinhead look of shaved heads and tattoos and supposed working-class behaviors like drinking and fighting. German skinheads even used the British flag as a sign of allegiance to skinhead culture.[16] All of this was organized around a "blood and soil" mythos that stressed German nationalism and pagan Norse roots. The casual violence associated with the skinheads was also exported. Skrewdriver band members and fans smashed windows and assaulted long-haired Germans during a tour in Germany.[17] In 1991, a skinhead gang shoved a Mozambican man off of a moving streetcar in Dresden, killing him; this was one of many assaults on immigrants by skinheads in Germany. In France in 1994, four skinheads left a National Front rally in Paris and pushed a Moroccan man, Brahim Bouarram, into the Seine as he was walking along its bank. Bouarram drowned as they watched.[18]

When the National Front imploded, in part because some of its members wanted to broaden its popular appeal by moving away from overt racism, Donaldson, along with several other white power musicians, created a skinhead music production organization in 1987 called Blood & Honour, named after the slogan inscribed on the blades of Hitler Youth knives. In contrast to the National Front, Blood & Honour pushed music as its main brand, with politics coming in through the back door. By the early 1990s, Blood & Honour, which also came to be known for its glossy magazines, had 30,000 members worldwide.[19]

Donaldson died in a car accident in 1993, though conspiracy theorists quickly claimed that the Jewish-controlled British government had killed him. Even before the crash, Donaldson had seemed to be withdrawing from the white power music scene, playing fewer concerts and passing on some of his Blood & Honour responsibilities. He had served short terms in prison for assault, and he told friends he did not wish to go behind bars again. His concerts had to have elaborate security procedures; even with these in place, the concerts were often canceled or had fans fail to show up due to confusion as to where to go and what the passwords were. In addition, Donaldson's right-hand man and fellow brawler, Nicky Crane, who had long been a secret homosexual (and had even appeared in several gay porn films), revealed it on television—a tremendous betrayal for Donaldson, who declared homosexuality "a perversion."[20]

The National Front had recruited soccer hooligans to protect its rallies, naming the new force Combat 18. Inspired by *The Turner Diaries,* the "18" in the name stood for the first and eighth letters of the alphabet, *AH,* for Adolf Hitler.[21] Combat 18 sought to take over *Blood & Honour* magazine and released white power albums with other bands and labels. They even exploited Donaldson's image, naming one label "ISD Records" after the singer's initials. Yet Combat 18 would have its fall, too, as musicians rebelled over the cut it was taking out of their profits. The infighting over control even led to assaults and attempted murder, with Combat 18 members eventually going to jail after attempting a mail-bombing campaign.

Skinheads saw themselves as street warriors, and they often adorned themselves with Viking berserker or Waffen SS tattoos. Skrewdriver sang of a final battle where "with gleaming swords and shining shields / Our flags we proudly wield."[22] Because of this warrior image, the skinheads saw themselves as men of action rather than ideologues. "Politicians think they can sort problems out by talking. We act more violently," said one skinhead.[23] They also embraced *The Turner Diaries,* which fit their predilection for action over specific ideologies.[24] Many members rejected Christianity because of its emphasis on meekness and nonviolence, instead embracing Odinism or other Norse mythology. For most skinheads, Nazi imagery was more about a coolness factor than any particular association with the specifics of National Socialism.[25]

The skinheads were more *against* their enemies than they were *for* any particular plan of action. The Italian skinhead motto "No to drugs, no to immigrants, no to communists, and no to gays" summed up their logic. Similarly, Combat 18 called for shipping "all non-whites back to Africa, Asia, or Arabia alive or in body bags," as well as the killing of Jews, homosexuals, and white race mixers. The movement embraced heterosexual masculinity, rejecting women's rights and abortion.[26] Much of the skinhead violence was against those who didn't fit their tough working-class self-image. In the United Kingdom, this included "Paki bashing" (attacks on South Asian immigrants) and "queer bashing," not only of open homosexuals but also of men who did not fit the stylized skinhead image of a working-class male.[27]

Around the world, skinheads, the KKK, the National Alliance, and other groups and parties were using white power music in their rallies, and white power concerts became a place to recruit new members.[28] Bands like Skrewdriver helped white supremacists recruit new members, exposing listeners to the ideas—and also the lifestyle—of the white supremacist world. An article in *Blood & Honour* noted that white power musicians "write and perform songs as instruments of mobilization." One U.S. white supremacist rocker (who later rejected racism) called music a "gateway drug" for young people to join the movement.[29] Tom Metzger, who led WAR, focused on recruiting younger members to the cause, labeling them "shock troops" for the revolution, and organized America's first hate rock festival, Aryan Fest. In 2000, the Hammerskins hosted Hammerfest 2000 in Atlanta, Georgia, drawing in fans from Austria, Canada, Ireland, and other countries, as well as all over America.[30] Resistance Records, a leading label run by the neo-Nazi National Alliance and its leader, William Pierce, until his death in 2002, claimed: "White Power music is the soundtrack of the white revolution."[31]

Music was a fun way for white supremacists to get pumped up, helping sustain enthusiasm and mobilize the community. As one researcher of the neo-Nazi movement put it, "it's Mein Kampf to a 4/4 beat."[32] At a concert, whether a small one at a local bar or a large white power music festival, fans developed a sense of comradery and met others in the movement who lived outside their home areas. They also became exposed to racist imagery, with Union Jacks, swastikas, and proapartheid imagery all mixed together. A believer could bond over beers while busting knuckles with his fellow concertgoers, doing the "Sieg Heil," and shouting at the stage—the specifics are different for the white power world, but the bonding is a familiar feeling to anyone who has attended a rock concert. "What a great show!!" one activist recalled; "after [the] speech I was ready to take on every jew in the land with a stick." Another white supremacist commented: "and here I thought we were alone LOL."[33]

Casual violence was also part of the scene. In July 1981, Hambrough Tavern, located in the Little India section of Southall, near London, hosted an Oi! concert.[34] Outraged by the racist bands playing and the presence of "Paki-bashing" skinheads, thousands of young Asians gathered outside the tavern to protest. Skinheads attacked the protesters with bricks and clubs, chanting "Kill the Pakis," and the protesters threw gasoline bombs into the tavern, burning it to the ground. At least 120 people, including 61 police officers, suffered serious injuries.[35] The Thatcher government sought to ban white power rock; predictably, this made its popularity soar.[36] Germany had a similar experience when it banned the Nazi rock group Störkraft in the early 1990s, catapulting a minor group into a household name—to the extent that, as one observer noted, "practically every fourteen-year-old in the country had to get an album by this 'ultra-hard' band if he didn't want to be totally uncool."[37]

Immigrants, the Black community, gays, leftists, and other supposed foes were all targets of the skinheads' violence, with much of the day-to-day danger on the streets.[38] Most of this violence was opportunistic; in their eyes, it was a fight, not a terrorist attack. Despite skinheads' anti-Semitism and antigovernment views, they were more likely to attack minorities who just strayed into their path—Turks in Germany, Roma in Hungary, Asians in the United Kingdom, and North Africans in France—using bats, knives, and boots. Spray-painting mosques, synagogues, Jewish cemeteries, and refugee shelters with racist graffiti was another popular pastime. In the late 1980s and early 1990s, skinheads were linked to 40 murders—some were against supposed racial enemies, but there was also considerable skinhead-on-skinhead violence.[39]

The music reflected, but also conveyed, a particular ideology that helped define the broader skinhead movement. As with Skrewdriver, most white power rock groups' lyrics were simple. Sociologists Ugo Corte and Bob Edwards contend that the music helped frame white power ideals, expressing them to members of the movement in easily digestible ways. The music denigrated other races and had anti-Semitic, antigay, antileftist, and antifeminist themes. At the same time, contrasting with this negativity, the music pushed the glory of the white race and promised a revolution to overthrow the existing order.[40] Bound for Glory, an American group, foretold a "hate train rolling leaving wreckage in our path." Aggressive Force sang: "It's okay to be White."[41] The band No Remorse sang: "Jew-boys need cyclone [i.e., Zyklon] B / queer-boys need cyclone B / nigger boys need cyclone B."[42] Both organizers and fans contrasted white power music to MTV and other popular outlets that promoted hip-hop and groups with liberal values, portraying them as The System brainwashing youth through music.

Various Blood & Honour chapters, Combat 18, and other white power organizations—including, indirectly, the National Front—also earned hundreds of thousands of dollars per year from sales of white power music.[43] In

1999, Interpol estimated that the white power music industry was generating more than $3 million a year. The real profit may have been even higher than this, as a black market thrived in some countries where the music was illegal. In addition to direct sales, bands and distributors often sold badges and other movement paraphernalia.[44] White power rock groups and their backers fought over this gold mine, firebombing one another's stores, mailing letter bombs, and otherwise using violence to attempt to control the movement and compete for profit.[45]

Over time, the white power music scene in Britain faded, and the momentum of the skinhead movement shifted to continental Europe and the United States. In addition to the ties Donaldson forged between the United Kingdom and Germany, U.S.-based Resistance Records purchased Nordland Records in Sweden, giving the U.S. label access to a country with a huge white power music scene.[46] By the late 1990s, Sweden's Ragnarock Records (run by Blood & Honour) and Panzerfaust (run by the Hammerskins in the United States) emerged as players in the white power music industry.[47] In Germany, Landser (previously called Endlösung: Final Solution) released "The Reich Will Rise Again" in 1992 and was later the first German band to be banned as a criminal association. Hundreds of white power music festivals took place in Germany in the late 1990s.[48] Music also helped spread the white power scene to Eastern European countries, where the end of communist dictatorships allowed skinheads and other white power groups to flourish. A Czech intelligence report, for example, found that groups like Combat 18 and Blood & Honour chapters openly sponsored concerts and recruited in the Czech Republic.[49] By the late 1990s, there were around 70,000 skinheads in over 30 countries. The groups themselves were really bands of like-minded (and like-dressing) individuals; there was no formal membership for those in the movement.[50]

In the United States, white power music took off in the 1990s, with groups such as Bound for Glory, Bully Boys, and Aggravated Assault making their mark.[51] For several years, the Hammerskin Nation (which took its name and the crossed hammers in its logo from the Pink Floyd movie The Wall) emerged as the leading skinhead group in the United States, spawning chapters in Europe, Canada, Australia, and New Zealand. It even had its own white power music company, Panzerfaust Records, with an associated internet presence.[52] All of this occurred at a time when the Klan and various neo-Nazi groups were in decline, creating an opening for a new brand of hate in the United States.[53]

The internet made the music scene even more transnational and, for a while, more lucrative. Racist music might be recorded in Europe, pressed onto a CD or other form in America, and then sold around the globe. Internet radio stations meant that music from one country was available anywhere.[54] When the internet began to spread, it allowed white power music companies to sell CDs, t-shirts, and other wares directly to supporters, bypassing traditional music stores, which usually refused to sell white power music.[55] Spotify, iTunes, and other online services allowed white power musicians to hawk their wares for years before finally cracking down.[56] Web-based sales hubs enabled users from around the world to easily find and purchase white power music. The internet also made it far easier to publicize even small concerts and to circumvent national bans on particular groups or songs. White power group fan websites also became centers for conversation and thus for recruitment and radicalization, as young visitors came for the music but stayed for the community and hate talk.[57] One white power music official claimed that, beginning as far back as 2004, he regularly emailed with young teenagers who came across his group's site, sending them literature and music. According to this official, "they watch the music videos, they listen to what we're saying, and it's like they just soak it up."[58] At the Unite the Right rally in Charlottesville, Virginia, white supremacists wearing Skrewdriver t-shirts were among the demonstrators.[59]

The internet, however, as it did for all musicians, also proved a two-edged sword. It enabled global, rapid distribution but also led to piracy—a particular problem for a movement that was always short of funds and whose members did not trouble themselves over the details of the law. In addition, services like Spotify and Amazon sucked away the white supremacist music and book industry from labels controlled by neo-Nazi groups like the National Alliance.[60] Profits plummeted as a result.

Many governments, especially in Europe, banned white power music groups outright. Antiracists went to white power concerts to protest and try to disrupt them and urged boycotts of bars and other venues that hosted the groups. To counter this, white power groups often had private concerts to exclude opponents. Security was tight: attendees might have to have a known local member vouch for them, display Aryan tattoos or other symbols, or otherwise prove their bona fides.[61] This security made it harder to attract new recruits and otherwise broaden the movement.[62] In general, white power music promoters tried to portray their efforts as countercultural: their "artists," they claimed, were forgoing millions of dollars by sticking to their beliefs and refusing to go mainstream. Indeed, they claimed to be facing a broader conspiracy to block access to the movement.[63]

To avoid being banned by governments or alienating broader audiences, the bands learned to calibrate the level of vitriol they expressed. Groups that pushed the neo-Nazi theme too hard, for example Swastika and Final Solution, often turned off potential audiences. In addition, they ran afoul of hate speech laws in countries like Canada and Australia and Holocaust denial laws in many European countries, limiting their ability to perform and sell music. In contrast, groups with tough-sounding but vaguer names, for example Fortress and Nemesis, fared better, as did those who stressed the defense of white people and what they considered "self-love" over explicitly racist stances. A few groups even achieved remarkable commercial success. The Swedish band Ultima Thule, which played songs in the 1980s extolling national pride to skinhead audiences but claimed to reject racism and Nazism, had three gold albums and one platinum one. They were also the first Swedish group ever to have three albums in the country's Top 20 at the same time.[64]

A Changing Europe

In the 1980s, the export of white power music from the United Kingdom to the rest of the world, and the emergence of a global skinhead movement, occurred against the backdrop of a changing Europe. As in the United States, the end of the communist governments in the former Soviet Union and Europe reshaped the white supremacist movement in Europe, with traditional anticommunism becoming less important and issues of race and immigration coming to the forefront. In addition, much of the new energy for the white supremacist movement was found in Eastern Europe and the former Soviet Union, where the oppressive control of communist governments was now lifted.

Russia itself developed one of the most active white supremacist movements in the world. Even in the Soviet days, the Russian nationalist Pamyat movement blamed a secret war by Jews and Freemasons for Russia's problems.[65] Membership ballooned with the collapse of the Soviet Union. A splinter of Pamyat, Russian National Unity, had 2,000 members with over 100 local cells by the end of 1994. The National Socialist Society in Russia targeted "dark-skinned migrants," murdering at least 27.[66] The skinhead movement became particularly popular in Russia, with the number of adherents peaking at over 60,000.[67]

On paper, Germany's laws against anything smacking of Nazism were tough and, by American standards, extreme. It was, and is still, forbidden to display a swastika or other Nazi symbols, with exceptions made for areas such as art and education.[68] Nevertheless, remnants of the country's Nazi past popped up. In the early 1970s, members of the banned group Wehrsportgruppe Hoffmann (Hoffmann Paramilitary Sports Group) murdered several Jews, including shooting a Jewish publisher and his lifelong companion in their home. The most lethal terrorist attack in Germany was the September 1980 Oktoberfest bombing, which killed 12 people and injured over 200. Gundolf Köhler, who had trained in Hoffmann Group camps, conducted the attack and died when the bomb detonated prematurely. Hoffmann himself was arrested but released, as investigators initially believed that he had no direct link to the bombing, though later evidence strongly suggested that organized neo-Nazis were involved.[69]

Despite the death toll from these attacks, German intelligence and law enforcement still largely focused on radical left-wing groups like Baader-Meinhof. Even after the bloody Oktoberfest bombing, authorities dismissed Köhler's attack as the work of someone who was mentally ill rather than a terrorist who was part of a broader community.[70] Germany's initial response to the skinheads years later was also half-hearted, in part due to the pressing needs that came with German reunification; the government quickly released skinheads who participated in mob violence, failed to investigate murders, and otherwise refused to take the problem seriously.[71]

Unification changed the politics of Germany and created openings for extreme right-wing parties and groups. Even before the Berlin Wall fell, East Germany had had a vibrant far-right movement, with one police estimate in 1987 claiming the existence of 15,000 neo-Nazis there. Communist authorities denied any neo-Nazi presence and dismissed the East Germans who attacked guest workers from Cuba and Angola as "rowdies" who had fallen under corrupt Western influence.[72] Now free to organize in the former East Germany and spread their message, skinheads surged in numbers.[73] In some areas, extreme right-wing parties did well in state-level elections, playing down their images as ruffians in order to enter mainstream politics.[74]

After Germany's unification, the government made it easier for immigrants to obtain citizenship, and by the mid-1990s, nearly 2 million Turks lived in Germany.[75] Right-wing voices blamed immigrants for drug trafficking, rape, and violent crime in general. Neo-Nazis sought to create "Germany for Germans." They vandalized Jewish cemeteries and firebombed or threatened residents at immigrant housing complexes.[76] Skinhead music groups made open references to the Third Reich, with bands like Stuka, in its song "Parasiten," warning: "soon the asylum seekers will be our masters."[77]

As the German and British experiences suggest, antiimmigrant sentiment became an important part of the white supremacist movement in Europe as immigration changed the face of Europe as a whole—at first in small ways and over time in big ways. In almost every country in Western Europe, the number of foreign residents surged from the 1950s to the 1970s. In Germany, for example, the number rose from around 1 percent of the population in 1950 to 5 percent in 1970.[78] In 1973, Jean Raspail authored *The Camp of the Saints,* depicting a world where hordes of migrants overran Europe. The novel embodied the fears of European white supremacists.

No white supremacist–affiliated political group ever gained significant power directly during this period. However, because Europe's political systems are parliamentary, there were a surfeit of small parties looking for political niches or appealing to relatively small slices of the electorate in order to have a voice and gain influence.

When far-right groups made gains, it often had less to do with sudden changes in public opinion and more to do with the status of existing, more mainstream parties and their ability to redress grievances that concerned potential far-right supporters, particularly around immigration. At first, more mainstream parties often failed to anticipate such issues, but as protests and violence grew, the parties recognized opportunities and exploited them, diminishing opportunities for the violent far right.[79] Indeed, conservative movements that sought to embrace politics at times rejected the far right, limiting the radicals' access to recruits and money—as happened in Italy when the Italian Social Movement purged individuals tied to New Order, a violent terrorist group active in the late 1960s and early 1970s.[80]

All Scandinavian countries saw a surge in racist violence, with immigrants being particular targets, in the late 1980s and early 1990s.[81] Antiimmigrant sentiment flared from time to time, entering mainstream as well as radical circles. This sentiment resulted in numerous instances of low-level violence against immigrants, including arson attacks on refugee centers, damage to mosques and synagogues, and verbal and physical harassment of immigrants, in addition to lethal violence.

The 9/11 terrorist attacks and subsequent jihadist mass-casualty attacks in Spain in 2004 and London in 2005 fit neatly into the evolving ideas and demographic changes that were alarming much of Europe. The jihadist threat to Europe was quite real: groups like Al Qaeda and ISIS conducted major attacks in Belgium, France, Spain, and the United Kingdom, as well as smaller attacks in Germany, Italy, Norway, and other countries. At the same time, death threats against the cartoonist who mocked the Prophet Muhammad and the murder of the gay anti-Islam Dutch filmmaker Theo Van Gogh fostered a sense in the broader public that Islam was a danger to multiculturalism, free speech, and other liberal European values. All of this added a national security element to what had long been an economic and social grievance. The English Defense League, a social movement that emerged in 2009 out of soccer hooligans, began holding violent rallies in 2009 as part of the "struggle against global Islamification" and claimed that Muslim migrants were bringing terrorism and "rape jihad" into the United Kingdom.[82] Such claims rose and fell in popularity but usually surged after a significant jihadist attack.[83]

As in the United States, many distinct streams of thought began to merge. Yes, immigrants were terrorists, welfare cheats, and job-stealers, but the overall conspiracy was bigger than that. The left, it turned out, was responsible for destroying traditional values through multiculturalism at home and for further mongrelizing Europe via migration—and who controls the left but the Jews?

Few Spectacular Attacks but Constant Violence

High-profile attacks akin to the 1980 Oktoberfest bombing, not to mention the 1995 Oklahoma City bombing in the United States, were rare to nonexistent in Europe for most of the 1980s, 1990s, and 2000s. The number of lethal attacks in Europe peaked in the early 1990s and, except for a brief surge at the end of the 2000s, has largely declined since that time. (See figs. 3.1 and 3.2.) After 9/11, this decline meant that the focus on jihadist attacks seemed sensible given the hundreds killed at the hands of jihadists in Europe during this period. Yet those who were looking saw that the seeds of future trouble were sprouting.

In Germany, nearly 200 people, mostly foreigners, died from right-wing extremist violence from 1945 to 2019, though much of it was low-level and

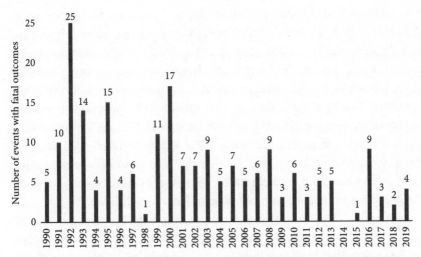

Figure 3.1 Number of deadly right-wing attacks in Europe, 1990–2019. N = 208.
Source: Jacob Aasland Ravndal, Sofia Lygren, Anders Ravik Jupskås, and Tore
Bjørgo, "RTV Trend Report 2020: Right-Wing Terrorism and Violence in
Western Europe, 1990–2019," C-REX Research Report No. 1, C-REX—Center
for Research on Extremism, University of Oslo (2020), 7, https://www.sv.uio.no/
c-rex/english/topics/online-resources/rtv-dataset/rtv_trend_report_2020.pdf.

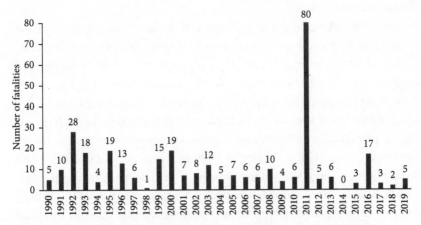

Figure 3.2 Number killed in right-wing attacks in Europe, 1990–2019.
N = 2019. *Source*: Jacob Aasland Ravndal, Sofia Lygren, Anders Ravik Jupskås,
and Tore Bjørgo, "RTV Trend Report 2020: Right-Wing Terrorism and Violence
in Western Europe, 1990–2019," C-REX Research Report No. 1, C-REX—
Center for Research on Extremism, University of Oslo (2020), 7, https://www.
sv.uio.no/c-rex/english/topics/online-resources/rtv-dataset/rtv_trend_report_
2020.pdf.

was not captured in many terrorism statistics. Some experts (often using different definitions and counting procedures) put the figure higher, and most of these deaths occurred after reunification.[84] In 1991, skinhead mobs armed with clubs and Molotov cocktails attacked areas housing workers from Mozambique and Vietnam. In 1992, Germany suffered almost 2,000 neo-Nazi attacks, mostly assaults and vandalism.[85] German intelligence reports that, between 1991 and 1994, there were almost 1,500 arson attacks against refugee shelters in Germany.[86] The attacks terrified residents, and the perpetrators boasted to one another that the threat of burning people conjured up images of the Holocaust.[87] Most attacks killed no one, but some firebombings led to the deaths of residents, including children.[88]

In August 1992, a series of antiimmigrant riots in the Lichtenhagen district of Rostock shook Germany. The rioters' initial target was an overcrowded shelter where Roma refugees lived in squalid conditions, with local authorities ignoring their plight. Chanting, "Germany for the Germans! Foreigners out!" hundreds of skinheads and other thugs gathered, throwing stones and later attacking the refugees with baseball bats and firebombs. Thousands of Germans stood by and watched, with many cheering on the rioters. The violence then spread to a nearby building housing Vietnamese immigrants. Authorities were slow to respond, and some were later accused of sympathizing with the rioters.[89]

More organized and lethal violence also occurred. In the 2000s, three members of Germany's neo-Nazi National Socialist Underground conducted a series of attacks with guns that killed 10 migrants, mostly Turks; bombed a grocery store owned by an Iranian family; and used a nail bomb on a busy street where migrants often shopped, injuring 22. They also shot and killed a police officer and wounded her colleague.[90] The attackers themselves were a three-person cell, but they drew on supporters from other groups, for example a German branch of Blood & Honour. These neo-Nazis lived in safe houses of supporters, worked with forgers to get fake passports, and otherwise thrived as part of a broader ecosystem.[91] Despite the pace of this activity and the resulting death toll, the group went undetected for over a decade. Two of the three eventually died in a murder-suicide, while the third sent videos to the media claiming responsibility for the killings.[92]

German intelligence recruited informants among the neo-Nazis, and some of these had direct contact with the bombers. However, it appeared that the informants took intelligence money but did not provide vital information, leaving the government blind.[93] The head of Germany's domestic intelligence agency ensured that many of the documents detailing the role of informants in the neo-Nazi movement were shredded.[94] Even when the German government did investigate the right people, it focused only on the immediate attackers rather than the broader network. Part of this was due to the decentralized nature of German law enforcement, with each state focusing on its bit of violence rather than the federal police putting the pieces together.[95]

Though large-scale, spectacular attacks were lacking, the number of low-level attacks by skinheads and other white supremacists was stunning. The years 1992 and 1993 saw over 1,000 attacks on Turks and other immigrants in Germany. Extremists in France bombed an immigrant hostel housing North Africans near Nice, and, in 1995, National Front members shot and killed a 17-year-old Comoran boy as he was running to catch a bus.[96] In the United States, skinheads killed Black people, gays, immigrants—and other skinheads. They were responsible for almost 40 murders by the mid-1990s.[97] Far more common, however, were assaults and vandalism, often fueled by white power music and alcohol.[98]

Most of these attacks were not terrorism per se. Much of the violence was within the movement, with disputes over drug trafficking, fears that a member might be an informant, or personal differences that flared into violence. An Anti-Defamation League report from 2006 details a range of skinhead attacks, some of which were akin to common drunken gang initiatives, with skinheads looking for someone to beat up so they could claim to be a true member of a movement.[99] European terrorism scholar Daniel Koehler argues that this sort of violence could be called "day-to-day" terrorism, as the targets fit the skinheads' ideological stances, and they would often chant "Sieg Heil" or otherwise make their agenda clear. It was a form of local dominance, letting everyone know "they rule[d] the streets."[100]

Russia was notably more violent. The socioeconomic turbulence of the 1990s, increasing immigration and restrictions on political parties, and the spread of white supremacist discourse combined with the growth of the internet to increase radicalization. In 2001, a mob of several hundred skinheads carrying metal bars attacked foreign vendors in a Moscow street market while shouting racist slogans, killing three. Some wore the swastika-like insignia of the Russian National Unity movement. In 2007 and 2008, the Russian neo-Nazi National Socialist Society killed 27 Muslims in a series of attacks.[101] The SOVA Center for Information and Analysis, which tracks violence in Russia, found that from 2004 to 2010, neo-Nazis and racists killed over 500 people. Violence fell after 2011, however, especially as repression by the state increased following unrest in Ukraine in 2014.[102]

Data compiled by Jacob Aasland Ravndal and his colleagues, presented in figures 3.1 and 3.2, show both the number of deadly attacks per year in Europe and the number dead in these attacks. Ravndal's work includes all right-wing violence (as opposed to strictly white supremacy), but his data indicate that over half of the attacks were against ethnic and religious minorities, a common target of white supremacists. As expected, immigrants bore the bulk of the violence, but those who were born in Europe and the LGBTQ+ community also suffered considerably. Jews were targeted but less frequently.

The skinhead movement emerged from the broader punk, antihippie culture, and it is not surprising that it declined as it lost its novelty and as these forms of youth rebellion faded. Several major groups collapsed due to arrests and infighting, sucking energy from the cause. By the late 2000s, the skinhead movement was in decline in both Europe and the United States, though it remained potent.[103] Some white supremacist leaders had advocated blending into society, essentially infiltrating it, rather than standing out like the skinheads. As the movement declined, the alt-right emerged around 2015, with an in-your-face, internet-savvy approach that competed directly for the attention of young males who might otherwise have become skinheads.[104] In the words of Heidi Beirich, "skinheads were replaced by the polo shirt and khaki pants crowd."[105] The internet also enabled other forms of counterculture, allowing individuals to follow a range of musical genres and pop culture themes.[106] As a result, some old groups, like the Hammerskins, persist, but few new ones are emerging.

Even in their heyday, skinhead groups quickly rose and fell, with hundreds of local chapters appearing and disappearing as arrests, infighting, and members simply growing up took their toll. Most skinhead groups had no ties to any broader national organization and simply dressed the part, went to white power concerts, and hung out with their friends. Some members were also part of other white supremacist groups, who tried both to work with and to compete against the skinhead movement.[107]

More organized groups, however, found it hard to work with the broader skinhead movement. Their embrace of drugs and alcohol was anathema to more puritanical white supremacists. Female skinheads, with their androgynous style and opposition to motherhood, were a particular problem.[108] The Klan, with its own distinct dress mode and tradition, never fit the skinhead vibe. Aryan Nations, White Aryan Resistance, and other groups tried to tap into the movements' pool of members; however, they often proved impervious to direction from on high. Some skinheads even stabbed and beat a leader of White Aryan Resistance when he tried to organize for the revolution.[109]

At a private conference in 2002, leaders of the neo-Nazi National Alliance William Pierce and Erich Gliebe called skinheads "freaks," "morons," and "hobbyists." The SPLC acquired a recording of the speeches and publicized it. Skinhead outrage was intense; as one wrote on a website: "you elite cluster fucks alienate us." The spat also hurt the sales of Resistance Records, which the National Alliance ran and which marketed white power music to skinheads, depriving the neo-Nazi group of one of its key sources of income. This public relations disaster, which made it difficult for Gliebe to consolidate power after Pierce died, led to the decline of the movement and its splintering in 2005 with the creation of the National Vanguard by disaffected neo-Nazis.[110]

Making the job easier for law enforcement, skinheads—with their propensity to fight, racist tattoos, shaved heads, and steel-toed Doc Martens boots—proved easy to identify and arrest.[111] Despite this risk, giving up their look in the name of security was difficult for many skinheads, as such style is often part of the attraction of the cause, giving them a community and an identity.

For all the drama of skinheads and their attacks on migrants, Europe seemed a sideshow of white supremacy in the post–World War II era compared with the United States, with no high-profile attacks like the Oklahoma City bombing. Today, however, Europe is front and center, with a range of groups and individuals producing a steady stream of attacks.

Much of this energy came from the worst white supremacist terrorist attack in European history, which occurred in Norway in 2011. The man who did this was not a skinhead, did not belong to a neo-Nazi group, and otherwise was not on the radar screen of either law enforcement or organized white supremacy. This man, Anders Behring Breivik, offered a model for aspiring white supremacist terrorists that remains powerful to this day.

4

Europe

The Return of the Knights Templar

Anders Behring Breivik helped propel Europe into the forefront of white supremacist violence because he feared a Muslim takeover of Europe and blamed left-leaning political leaders for allowing Muslim immigration. According to his worldview, Marxism, multiculturalism, and Muslim migrants were all part of one big conspiracy. On July 22, 2011, at about 3:25 in the afternoon, Breivik detonated a car bomb—similar in design to that used in Oklahoma City—in downtown Oslo at the heart of a complex of government buildings, killing eight. He then traveled to the island of Utøya, where around 600 teens and their adult minders were attending a summer camp run by the Workers' Youth League, the country's largest youth political organization, which is affiliated with Norway's left-leaning Labor Party.[1] Utøya is known throughout Norway as an idyllic getaway for left-leaning youth, and all the major political figures in the Norwegian Labor Party had spent time there.[2] There, Breivik dressed himself as a police officer and systematically shot the young attendees, killing 69 of them while declaring: "You are going to die today, Marxists!" Hundreds more were wounded in the two attacks. He also sought to kill former prime minister Gro Harlem Brundtland, but she had left the island shortly before he arrived.

Until this attack, post–World War II Norway had seen little right-wing and white supremacist violence. What limited violence there had been peaked in the late 1990s as left-wing and right-wing militants increasingly escalated attacks, culminating in the murder of 15-year-old Benjamin Hermansen, who had a Norwegian mother and a Ghanaian father, in 2001 because two skinheads thought he was a foreigner. In contrast, Breivik's attacks were devastating; however, as horrific as the death toll was, it easily could have been worse. A Norwegian commission that investigated the attacks noted that if the bomb at the government complex had gone off a few hours earlier, as Breivik had planned, far more people would have died.[3]

Breivik also took advantage of the internet to publicize his ideas—an approach that became a staple of attacks that followed. Before the attack, he collected the email addresses of far-right figures and sent out a massive manifesto (1,500 pages in all) to 1,002 recipients whom he believed might be sympathetic.[4] In his tome, Breivik portrayed European whites as victims, both of Islam and of an establishment determined to destroy traditional values, using this accusation to justify violence. Much of the manifesto rambles: he imagines a European civil war lasting for generations, ending only in 2083. In that year, Europe would be Christian and free of Muslims, Marxists, and feminists. He proclaimed himself a member of the refounded Knights Templar, a medieval Christian order that waged war against Muslims during the Crusades. Although Breivik's targets were Norwegian, his audience was European, and he saw Muslims as a problem for white European civilization broadly, not just his own country. He claimed that numerous other members exist, although, conveniently, for "security reasons," he did not divulge their names.

After embracing radical white supremacist ideas, Breivik consumed racist online content at the white nationalist site Stormfront, as well as at the Scandinavian far-right forum Nordisk.nu, which reinforced his extremism. Unlike many later would-be terrorists, Breivik did not publicize his intentions online as he radicalized or otherwise reveal his plans in advance. Indeed, his online rhetoric seemed to match that of numerous other far-right voices.[5] He also stayed away from, and even seemed to scorn, other Norwegian white supremacists who acted on the street, whom he saw as ignorant. His extremism was purely virtual until he attacked.[6]

Breivik learned from The Order and similar groups, recognizing (correctly) that in acting alone he was less likely to be detected by security forces.[7] Although a staunch Islamophobe, he also learned from jihadist groups, studying Al Qaeda attacks and learning about explosives from the English-language jihadist magazine *Inspire*.[8] He even praised the effectiveness of "martyrdom" in his manifesto.[9]

As a result of these precautions, Breivik's attacks caught Norwegian security services flat-footed. A subsequent investigation found that the Police Security Service had had a chance to detect him because he was on a list of people who had purchased chemicals and explosives and he had at times purchased too much, perhaps detectable as a particularly menacing action had the list been crosschecked to reveal his weapons purchases; however, numerous other individuals purchased more than their share of chemicals and explosives, and he did not stand out. Altogether, even in hindsight, there were relatively few indicators.[10]

Breivik hoped his attack would not only punish the "cultural Marxists" but also draw attention to his cause and manifesto. As Åsne Seierstad, a journalist who wrote a brilliant account of the attacks, noted, Breivik described his murders as a "book launch."[11] Mass audiences had ignored his writing in the past, but he knew it would be read if he became famous—even if this fame came from killing people.[12] He also hoped that the government would crack down on the right in general, further radicalizing it.[13] Nor did the nightmare end after the attack: he saw his trial as a "propaganda phase" for his operation and attempted to turn it "into a theater."[14]

More than any other living white nationalist, Breivik's impact would be felt around the world—not just because of his ideas, but as a model for action. In bombing Oslo, Breivik saw McVeigh's attack on Oklahoma City as a model; however, it was his own innovation with the mass shooting at Utøya that would prove a more enduring legacy.[15] The attack resembled the first-person-shooter video games Breivik had immersed himself in for years prior to turning to terrorism. Prize-winning Norwegian novelist Karl Ove Knausgård contends that Breivik's self-image as a Knight Templar crusader battling Islam, along with his claim to be part of a nonexistent organization, "resembles role-playing, rather than political terrorism."[16]

Breivik's inspiration can be seen again and again in the years that followed his mass murder, including an attack in Moscow in 2012 that killed six, the attack in 2014 on the Overland Park Jewish Community Center and nearby retirement community in Kansas (three deaths), the 2017 Aztec High School shooting in New Mexico (two deaths), the murder of British Labour parliamentarian Jo Cox, and attacks in the United States in 2019 on a Walmart in El Paso (22 deaths) and a synagogue in Pittsburgh (11 deaths), among many others.[17] Christchurch shooter Brenton Tarrant would claim Breivik inspired him; indeed, Breivik's style would be evident in Tarrant's manifesto posting and shooting spree. Breivik also inspired numerous bloggers and social media commentators, who embraced his hostility to Islam, support for white power, and anger at feminism.[18] In video game parlance often used by younger extremists, Breivik had a "high score," and "Going Breivik" would come to mean a full commitment to the cause.[19]

Responding to a Changing World

Breivik's attack occurred at a time when Europe itself was in crisis. The 2008 financial shock shattered confidence in traditional ideas about the economy and the parties that championed them. To help their countries through the disaster, center-right and center-left parties often came together. This allowed unpopular but necessary reforms to go through; it also allowed more extreme parties to position themselves as the alternatives to those in power, which they did in France, Austria, Hungary, Italy, Spain, and Greece, among other countries.[20] In many countries, both the left and right extremes grew stronger, taking advantage of the economic crisis and the subsequent decline in living standards to push grievances about a range of issues, from immigration to political elitism.[21]

The specific concerns of the most extreme of these groups vary, from the presence of North Africans in France to that of Turks in Germany, Pakistanis in the United Kingdom, and so on. However, the "enemy" groups are usually people with darker skin, and most are Muslims. Many European white supremacists push a dark vision of "Eurabia," a hypothetical Europe that is overrun by Muslim immigrants and refugees who in turn outbreed European whites. In doing so, the newcomers broaden the caliphate, subject white Europeans to Islamic law, and force them to convert.[22] Breivik discussed Eurabia in the manifesto he released when he went on his killing spree.

In some countries, such as France, white supremacists remain a minority within the extreme right, with much of the overall extreme right focusing on traditional nationalism, opposing, for example, the European Union and the spread of U.S. culture.[23] Jews still remain a concern for European white supremacists, though not as much as migration.[24] As Rafal Pankowski of the Never Again Foundation in Poland has noted, there have been relatively few attacks on Jews there, but that is because not many Jews remain in Poland. Indeed, vandalism against Jewish graveyards and monuments to victims of the Holocaust is common.[25]

In the post-9/11 world, and in the aftermath of horrific jihadist attacks in the United Kingdom, France, Spain, and other countries, popular fears for their security involving jihadist terrorism have melded with traditional tropes about immigrants, especially concerning jobs and crime, and a dash of anti-Semitism is common as well. The neo-Nazi Blood & Honour, for example, began in the United Kingdom as a racist skinhead group with an anti-Semitic bent but has increasingly focused on Muslim migrants. One of its successor groups, Combat 18, calls for a "whites-only" United Kingdom and for shipping "non-whites back to Africa, Asia, Arabia, whether alive or in body bags," as well as executing "Queers," "race mixers," and "all Jews who have actively helped to damage the white race," and putting the rest in camps.[26] Attacks have often involved arson; mosques and refugee centers have been common targets. Car rammings have also become increasingly popular, and white supremacists at times have even attacked politicians deemed to favor immigrants.[27] Ideas have also became increasingly European and even global, as they move in and out of different countries among activists connected via social media.[28]

Given this focus on immigration, ethnic and religious minorities, many of whom are immigrants or children of immigrants, have been especially likely to suffer attacks. Data from Jacob Aasland Ravndal, Sofia Lygren, Anders Ravik Jupskås, and Tore Bjørgo indicate that in 2019, ethnic and religious minorities suffered four times as many attacks as any other demographic category (fig. 4.1), with Muslims and Black victims the majority within that category. Much of the violence was not high profile; beatings and various assaults were far more common than bombings or gun attacks (fig. 4.2).

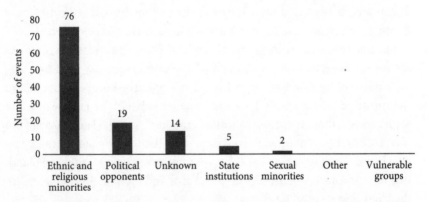

Figure 4.1 Targets of right-wing violence in Western Europe, 2019. N = 116. *Note*: All but two of the events with "unknown" target group concern "preparations for armed struggle." *Source*: Jacob Aasland Ravndal, Sofia Lygren, Anders Ravik Jupskås, and Tore Bjørgo, "RTV Trend Report 2020: Right-Wing Terrorism and Violence in Western Europe, 1990–2019," C-REX Research Report No. 1, C-REX—Center for Research on Extremism, University of Oslo (2020), 15, https://www.sv.uio.no/c-rex/english/topics/online-resources/rtv-dataset/rtv_trend_report_2020.pdf.

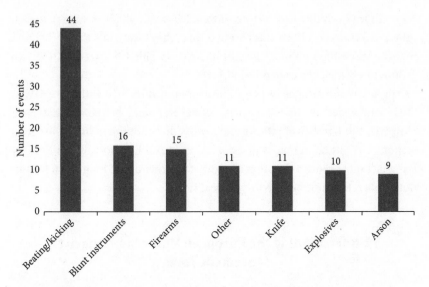

Figure 4.2 Weapons used in right-wing attacks in Europe, 2019. N = 116.
Source: Jacob Aasland Ravndal, Sofia Lygren, Anders Ravik Jupskås, and Tore
Bjørgo, "RTV Trend Report 2020: Right-Wing Terrorism and Violence in
Western Europe, 1990–2019," C-REX Research Report No. 1, C-REX—Center
for Research on Extremism, University of Oslo (2020), 16, https://www.sv.uio.
no/c-rex/english/topics/online-resources/rtv-dataset/rtv_trend_report_2
020.pdf.

Concerns about Muslim immigrants, and about Muslim residents and
citizens in general, surged with the increase in attention on ISIS in 2014
and 2015, in part due to the group's beheadings and spectacular terrorist
attacks, including the killing of 130 people in a series of attacks in Paris in
2015. This increased jihadist terrorism occurred as Muslim refugees fleeing
Syria poured into Europe, creating fears of terrorism in many countries and
leading to a dramatic increase in arson and other attacks on refugee facilities. Many of these attacks, though, were against empty housing facilities or
were otherwise nonlethal and were perpetrated by individuals who simply
did not want refugees moving in but were not tied to a broader political
movement.[29] In Germany, there were fewer than 20 attacks on refugee sites
in 2011; this number grew to almost 250 in 2014 and skyrocketed to over
1,500 attacks on such sites in 2016 and 2017.[30] Southern Europe—where
right-wing attacks were antileftist, not white supremacist, before the migration crisis—now saw a surge in attacks on immigrants as refugees sought

haven in these countries.[31] White supremacists and jihadists validated each other: extremists on both sides argued that "they" were out to get "us" and that the traditional political system had clearly failed.[32] That said, the two groups rarely attacked each other directly.[33]

Migration and refugee flows to Europe plunged in 2020 with the COVID crisis and a decline in the ferocity of several wars in the Middle East. However, the number of attacks and arrests did not immediately plunge in response. White supremacist grievances, and resulting motivations to carry out attacks, are more a function of abstract *perceptions* of long-term trends, not actual reflections of year-to-year realities.

Understanding the European White Supremacist Movement Today

Often the reality of a country's demographics has little to do with the white supremacist agenda. Pankowski has described Poland as having "anti-Semitism without Jews" but also, given the paucity of Muslims there, "Islamophobia without Muslims." He notes that in the 2015 elections, fear of Muslims became an important political issue, with leaders competing to portray themselves as the most hostile to Muslims: as there were few actual Muslims in Poland, the hate crimes that did occur often were because of a mistaken identity, for example a Latin American or Italian tourist being assaulted after being mistaken for a Muslim.[34]

Lone-wolf attacks are also increasingly the norm in Europe, as in the rest of the world. In 2019, an attacker tried to attack a synagogue in Halle, Germany, on Yom Kippur but was foiled by the security system. Yet he still shot and killed a woman passing by and then opened fire on a nearby kabob shop, killing a person there. That same year, in Bærum, Norway, a man shot his stepsister and then forced his way into a nearby mosque. Prayers had ended, and only three people were present; after the shooter shot a hole in the door, through which he entered the mosque, he failed to kill anyone before the few remaining worshipers subdued him.[35] Neither attacker was particularly skilled or prepared; with training, both could have killed far more. Lone-wolf attacks often mix personal grievances with white supremacist ideas swirling around the internet. The Halle attacker, for example, blamed his lack of sexual partners on foreigners and feminism, which he claimed were both a Jewish plot.[36] A study of attackers in Germany found that most were not known to security agencies or tied to known groups but acted impulsively, motivated by an idea of "resistance" to immigration and other supposed evils but with no real ideological depth.[37]

Ideas regarding immigration mixed with concerns about other enemies, ranging from Jews to socialists. The Identitarian movement, embodied in Generation Identity, which emerged in France in 2012 and has chapters in at least 14 countries, pushes the idea of a European identity that excludes immigrants.[38] The movement is youth-dominated, and many of its leading lights go on to play roles in right-wing, antiimmigrant political parties.[39] Generation Identity portrays itself as preserving European identity and defending freedom of speech in the face of a politically correct elite. It also calls for repatriating illegal immigrants, securing borders, and otherwise trying to stop most immigration.[40]

In Europe, movements like Generation Identity, which have an online presence that is far more influential than their on-the-ground visibility, are part of a mainstreaming effort, serving as a bridge between violent white supremacists and mainstream parties, often with a particular focus on immigration and refugees. Identitarians embrace the "Great Replacement" theory and reject the values of diversity; some describe them as essentially rebranded skinheads who dress better and are better educated. Unlike the most extreme groups who believe they are in the middle of a race war, the Identitarian movement calls, rather euphemistically, for "remigration," which, in reality, would entail a mass deportation of European residents— many of them citizens—with migrant backgrounds.[41]

As such rhetoric suggests, Generation Identity does not openly endorse violence, though it flirts with it by operating training camps in rural France, supposedly for self-defense.[42] Its members prefer provocative rallies and stunts, for example, hosting a wine and pork feast that is meant to exclude French Muslims. The movement also favors extralegal tactics: its members have occupied the site of a future mosque, erected a blockade to prevent migrants from entering France via Italy, and set tires on fire at the edge of refugee camps.[43] Because its leaders claim to reject violence, they are better able to have a large presence on social media without interference; for example, Martin Sellner, the leader of the Austrian chapter, amassed tens of thousands of followers as he preached "the Great Replacement" on YouTube and Twitter and was able to resist calls for his banning until July 14, 2020, when Twitter finally terminated him.[44] Sellner even released a manual with the title "Media Guerrilla Warfare" to help content go viral. Another work,

"The Art of Red-Pilling," offers a step-by-step explanation of how to radicalize recruits. Red-pilling is a reference to the movie *The Matrix*, where consuming the red pill opens one's eyes to the grim reality of the world (in this case, white subordination) as opposed to living the false dream (equality). Sellner's guide advises starting a potential recruit's radicalization with news pieces, anecdotes over a beer, and other small steps before moving toward addressing broader grievances over gender equality and political correctness. From there, adherents can radicalize individuals further by moving them to Telegram and other encrypted sites where more disturbing ideas can be put forward. Christchurch shooter Brenton Tarrant gave money to Sellner's movement and other Identitarian chapters and exchanged emails with Sellner himself (though nothing in these emails suggests violence); Sellner also possessed a copy of Tarrant's manifesto when Austrian intelligence raided his home.[45] In March 2021, France banned Generation Identity as a political party for "incitement to discrimination."[46]

Generation Identity's ideas and style would influence Richard Spencer and other alt-right figures in the United States, as well as different movements throughout Europe.[47] Indeed, for violent groups as well, the internet enables ideas about targets and tactics to flow from the United States to Europe and back. *Siege,* an influential collection of white supremacist essays by U.S. ideologue James Mason, first published in the 1980s, in which he seeks both to draw in new recruits and to critique the movement's failures, is read in Germany and is consumed in the United Kingdom by a dozen groups, according to a British intelligence official.[48] In Sweden, *The Turner Diaries,* leaderless resistance, and other U.S. concepts have found purchase, and Swedish neo-Nazi groups, for their part, have established sister organizations in other Scandinavian countries.[49] The Order, the white supremacist group active in the United States in the early 1980s (with David Lane, among others, a member), inspired new groups decades later in Italy, notably New Order Vanguard, which targeted leftists and immigrants in 2014.[50]

Ukraine and its civil war have proven an important nexus. Hundreds of white supremacists from the United States and Europe have gone to Ukraine—at times fighting for groups allied with the government and at times for those allied with Russia—where they have gained combat experience and connections to other groups. The Azov Battalion, in particular, has recruited white supremacists from the West and cultivated relationships with the Atomwaffen Division (*atomwaffen* is German for "nuclear weapons"), the Rise Above Movement, and others. Veterans of Ukraine's wars have returned to their home countries to work with these and other groups.[51] Ukraine is also a source of weapons for European groups who do not enjoy the easy access of their American counterparts.[52] Christchurch shooter Tarrant even considered going to live in Ukraine.[53] Ukraine itself, however, is not a unifying factor: fighting there has given participants valuable combat experience, but the fact that volunteers have fought on opposing sides suggests the divisions in the movement.[54]

A number of European groups also have links to Russia, seeing its chauvinistic and authoritarian tilt as a model for their own anti-LGBTQ+, anti-feminist, and antiimmigrant agenda. Some members of Finland's Kohti Vapautta (Toward Freedom) neo-Nazi group received training from the Russian Imperial Movement.[55] Russia also has ties to the Greek far-right political movement Golden Dawn.[56] Members of the Nordic Resistance Movement, a neo-Nazi group in Sweden with chapters in Finland, Denmark, and Norway that exists on the edge of legality, trained in Russia under the Russian Imperial Movement and carried out bombings in 2016.[57] In 2020, the United States designated the Russian Imperial Movement as a terrorist group—the first such U.S. designation of a right-wing group. Russia tries to use these groups and the white supremacist cause in general to undermine the West, largely by increasing polarization, though Russian influence on the movement as a whole is limited, according to several experts I spoke to on this subject.[58]

The election of Donald Trump in 2016 also inspired many on the right, including white supremacists, in Europe. Leaders of both political and violent groups embraced Trump's antiimmigrant rhetoric at rallies and otherwise echoed his form of cultural nationalism.[59]

An Uneasy Relationship with Politics

Like their American counterparts, European neo-Nazi and other white supremacist organizations have a fruitful, but also uneasy, relationship with political organizations that share parts of their agendas but not their embrace of violence. Although it is tempting to draw a straight line between racist parties and racist violence, political organizations can also act as safety valves: when there is no peaceful way to express anti-immigrant or other grievances white supremacists champion through the political system, it can manifest in more support for violence.

Jacob Aasland Ravndal has found that the rise of antiimmigrant parties has offered political outlets for those who might otherwise be more extreme, and that there is a negative relationship between fatal violence and electoral support for antiimmigrant parties—"a clear negative correlation," he told me. He notes Sweden's vibrant and violent white supremacist community as one example. In Sweden, antiimmigrant discourse, even skepticism on economic grounds, is often branded as racist, with elites uniformly in favor of multiculturalism. Other experts I have interviewed have made similar observations about violence in the United Kingdom, Germany, and the countries they have followed closely.[60] Overall, antiimmigrant voices in Sweden have little electoral support. As a result, there are few legitimate outlets for those who are alarmed by immigration, making extreme alternatives more attractive and credible as defenders of national "values." Sweden, Germany, and the United Kingdom have seen considerable white supremacist violence but limited support for antiimmigrant parties at the polls, in contrast to France, which has a strong right-wing, antiimmigrant party in the form of the National Front. As the National Front began to mainstream itself in the 1990s, it began to police its membership to avoid anything smacking of neo-Nazism that might turn off mainstream voters. As Jean-Yves Camus, an expert on the French far right, notes, "the National Front acts as a shield against more extreme violence."[61] As Ravndal notes, it is harder to sell the idea that the system is stacked against you if you have a successful political party.[62] Having a small minority party with hateful ideas, however, is less dangerous in a multiparty parliamentary system than in a two-party presidential one, where that party could easily find itself in power.

In the last decade, Alternative für Deutschland (AfD) in Germany, Golden Dawn in Greece, Jobbik in Hungary, and Lega Nord in Italy have all exploited immigration to become important political players, at least temporarily.[63] Pan-European organizations, for example Patriotic Europeans against the Islamification of the Orient, also flourished for several years, holding large and at times violent rallies. These organizations claim that they are not racists but "cultural nationalists," but the end result is the same: they elevate European white communities and traditions above those of nonwhites.[64] White supremacist concerts have also increased; in Germany alone, the number surged from 55 concerts in 2014 to almost 260 in 2017.[65] In Germany, this influence spiked in 2015, when Chancellor Angela Merkel welcomed hundreds of thousands of refugees from Syria. The AfD, which initially had focused on criticism of the German government's aid to Greece and other countries in the aftermath of the 2008 financial crisis, then seized on immigration, declaring in its party manifesto that "Islam does not belong in Germany" and that Muslims are "a danger to our state, our society, and our values."[66] Embracing other racist tropes, the AfD also warned of a "small and powerful elite"—code for Jews—who were manipulating the country and rejected calls to commemorate the Holocaust, as all post–World War II German governments have done.[67] The AfD also warned of "Eurabia" in its electioneering.[68] Previously on the margins, the party became the third largest in Parliament in the 2017 elections and peaked at over 15 percent approval in 2018. The AfD used its access to funding and power to protect the extreme right rather than contain it.[69] Nor was the AfD alone in its success. In 2018, Lega Nord became Italy's third largest party, and its leader, Matteo Salvini, served as interior minister for over a year. That same year, Jobbik became the second largest party in Hungary's parliament, winning 26 seats.[70] The AfD also spawned imitators, albeit less successful ones, such as "Alternative for Sweden."[71]

In some countries, the violent and the more mainstream right wings have successfully merged. In Greece, the neo-Nazi Golden Dawn party won 18 seats in parliament in 2012 and held those seats in the 2015 election. Golden Dawn began as a fringe party in the 1980s, drawing heavily on soccer hooligans. Initially, Golden Dawn was openly racist and anti-Semitic, holding rallies displaying images of Hitler and adorned with swastikas. Over time, it moved away from boasting of its neo-Nazism, instead recruiting middle-class professionals as candidates who would be more reassuring and using Identitarian rhetoric and stunts, for example torchlight marches, to grab media attention. The group exploited Greece's financial crisis, denouncing foreign governments and decrying the supposed threat of immigrants. Yet, even as Golden Dawn sought respectability, its members posed as police and then beat migrants, damaged immigrant shops, assaulted left-wing parliamentarians, and attacked an Egyptian immigrant with a dog, among other outrages.[72] There were hundreds of assaults, perhaps more, in all. Police officers often stood by, and in a few cases joined in, as Golden Dawn members went on rampages—roughly half of Greece's riot control police voted for the party. Golden Dawn also sent a few select members, several hundred in all, to boot camps in the Greek countryside for additional training, intending to use them as assault troops. The Greek government began a murder investigation that eventually led to a multiyear trial of 69 Golden Dawn members and supporters, accusing them of organized crime and use of violence. Group leaders, not just a few fringe members, have been implicated in murders.[73]

The silver lining for Europe as a whole is that most far-right groups have failed at the polls or been unable to sustain their positions from election to election. The Nordic Resistance Movement, for example, received only a handful of votes in the 2018 Swedish elections and even fewer in the 2019 EU elections, although part of that weakness stemmed from the growth of extreme but less violent political movements like the Alternative for Sweden.[74] In 2015, Golden Dawn won 17 parliamentary seats; four years later, it won zero, as its involvement in violence alienated many voters.[75]

For far-right parties and social movements, violence often poses a dilemma, as it can alienate potential supporters and therefore limit the movement's growth as a whole.[76] For example, despite its incendiary rhetoric, the AfD avoided specific acts of violence and dissolved a faction known as Flügel (Wing) after German intelligence labeled it a threat to democracy. The AfD feared that if Flügel continued to operate, the party as a whole would face constant monitoring and other pressure.[77] Splinters are common as a result of these concerns. Nordic Strength split off from the Nordic Resistance Movement in 2019, in part due to the tension between being a violent revolutionary movement and a broader political organization.[78] When the English Defence League tried to tone down its openly racist, thuggish approach in 2011, a splinter formed (the Infidels), and the two clashed in the streets.[79] The English Defence League then had a "lethargic and alcohol-fueled almost comic collapse," in the words of one civil society organization that opposed it.[80] A September 2017 march in Essex attracted fewer than 10 people.

An Uneven Response

Many European governments became far more aggressive against terrorism as violence grew in their, using a mix of crackdowns and restrictions on assembly and speech. After Breivik's rampage, Norway established a new counterterrorism unit and allocated more resources to the problem.[81] In contrast to the United States, white power music sales are now banned in most European countries (though usually with little success).[82] In 2016, the British government declared National Action to be a terrorist group—the first time it had prohibited membership in a far-right organization since World War II—even though the group itself had not directly carried out any attacks.[83] Germany banned Combat 18 in 2020 after finding links between group members and the murder of proimmigration politician Walter Lübcke. In 2018, Britain banned Identitarian leader Sellner from speaking in the country. The number of arrests related to right-wing terrorism in the European Union nearly doubled from 2016 to 2017 and doubled again from 2017 to 2018.[84]

Because of the overlap between mainstream politics and white supremacist violence, however, some states continue to be lax in their responses, despite the dangers shown by Breivik and the increased violence in general. Many in the Greek establishment have focused more on leftist groups, which have also plagued Greece for many years, and been sympathetic to right-wing ones. Law enforcement failed to take seriously the danger Greece's Golden Dawn movement posed for many years, only focusing on it as it moved from the fringe to the center of national politics after the 2012 elections and escalated its violence.[85]

Even as white supremacist violence has mounted, though, many countries have focused on other threats. Germany, for example, has laws against state-threatening violence, which it has used against terrorist groups. However, these laws were designed to combat the left-wing terrorism that plagued Germany in the 1970s. Because the laws are designed for groups with hierarchies and clear plans, they proved harder to use against more amorphous right-wing groups. After 9/11, Germany's counterterrorism resources were focused against jihadists. When prosecutors did go after white supremacists, they often used charges related to criminal violence, which was enough to stop the perpetrators but did little to eradicate the broader networks.[86]

One bright spot is the relative difficulty white supremacists in Europe have in acquiring guns, at least compared to their American counterparts. Because acquiring guns is illegal or at least heavily regulated in most countries, white supremacists face significant criminal charges if they are caught trying to arm themselves. It also leaves them open to detection by police who are monitoring arms markets, even if the police are not directly focused on the white supremacists.[87]

The presence of white supremacists in the military and police has only recently received attention. Golden Dawn's infiltration of Greek police forces has contributed to police brutality against minorities.[88] In Germany, investigations in 2020 found hundreds of white supremacists in the military and police.[89] However, white supremacists within the German police forces have posted neo-Nazi propaganda and even used police databases to find information they have used to harass leaders of the Muslim community. During the 2015 migrant crisis, neo-Nazi soldiers pushed the narrative that the migrants, many from countries where German soldiers had fought, for example Afghanistan, would destroy the country. Most worrisome, white supremacists were caught preparing for the day when Germany's democracy will collapse and infiltrated one of the country's most elite special forces units, forcing the government to disband it in 2020. By then, the white supremacists had already siphoned off military-grade weapons ranging from silencers to plastic explosives.[90]

Despite taking the threat more seriously in recent years, most European countries have only devoted a fraction of the resources given to fighting jihadist terrorism to the white supremacist problem. Even when they have addressed white supremacist violence, most countries' security services have focused far more on the highest end of the violence and less on the day-to-day assaults and harassments against many minorities. In addition, cooperation with the United States and other countries is limited, despite the globalized nature of the white power movement. That said, the last few years have seen considerable progress, with almost all European countries acknowledging the greater threat and with many adding more resources to the fight.

The most difficult issue for European countries, as for the United States, is the question of what to do when extremists are linked to large political parties or government. In March 2021, it was revealed that Germany's domestic intelligence agency had intended to monitor the AfD, whichwhich won over 12 percent of the vote in the 2017 election, as a threat to democracy, only to have a German court quickly reverse the decision—the legal conflict remains ongoing.[91]

Part of the challenge for law enforcement and society as a whole is that white supremacist ideas can easily become interwoven with mainstream politics and with the political issues of the day, such as immigration and the rise of populist politicians like Donald Trump. The emergence of a new form of communication, social media, facilitates this interaction, enabling white supremacists to reach far greater audiences with their ideas and to show off their bloody methods. In 2019, Brenton Tarrant, who like Breivik was off the radar screen of law enforcement and not part of an existing group, took Breivik's tactics and ideas to the next level, becoming a global white supremacist sensation by livestreaming his mass murders.

5

Terrorism in Real Time

Social Media and the Spread of White Supremacist Violence

"All right," Brenton Tarrant says as he puts his Subaru in gear, "Let's get this party started." Minutes before, he has posted a manifesto to 8chan with a link to Facebook Live, promising to livestream "an attack against the invaders."[1] With his headcam running, he guns down 51 worshipers at the Al Noor Mosque and Linwood Islamic Centre in Christchurch, New Zealand. It is 2019. Muse Awale, a former religion teacher, was the oldest victim at seventy-seven. The youngest was Mucaad Ibrahim, a three-year-old his family described as "a Muslim-born Kiwi who was full of energy, love and happiness."[2]

Killing in the name of white supremacy was not new. Broadcasting the attack in real time, however, was innovative, and Tarrant's violence was camera-ready. The video begins as Tarrant drives near the Al Noor Mosque, with a Serbian nationalist song playing in the background. Yes, Tarrant had made a mix for his massacre: the music was an homage to the mass murder of Bosnian Muslims by Serbs in the early 1990s. Tarrant is wearing dark camouflage clothing that allows him to pretend to be the commando he imagines himself to be, complete with an Azov Battalion patch on his body armor.[3] He pulls his car into an alleyway to park and readies his vast array of guns, including two 12-gauge shotguns, two semiautomatic rifles, a .357 Magnum rifle, and a bolt-action .223 caliber rifle, as well as high-capacity ammunition magazines.[4] These are covered with stickers bearing the names of white power mass shooters, the number 14 in homage to David Lane's white supremacist mantra, references to Hitler, and other propaganda. Tarrant selects another gun, a shotgun, from his car trunk.

Carrying his weapons, Tarrant then walks to the mosque, where a man, later revealed to be Daoud Nabi—an Afghan refugee who found a haven in New Zealand in the 1970s—opens the door and greets him with "Hello, brother."[5] From now on, we see the barrel of a gun in the center of the image, as we would in a first-person shooter video game. Tarrant commences firing, stepping over bodies and taking a break only to retrieve more ammunition from his car. He kills 42 worshipers at the mosque. After the slaughter, he drives toward the Linwood Islamic Centre, running over a woman on the street after shooting her in the head as she cries for help.[6] Now, the headcam footage ends.

At Linwood, he kills another seven worshipers—the number would have been greater if Abdul Aziz Wahabzada, one of the worshipers, had not thrown a nearby credit card reader at him to distract him and then run out-side and ducked and weaved through the parking lot, miraculously surviving as he distracted the shooter. Tarrant apparently also planned to attack a third mosque. Police officers, however, saw his Subaru zigzagging through traffic with holes in its windshield and its hazard lights blinking. They forced him to the curb and, like Breivik, he did not struggle on arrest.[7] Tarrant told police he regretted he had not killed more people. He was eventually convicted of mass murder. Silent in the courtroom and still expressing no remorse, he be-came the first person in New Zealand's history ever to receive a life sentence without the chance of release.[8]

A subsequent investigation found that Tarrant "was well equipped to pre-pare, plan and carry out a terrorist attack." He had "perhaps no empathy," which meant he could "contemplate with equanimity large scale murder." He was an intelligent digital native, enabling him to use social media with ease, and he knew how to modify firearms by himself. He had no need to be close to other people, thus limiting possible "leakage" of his intentions that might have helped police and intelligence services.[9]

Indeed, it was almost impossible for the New Zealand government to have detected and stopped Tarrant. He planned his attack for almost three years before he struck, but in that period he gave away few clues of his plans. His father developed cancer from exposure to asbestos and killed himself; he willed the settlement money to his children, and Tarrant received over $300,000 as his share. He thus had no need to work or raise money for his attack, so he was able to prepare for it for several years while living a sol-itary existence. During that time, he does not appear to have had serious romantic or sexual relationships. He also traveled the world in the years be-fore the attack, spending time in countries like Ethiopia, North Korea, and Malaysia, as well as Ukraine, Serbia, and other countries of more interest to white supremacists. However, it does not appear that he met with white supremacists in these countries.

Unlike many would-be attackers who boast on social media and are detected, Tarrant was careful, particularly after he decided to strike, and he even tried to delete much of his digital footprint. Tarrant's mother and sister and a few acquaintances knew he was a racist, and he even gave money to racist antiimmigrant organizations and individuals, for example Martin Sellner, the Identitarian leader in Austria. However, he never received training or met known extremists in person. Even when he scouted out the mosques, he did so using a drone rather than going in person, and he did a virtual "walk-through" via a video posted by a tourist who had visited the mosque.[10]

Breivik was a model for Tarrant. Heeding the Norwegian's advice, Tarrant joined a rifle club to improve his shooting and went to a gym to bulk up. His attention to operational security also reflected Breivik's guidance, as did his obsession with the "optics" of the exercise to make sure it reflected well on the white supremacist cause as a whole. Tarrant took great care, for example, to clean his house, knowing it would eventually be investigated and publicized. Most important, the calm style of the mass shooting he carried out, going from target to target, followed Breivik. Tarrant even claimed in his manifesto that he was part of the same fake Knights Templar organization of which Breivik had purported to be a member.[11]

Tarrant's attack shows the power of social media for terrorists. He exploited both the most popular social media platform in the world, Facebook, and one of the most obscure, 8chan. A controversial website, 8chan portrayed itself as a free speech haven, and it was popular with conspiracy theorists, white nationalists, and other extreme voices before being taken offline in August 2019. (It has since come back as 8kun, hosted on a Russian hosting service.)[12] With the advance notice Tarrant provided, 8chan users were ready to download his Facebook Live video and save it for later rebroadcasting. He also uploaded his manifesto on MediaFire, ZippyShare, and other small file-sharing sites.[13]

The video, around 17 minutes long, began at 1:33 p.m. local time; while it was livestreaming, no Facebook user reported inappropriate content, which Facebook urges users to do in case of violence, child pornography, or other crimes. The first user report came in at 2:02 p.m., 12 minutes after the video ended, and police alerted Facebook to the video at 2:29 p.m. It was removed minutes later. In total, the original video was viewed fewer than 200 times during the live broadcast and approximately 4,000 times before it was removed.[14] Alex Stamos, a former head of security at Facebook now at

Stanford University, testified that Facebook's algorithms had difficulty recognizing the Christchurch massacre for what it was because it looked more
like a video game or a movie than, say, an ISIS beheading video.[15] And it was
that perspective that made the video particularly troubling, with Facebook
experts finding that the viewer had the perspective of the killer.[16]

In the first 24 hours after the shooting, Facebook blocked 1.2 million copies
of the video from being uploaded and removed another 300,000 that had
managed to slip through its outer defenses. Facebook initially permitted clips
of Tarrant's video that did not show bloodshed to stay up but later removed
all of the footage.[17] In addition, Facebook designated the shooting as a terrorist attack, so praising or supporting it was not permitted on Facebook.
Tarrant's account was removed, as were "imposter" accounts that individuals
claiming to represent him created.[18]

Facebook, in addition to trying to stop the spread of the video on its
own platform, coordinated with its partners in the Global Internet Forum
to Counter Terrorism, a partnership among the leading internet companies to share information on suspected terrorist activity and prevent related video and content from going from Facebook to YouTube to Twitter
and to other major platforms.[19] Reddit banned the main channel on its
platform where users were sharing the video.[20] As part of this cooperation,
Facebook "hashed" the original video, essentially giving it a digital finger-
print that allowed Facebook's artificial intelligence systems and those of
other platforms to better identify it. YouTube later reported that in the hours
after the shooting, videos of it were being posted at a rate of about one per
second, with users editing the size of the clips, adding additional footage, or
otherwise trying to fool the automatic censors.[21]

Despite these efforts, some users quickly downloaded and cloned, edited, and reposted the footage on mainstream sites and on fringe websites,
ensuring its continued availability. As Kate Klonick, a legal expert who
studies technology companies, argues, "Facebook did all you could possibly
do after Christchurch, and it was not enough."[22] Slightly doctored versions
of the video, for example, were further edited to make it look even more like
a first-person-shooter video game. These were then posted on Discord, an
easy-to-use site that enables users to quickly form groups where they can
communicate by chat, voice, and video. Discord was initially designed for
video gamers, but white supremacists also found its convenience attractive.[23]
Facebook claimed: "we saw a core community of bad actors working together to continually re-upload edited versions of this video in ways designed

to defeat our detection."[24] Links to the video showed up on numerous social media platforms, ranging from household names like YouTube and Facebook to less-known parts of the ecosystem, for example Kiwi Farms and Torrentz.[25] Several hundred thousand versions of the video were eventually uploaded.

Tarrant himself was a creature of social media, and it was on social media that he sought to make his mark. He claimed that YouTube videos were an important source of his beliefs on white supremacy.[26] Tarrant is not alone: Over 90 percent of Americans ages 18 to 24 use YouTube, more than any other online platform, and a *New York Times* investigative report found that radicals cite YouTube as the most frequent source of their inspiration to turn to extremism, a problem observed throughout the world.[27] Accordingly, Tarrant's manifesto was full of references to memes and in-jokes most of which only made sense to other users of the social media platforms he frequented. He clearly wanted to create a meme—a style and image that spreads throughout a culture, usually a joke that is applied to a video, text, or other cultural fragment that authors alter, often anonymously, as it spreads.[28] In benign contexts, memes have included things like a distracted boyfriend, calls for more cowbells, a grumpy cat, and Randall the Honey Badger doing a voice-over.[29] A few memes, however, have been more menacing. Dylan Klebold, one of the Columbine shooters, offered a template for future school shooters that made such attacks more likely to spread.[30] Hate groups often use memes, such as Pepe the Frog, to spread their ideas, employing a kidding-not-kidding vernacular—an approach that has spread to white supremacist discourse around the world.[31] Pizza baking is a reference to "putting another Jew in the oven."[32] Memes of cars running over protesters were widely shared by organizers and attendees of the 2017 Unite the Right rally in Charlottesville, in which a white supremacist did just that, killing a ocounterprotester, Heather Heyer.[33] Tarrant, on Facebook, expressed outrage that taxpayers were funding Muslim schools in New Zealand but then noted that "it makes them all gather in one place." He quickly inserts "JK JK JK" (short for "just kidding") to show he is not serious, but extremists like him often do so to claim deniability while showing that they are indeed considering action.[34]

The causes and grievances Tarrant put forward in his manifesto placed him squarely at the heart of global white supremacism today. Titled "The Great Replacement," his manifesto drew on some of Breivik's themes but also echoed the ideas of the French Identitarian movement, which claims (with at best selective or, often, invented facts) that Muslims and other foreigners were, through a mix of high birth rates and immigration, supplanting white culture in Western countries. Although an Australian who carried out an attack in New Zealand, Tarrant saw himself as a European: "The origins of my language is [sic] European, my culture is European . . . my identity is European and, most importantly, my blood is European."[35] Indeed, Tarrant claims that he self-radicalized in 2017 after the April 7 terrorist attack in Stockholm, when a rejected asylum-seeker from Uzbekistan who claimed allegiance to ISIS drove a truck into a crowd, killing five, including Ebba Åkerlund, an 11-year-old girl whose name Tarrant painted on one of the guns he used in the attack. He also claimed that during a trip to France, he had watched "invaders" at a shopping mall and had an epiphany that violence was necessary—a vision reinforced by attacks like Breivik's and others in Europe that showed him the path forward. That same year, antiimmigrant candidate Marine Le Pen lost the French presidential election, and Tarrant believed that democratic politics would not work to stop immigration.[36] Nor was his vision confined to Europe. He also praised a 2017 mosque shooting in Quebec City and described himself as a fan of Dylann Roof, as well as Donald Trump.[37]

Tarrant proved a harbinger of things to come and, as with Breivik, entered the white supremacist pantheon. On sites like Telegram, favored by many radical white supremacists because of its emphasis on encryption and privacy, fans churn out memes and videos in praise of Tarrant and call for others to "do a Tarrant."[38] Video games are modified to enable the player to pretend to be Tarrant and go through mosques in Christchurch shooting people. Tarrant's manifesto, despite efforts to take it down, was eventually translated into French, German, Ukrainian, and at least a dozen other languages.[39]

Most important, Tarrant's mix of shooting and livestreaming has been emulated more and more. In April 2019, a 19-year-old man yelling anti-Semitic slurs shot worshipers at the Chabad of Poway synagogue in California, killing one and wounding several others. Inspired by Tarrant, he too left behind a manifesto and tried to livestream his attack, but his camera malfunctioned. In August 2019, a Norwegian man attacked a mosque in Bærum, taking inspiration from Tarrant.[40] In October of the same year, in Halle, Germany, a man attacked a synagogue during Yom Kippur services, publishing a link to Twitch to livestream footage from his helmet-mounted camera.[41] On April 11, 2020, a Texan right-wing terrorist started to livestream on Facebook as he drove around and looked for police officers to ambush.[42]

Social media platforms are now counterterrorism battlegrounds. Killers like Tarrant become more radicalized there and seek to radicalize others through their words and achievements. At the same time, most social media companies are stepping up their efforts to fight white supremacy, and government officials often detect, and stop, potential terrorists with information gleaned from social media.

White Supremacists and Technology

White supremacists have been early and eager users of the internet and other forms of communications technology. William Pierce, in addition to promoting white power rock, issued a constant stream of newsletters and other propaganda, and WAR leader Tom Metzger had a cable access program. Such efforts, however, reached few people, and it was expensive to print and mail large amounts of propaganda. Extremism expert J. M. Berger notes that from most of the 1970s through the 1990s, social norms against white supremacy, views of the mainstream media, and Federal Communications Commission regulations kept white supremacists isolated and hidden from most Americans. Racism, anti-Semitism, and other forms of hatred remained common, but Berger notes that it was often not fully articulated, and there was no ideology behind most of it that demanded acting against persons of other races.[43]

As early as 1984, Louis Beam established Liberty Net for Aryan Nations. Anyone around the country with a modem could dial up and gain access to white supremacist propaganda and information about Aryan Nations meetings. "The computer offers, to those who become proficient in its use, power undreamed of by the rulers of the past," Beam predicted.[44] In keeping with the networked nature of the movement as a whole, Beam also posted details about other white supremacist groups, enabling individuals to enter the broader ecosystem, not just Aryan Nations.

Successors played a similar multipurpose role of introducing individuals to the broader movement. In the early 1990s, the information ecosystem consisted of faxes, toll-free numbers, videotapes, and computer bulletin boards, and it adjusted as technology did.[45] However, few people saw these videos or were otherwise part of this community, and its leaders had a hard time reaching bigger audiences.[46]

The internet began to change all this, at first slowly and then dramatically. Stormfront, one of the longest-lasting internet forums for white supremacists,[47] began in 1995 as a standard website and transitioned into an interactive message board in 2001. This was a shift from typical websites, and this message board became the first form of participatory social media for white nationalists, creating a feeling of community among members.[48] Stormfront had a library of white nationalist documents, a letters page, a range of racist cartoons, and links to groups like Aryan Nations and the National Alliance. Groups often monitored Stormfront for new users and tried to recruit them.

As of 2000, one study found that there were "several hundred white supremacist sites" online and "virtually all of the major white supremacist organizations [were] represented on the internet."[49] The websites ranged in sophistication and material: some contained just a few paragraphs of informational content, and others hosted music and graphic downloads, merchandise for sale, discussion groups, and more. Other sites even provided services like a "whites only" dating site or offered racist video games and music.[50] Some websites took on an "academic" tone, for example some were Holocaust revisionist sites; others had much more virulent racist and anti-Semitic content. Four of the most central websites were Stormfront; Zundelsite, a Holocaust revisionist site; Resistance Records, a producer of white power music; and the National Alliance, an overtly neo-Nazi organization. Hosting sites of different ideologies, groups, and styles, the internet at this stage helped develop a "cyber community" and a defined online network of white supremacists, with websites linking to other sites that shared ideologies or goals.[51] Computer bulletin boards and online discussion groups also existed alongside these more passively consumed websites.[52] As white supremacist terrorism expert J. J. MacNab contends, the accelerant of so many right-wing movements "is the internet."[53]

Terrorists of all stripes were quick to recognize the value of Facebook, YouTube, Twitter, and other social media platforms. In 2004, an obscure Iraqi jihadist named Abu Musab al-Zarqawi seized the limelight by posting videos of himself beheading a U.S. hostage in Iraq, publicity that made him a jihadist superstar (Ttactics he group he founded would later go on to perfect these tactics in its incarnation as ISIS.). ISIS and similar groups posted videos of their accomplishments on the battlefield, used email and various chats to direct operatives, and otherwise exploited new technologies to further their cause.

Social media allows both groups and individuals to quickly, and cheaply, spread their messages. The technologies involved are simple to use, and members can quickly trade best practices, ranging from how to set up a virtual private network to how to use more anonymous email accounts.[54] On social media platforms, individuals can upload videos and manifestos, communicate with friends and admirers, and otherwise build an organization and spread their cause—all for free. In the white supremacist world, James Mason's writings in *Siege*, for example, are promoted on Facebook, YouTube, and Twitter, as well as more tolerant sites like Gab.[55] 8chan, too, served as the sole platform for QAnon, a strange pro-Trump conspiracy theory community that claims there is a "deep state" of corrupt government officials working to undermine the president. The theory gained significant support on 8chan and spread to other platforms, such as Twitter. QAnon then gained enough traction to act offline and become a real-world political movement, with several supporters successfully running for office.[56]

Social media have also reordered the white supremacist universe, just as it has politics and the media in general. Older organizations like the Klan, already in decline, have proved far less social-media savvy than other white supremacist organizations and alt-right figures like Richard Spencer. New stars can more easily arise, and many of them cross borders, attracting followers around the world. At times, absurdity can arise from such online stardom. One neo-Nazi Feuerkrieg Division "commander" from Estonia, for instance, turned out to be a 13-year-old boy whose anonymity online enabled him to play a major role.[57]

The violent fringe of white supremacy regularly interacts with the broader right-wing and white supremacist online ecosystem, including alt-right figures who are pro-Trump and claim they are merely true conservatives and "alt-lite" figures who revel in mocking liberals. Most of these figures are young and internet-savvy. They use jokes and sarcasm to lampoon the social justice community, feminists, and other villains—and they have flourished. As one leading conspiracy theorist noted several years ago, "I'm not sure the left understands the monumental ass-whupping being dished out to them on YouTube."[58]

Most white supremacists are constantly cash-strapped, so the free nature of the platforms they use is especially important. Indeed, some even use them to make money. To encourage compelling content, platforms like YouTube give the creators of popular videos payment—monetization—to feed consumers' endless appetite for the platform's videos. For instance,

Yuya, a beauty vlogger, has approximately 20 million followers and makes about $74,000 to $100,000 a month. Likewise, at age eight, Ryan Kaji, who has a channel centered on reviewing toys, drew in an income of $22 million in a single year.[59] Although most YouTubers do not receive nearly as much advertising revenue because they do not draw in as many views, some white supremacists use this monetization to raise money to sustain their propaganda and have earned thousands of dollars doing so.[60]

Terrorists, like extremists of all sorts, also enjoy social media because they can create their own narratives. For years, national newspapers, network news, and other traditional media acted as gatekeepers: even though terrorists depended on the media for publicity, coverage of their actions was usually negative. Today, white supremacists can take a world event, such as the 2020 Black Lives Matter protests following the murder of George Floyd, and frame it as left-wing and Black violence run amok. For instance, on the day of a June 2020 Black Lives Matter protest in Harrison, Arkansas, a town known for being a white supremacist haven, a rumor spread that busloads of Antifa protesters were on their way to burn Harrison to the ground. The rumor fired up "militia types" to come out to the town square with bulletproof vests and military-style rifles. After the fact, a KKK leader gave a sermon online that referred to such protesters as "cultural terrorists" and encouraged confrontation with them, explaining that the protests were "designed to create hatred for law enforcement . . . because law and order is one of the most fundamental characteristics of a white society."[61]

White supremacist groups can also add fake or misleading content, as when a Twitter account called @Antifa-US run by white supremacists posing as antifa, in order to stoke racial tensions, tweeted on May 31, 2020: "tonight's the night . . . we move into the residential areas . . . the white hoods . . . and we take what's ours."[62] Even beyond such clever manipulations, white supremacists can take individual incidents of real Black-on-white violence, crime by Latinos, financial fraud by Jews, and so on to "prove" their broader arguments. Isolated examples are presented as broader trends, and as this mindset takes hold, further examples reinforce it. Even mistakes can help. When a white supremacist ran over Heather Heyer, the antiracist counterprotester, in Charlottesville, a reporter tweeted out the initial reaction of two police officers that the driver of the car acted only out of fear of the counterprotesters. The reporter later deleted the tweet after admitting the officers had no firsthand knowledge of the car attack, but the initial tweet, and even its deletion, fueled far-right conspiracy theories that the crash had been an accident.[63]

Social media also allows for endless individual creativity. In essence, this advantage allows the bypassing of a constant white supremacist weakness—their lack of organization—and plays to their strong networks and popular causes. As a result, many individuals not affiliated with particular groups provide propaganda for the broader white supremacist movement. The Boogaloos, for example, have used social media to popularize their cause, spread their memes (such as wearing Hawaiian shirts), and otherwise attract followers, but they have done so in a bottom-up way, without any top-level coordination.[64] Indeed, the Boogaloos' very name is an example of how memes take on a new life in the white supremacist world. The term comes from the 1984 film *Breakin' 2: Electric Boogaloo*: the meme involves replacing the first part of the term, as when George W. Bush was elected: "Bush 2: Electric Boogaloo." The antigovernment (though not always white supremacist) Boogaloo movement took this to refer to the anticipated next American civil war, and the joke became the name of the movement, along with similar terms ("big igloo") and the use of Hawaiian shirts ("big luau").[65]

Videos are particularly important, which is why Facebook Live was so integral to Tarrant's plan. Videos are more visceral than words, and many of those radicalized cite online videos as essential to the process. In addition, through videos, potential recruits learn the jargon of white supremacy—not just how to think like a white supremacist but how to act like one.[66] –

At the same time, however, it is important to recognize that the real world, and its interaction with the online sphere, still plays the most important role in radicalization. Acquiring some hard skills, such as handling explosives, is facilitated by in-person instruction. Even more important, without discounting the reality of online relationships, in-person ones tend to be stronger and more sustained, as well as less vulnerable to online eavesdropping.

Although the amount of propaganda online has exploded and seems to always be increasing, it does not directly correlate with increases in violence. Indeed, as one online radicalization expert noted, there is an automatic assumption that all violent propaganda works, when much of it has a poorly crafted message, a bad messenger, or both. There is "a lot of shit terrorist propaganda that does not go viral."[67]

Music has also always been important to the modern white power movement, and now groups use social media to spread it. One 2020 journalistic investigation found more than 120 Facebook pages belonging to white power rock groups. On the pages, neo-Nazi groups with names like Kristallnacht and Les Camps de la Mort (The Death Camps) have, via Facebook, uploaded their music, posted notices about coming performances, and advertised merchandise.[68] YouTube, too, has a large amount of white power music on its platform.[69]

In addition to propaganda of various sorts, social media also helps terrorist groups organize themselves. Most social media platforms have both a public-facing side and a private side. Facebook, for example, has both "pages," where groups can post propaganda, and "groups" and Facebook Messenger, where they can organize followers. For Twitter, the general timeline is used for propaganda, but direct messages can be used to organize individuals. Social media expert Megan Squire points out that platforms, like Telegram, that are encrypted and allow for an easy back-and-forth between public and private channels are especially dangerous.[70]

Groups usually use a combination of public and private functions. White supremacists, in contrast to ISIS, use the outward-facing side of Telegram as well as private chats, churning out memes, sharing files, and sending videos to followers.[71] A study of the Soldiers of Odin, a vigilante network, showed that they used open pages to publicize their activities to both activists and new recruits. These open pages were more "sanitized," according to one study, while closed sites were used for networking among existing believers and co-ordinating activities.[72] Discourse on the closed sites was more extreme.

The virtual and real worlds combine. On Facebook, groups might urge new recruits to meet with local talent spotters or organize real-world rallies designed to intimidate Muslims or immigrants.[73] In these in-person settings, they are then further radicalized. The alt-right, a relatively newer form of white supremacy, was largely organized and spread online and provides an illustrative example of the shift from online radicalization to real-world vi-olence. Trump's 2016 election emboldened white supremacists across the board, who began meeting more in the real world through various rallies, conferences, protests, and counterprotests. The largest event, the 2017 Unite the Right rally in Charlottesville, was mostly organized and publicized by the alt-right online, with organizers using less-known services like Discord to coordinate.[74]

Social media also plays a vital role in self-radicalization and inspiring lone actors, a phenomenon far more common for white supremacist violence than for jihadists and other types of terrorists.[75] Heidi Beirich recalls that around the time of Dylann Roof's attack, if you searched for Martin Luther King, Jr., on Google, the top hits were all white supremacist sites like Stormfront.[76] Because most users are anonymous, the platforms encourage even more extreme discourse, as users feel immune from the consequences of their words. In the past, almost all radicalization involved significant face-to-face interaction, but starting in 2015, far more violence has involved online-only radicalization.[77]

In addition to radicalization and recruitment, social media allows white supremacists to harass and troll their enemies.[78] A favored white supremacist tactic—one their left-wing foes also use against them—is to "dox" their enemies.[79] This involves finding private information about an individual, such as a home address, and then publishing it online, implicitly (and at times explicitly) calling for real-world violence against them or other harassment. At times, white supremacists and other haters simply try to overwhelm a person or site with hateful comments—in 2019, Facebook had to shut down the livestreaming of a congressional hearing on white nationalism because of the volume of hostile comments.[80] National Action, a British neo-Nazi group, also targeted Luciana Berger, a member of Parliament, in what it called Operation Jew Bitch, spamming her with endless tweets.[81] (It is common for female minorities to suffer far more online harassment abuse than their male counterparts.)[82]

White supremacists today employ an ironic style to attract recruits and protect themselves from being blocked by social media companies, often claiming that their hateful remarks are just edgy jokes. The *Daily Stormer*, for instance, published a style guide, which calls for a "humorous, snarky style" while noting that the "Prime Directive" is to "Always Blame the Jews for Everything" and that "Women should be attacked" as well.[83] Supposedly humorous memes are also common, such as the anti-Semitic "Happy Merchant" meme that pictures a gleeful, hooked-nose Jew, into which white supremacists have inserted various captions.[84] Another meme pictures James Alex Fields, Jr., in Charlottesville, driving his car into a crowd described as protestors with the caption "You have the right to protest, but I'm late for work."[85] 8chan users have been known for "shitposting," deliberately inserting provocative material into posts in order to draw attention and spark a reaction, regardless of whether the user believes the material or not. Indeed, it is a mistake to read too much into Tarrant's manifesto and the writings of many other white supremacists, as much of what they write is an attempt to troll their readers and draw media attention to their cause.[86] Tarrant, for example, paused before beginning his killing spree to tell viewers: "remember, lads, subscribe to PewDiePie"—a reference to a Swedish YouTube entertainer and an in-joke for those who live in the social media world. This sort of reference allowed Tarrant and others to tap into broader cultural conversations and laugh their way into expanding their audience. Tarrant also claimed to seek to provoke a debate about gun control in the United States in order to worsen polarization and encourage a civil war.[87]

Although the white supremacist movement has always had global aspects, social media puts all this on steroids. White supremacist watcher Heidi Beirich observes that when she began watching this community in the late 1990s, concerns were local: Mexican immigrants in the U.S. Southwest, Jews in the Northeast, and so on. Now, there is far more a shared narrative, focusing on white genocide and the Great Replacement, with believers all around the globe adhering to, and building up, the message.[88] Groups like the Soldiers of Odin have used Facebook to connect their organizations and members in Canada, Finland, and Sweden.[89] Ideas like white genocide and the Great Replacement have achieved greater global convergence, allowing white supremacist ideologues to knit together a scattering of grievances into a common cause. Globalism can be overstated: most groups remain national or local, and even those with global connections are not unified. Ideas, however, flow freely across borders today. The Great Replacement, which came out of the French Identitarian movement, inspired not only Tarrant but also two attacks on American synagogues in 2018 and 2019; a 2019 attack on a Walmart in El Paso, Texas; a 2019 attack on a synagogue in Halle, Germany; and 2020 attacks on shisha bars in Germany targeting Muslims who frequented them.[90] Canadian neo-Nazis warn that multiculturalism "is the displacement, marginalization, and eventual destruction of the host population—The White Race!!!"[91] White supremacists can also share the tactics for attacks and try in other ways to make one another more effective.

Social media makes grievances far more visible and plentiful. What once would have been buried in local news or coverage confined to one country is now available for the world to see. A single action—a minority man who rapes a white woman or a jihadist terrorist attack that screams for vengeance—is now put forth for all to see as proof of that community's overall guilt. A supposed threat to whites in one country can be extrapolated to others: for example, legislation in South Africa that could hurt white farmers generated spikes in discourse among white supremacists in the United States and Europe.[92]

In so doing, social media has disrupted the terrorism landscape. The old guard of the KKK and skinheads are not usually proficient at creating memes or exploiting the latest form of social media.[93] As a result, they are being left behind as the white supremacist world evolves. As Cassie Miller of the SPLC argues, "anyone with a bit of charisma has an enormous platform to spread ideas."[94]

Social media has thus changed the movement as a whole. Social media's bottom-up nature makes it hard for anyone to control the narrative, a particular problem for the already decentralized white supremacist movement. As a result, new ideas regularly enter the mix, many of them linked to conspiracy theories. In both the United States and Europe, a common set of ideas are emerging centered around themes linked to the Great Replacement. These are less tied to particular organizations and more about a common set of narratives shared within the broader white supremacist ecosystem. These involve the "replacement" of traditional society with foreigners, a plan that Jews and a globalist elite purportedly orchestrate. Multiculturalism, feminism, and LGBTQ+ rights also further undermine traditional values in white supremacists' eyes.[95]

Social media is also changing gender views. In the past, Lane and others saw themselves as knights defending white womanhood. Now, the toxic anti-female part of the internet is stronger, and white supremacists often call for rape or otherwise glorify violence against women. They often overlap with the "involuntarily celibate" (incel) community, who blame females for not having sex with supposedly undesirable white males.[96] Squire, who tracks white supremacists on social media, finds that misogyny is "almost foundational" to the white supremacists of today, with almost all those she tracks displaying hostility to women.[97]

Social Media Companies' Mixed Responses

Social media companies have made progress in trying to stop violent and hateful users like Tarrant. Inadvertently, however, social media platforms themselves often help white supremacists and other extremists in other ways. Part of this is technical. A Facebook team warned in a leaked internal publication: "our algorithms exploit the human brain's attraction to divisiveness," meaning that viewers are more likely to promote content like white power as a result. An internal Facebook study from 2016 found that "64%

of all extremist group joins are due to our recommendation tools," with "Groups You Should Join" and "Discover" algorithms being particularly important.[98] Dylann Roof claims he began his journey into white supremacy by Googling "black on white crime." This led him to the hate group Council of Conservative Citizens, one of the top results, where he found white power propaganda.[99] Similarly, a 2015 study of YouTube found that viewers seeing one piece of white supremacist content were likely to be recommended to other pieces of white supremacist content, "leading to an immersion in an ideological bubble in just a few short clicks."[100] For the average user, more than 70 percent of the time a user spends on YouTube is watching videos generated by the video recommendation algorithm. Despite YouTube's subsequent efforts to solve this problem, the recommendation algorithm continues to suffer from similar problems.[101]

This is in part because YouTube's business model, and that of many other companies, depends on keeping people glued to their screens so they can sell advertisements, and salacious and provocative content helps do this.[102] This makes provocative white supremacist content harder to remove than jihadist content because it interacts with a far broader, and thus more profitable, audience. The company officials who are focused on safety and content moderation and are genuinely trying to fight extremism have far less power than the same company's marketers, who are focused on selling data and growing the user base. Indeed, as one government counterterrorism official noted, "We shouldn't expect anything from these companies. They don't give a shit."[103]

In addition, a small number of hyperusers enjoy considerable influence in determining the content other users see. Because many extremists are extremely active online, they drive content far more than their numbers would suggest. In addition, white supremacist accounts are often private, anonymous, or hidden from the public, making it hard for outsiders to know who is responsible for what. This allows hyperusers to drown out less active users, even though a closer look at some of these accounts shows they are created to manipulate the platform. Some appear to be active on the platform as much as 20 hours a day, suggesting either that teams of people working in shifts manage them or that they are automated accounts.

Social media companies also face difficulties because the amount of genuinely dangerous content and users is small, so it is easy to miss them or to use too heavy an approach—one that removes or blocks well-meaning users. Twitter found, for example, that 70 percent of the views of the Christchurch footage on its platform were from news organizations and individuals who condemned the attack. Taking down these users would be unfair.[104] In addition, many social media technologies are a boon to human rights activists and other positive social change agents. The growth of the Black Lives Matter movement, for example, owes much to livestreaming technology, which has captured police abuses in real time.[105]

The social media companies are also global, compounding the challenge. What is offensive with regard to nudity in France, say, differs from that in Pakistan; and the acceptability of hateful language also varies, with some countries far more sensitive than others, one technology executive told me.[106]

In response to these and other problems, some changes have occurred. Leading companies like Facebook, Twitter, and YouTube have changed their policies, prohibiting content that "dehumanizes" other groups or justifies discrimination and broadening their focus on, and rules about, stopping a wider swath of violent groups, not just those formally designated as terrorists.[107] On Facebook, publishers who push false news are promoted on the platform less often, and the role of hyperusers has been slightly reduced. In response to criticism, Facebook has become more aggressive against white supremacists, adopting an explicit ban against praise for white supremacists and prohibiting the harassment of civil rights activists.[108] As events like the 2017 Unite the Right rally have showed the power of these groups, Facebook has increased the number of groups and individuals it bans. It has also incorporated more civil rights principles into its advertising system and product development; removed users like Richard Spencer who have tried to put an acceptable veneer on racist ideas; and banned posts that allege that a racial group as a whole is a threat or will take over the political system or put up other white supremacist tropes. Facebook has also changed its newsfeed content selection algorithms to encourage higher quality information, and in 2019 YouTube banned videos endorsing neo-Nazism and white supremacy.[109] In March 2019, Facebook claimed that its automated systems could delete 65 percent of hate speech before it appeared on the platform; by March 2020, this figure was at almost 90 percent.[110] Twitter claims that the vast majority of terrorist content is taken down quickly through its algorithms.[111] These companies deserve credit for moving forward. As Richard Spencer lamented, "at one point, say two years ago, Silicon Valley really was our friend. . . . What has happened in terms of the Silicon Valley attacks on us are, just, really bad."[112]

Other companies have taken a range of intermediate steps. YouTube, in particular, has tried to develop a menu of options. For posts that do not openly violate its terms of service guidelines but are still, in the company's polite words, "controversial," they have removed the "likes" and "comments" features and taken such posts out of the company's recommendations algorithm to minimize their impact.[113] YouTube also demonetizes, and does not allow advertising related to, these "controversial" videos, trying to remove the financial incentive to post such content.[114]

Many technology companies start with a "whack-a-mole" approach, removing offending content when it pops up and then repeating the process as necessary. If the user repeatedly puts up dangerous content, they may remove the user from their platform and purge all the user's content. The user, in turn, may create a new account, and the process can start up again.[115] However, as online radicalization expert Maura Conway contends, if you take whack-a-mole seriously enough, white supremacists reach a tipping point where they find it hard to stay on a platform, "with their accounts lasting minutes, rarely days." As Conway points out, their followers no longer know where to find them. They can shift platforms, but every time they do, they lose followers who do not use the new platform. They often end up with fewer followers, albeit more virulent members, on small platforms that overall have few members.[116]

Over time, the few extremists who migrate to obscure platforms become highly vulnerable to law enforcement monitoring and arrests. Conway notes that white supremacists are often bad at hiding online, leaving a trail that is easy to follow. Their rhetoric may grow more virulent, but it is easy for law enforcement to monitor them, as users are now "corralled in specific places."[117] Similarly, Berger notes that, even without law enforcement attention, private groups like Antifa and Bellingcat regularly track white supremacists online.[118]

The simple step of kicking groups and individuals off social media— "deplatforming" them—can be surprisingly effective. As Squire points out, if groups are not on mainstream platforms, it is harder for them to appear normal to those they seek to recruit who have not yet drunk the Kool-Aid. In addition, new platforms like Gab and 8chan are often technically and aesthetically cumbersome and unfamiliar to new users—there is a reason people prefer Facebook and Twitter. Finally, after deplatforming, users cannot troll their enemies as effectively, depriving them of one of their most important tactics.[119]

Deplatforming grew after Charlottesville, and social media companies became less committed to a laissez-faire approach to discourse on their platforms. The rally itself drew white supremacists of all kinds, with over 500 attendees. In addition to the killing of Heather Heyer, people of color were beaten and counterprotesters were attacked. All this made for bad publicity for the social media companies, whose permissive approaches toward the right stood in sharp contrast with their policies toward jihadist organizations. Their own workforces, diverse and leaning progressive, also highlighted the hypocrisy. After the neo-Nazi *Daily Stormer* mocked the death of Heather Heyer, many platforms took it and other similar sites down. Apple and PayPal banned the selling of white supremacist merchandise on their sites, and Spotify moved to stop sales of white power music.[120] Many began, finally, to enforce the antihate portions of their terms of service. Facebook has thrown various Combat 18 branches off; Twitter has deplatformed English Defence League cofounder Tommy Robinson and Generation Identity leader Martin Sellner; and Facebook, Tumblr, and other companies have suspended various English Defence League chapters. PayPal has denied the group access to its services. Facebook, YouTube, and others have suspended numerous accounts linked to Generation Identity. YouTube has kicked off numerous accounts associated with the Nordic Resistance Movement. Many of these white supremacist groups and public figures have lost support and seen themselves marginalized as a result of these social media bans.[121] As one technology company expert told me, "removing a bullhorn from a provocateur can be very successful."[122]

Deplatforming grew even further after the January 6, 2021, insurrection at the U.S. Capitol, when white supremacists, along with a range of conspiracists and antigovernment extremists, were thrown off major platforms and an entire platform they used, Parler, was taken off Amazon Web Services. Discord, long used by white supremacists to communicate, removed a pro-Trump community from its server. In a sign of how platforms are more aware of the risks, Discord officials noted that while the 2017 Unite the Right rally had used Discord without interference, this time the company monitored potentially dangerous users in real time and blocked insurrectionists from using several of its channels in the leadup to the attack.[123]

Deplatforming has to be balanced against free speech concerns, but these can be overstated. When President Trump, Tommy Robinson, or a nameless white supremacist is kicked off Twitter or Facebook, the individual still has the right to speak to their neighbors, go to meetings, or write a racist screed. Removing them from social media only reduces the scope and scale of their audience. In addition, because white supremacists harass and dox online, removing them allows for a healthier information ecosystem for others,

especially women, minorities, and other frequent targets of white supremacist vitriol.

Other sites can simply refuse services to white supremacists. During
the Charlottesville rally, AirBnB "dehomed" white supremacists, canceling
their contracts for the homes they rented while seeking to attend the rally
(while reimbursing the renters to avoid punishing them).[124] Denying services—when hosting and routing services like GoDaddy and Amazon Web
Services stop white supremacist groups from having robust presences online—is effective. Payment processors like Venmo or PayPal also play an important role.[125] After the Pittsburgh synagogue shooting, for example, Gab's
web hosting provider refused to continue hosting the site, and it temporarily
went offline as a result. GoDaddy similarly gave Gab 24 hours to find a new
domain name hosting service, and PayPal and Stripe suspended Gab's account and transfers to its account, respectively.[126] Following Charlottesville,
GoDaddy and Google Domains stopped hosting the *Daily Stormer*.[127] Many
white supremacists had to pivot to cryptocurrency as they lost access to
PayPal, credit card companies, and other traditional means of financing.[128]

Services like Cloudflare that protect websites from denial of service attacks
can also withdraw their protection, leaving white supremacist websites vulnerable to left-wing or other vigilante hackers conducting such attacks, which
flood sites with false traffic until they crash. Cloudflare once protected at
least 48 hate websites, including the *Daily Stormer* and Stormfront. However,
after the Charlottesville rally—following pressure from peer companies,
employees, and social media—Cloudflare removed the *Daily Stormer*'s account from its services. However, Cloudflare's CEO eloquently warned that
he and other CEOs should not have the power to decide which voices are
legitimate. The company's ambivalence toward the *Daily Stormer*, and the
CEO's commitment to free speech, illustrate the tensions tech companies
dealing with white supremacists face between free speech and preventing the
spread of hate.[129]

Facebook and other social media companies have historically focused on
countering jihadist groups rather than white supremacists and, as such, they
were less able to respond to attacks like Tarrant's. This is largely a legacy of
the struggle against the Islamic State. When that group emerged on the world
stage in 2014, Facebook and other companies, at first, largely ignored it. After
criticism grew following the posting of ISIS beheading videos and the 2015
ISIS Paris attacks, among other outrages, some companies tried to preemp-
tively block content and remove users associated with designated terrorist

groups like ISIS, but they also wanted to reassure constituencies dedicated to free speech. In this context, the U.S. government designation of ISIS as a terrorist group was important, as it gave a legal imprimatur, and political cover, to a decision to restrict content from some users but not others. In the United States, in particular, however, the government does not designate domestic terrorist groups (as most violent white supremacists would be classified), largely because the First Amendment prohibits restrictions on political speech and assembly, and administrations have feared that such a list could easily become political. In addition, as of early 2021, only one right-wing group, the Russian Imperial Movement, was officially declared a terrorist group (in this case, by being designated as a Specially Designated Global Terrorist Entity), despite there being many such groups abroad. In contrast to the case of jihadist terrorist organizations, there is no formal U.S. government list social media companies can use, though some democratic governments like Canada have become more aggressive in listing right-wing sgroups, including white supremacists. Facebook and other large organizations also have their own lists.[130]

Yet social media companies still do not treat white supremacist groups as they do jihadists, and they often wait until after a problem is manifest before acting.[131] When presented with internal findings about how Facebook's algorithms were helping extremists, Facebook executives downplayed the dangers and watered down the solutions. As technology expert Hany Farid notes, companies like Facebook market the precision of their data when it comes to advertising but deny it when it comes to identifying extremists. "Why are they so good at targeting you with content that's consistent with your prior engagement, but somehow when it comes to harm, they become bumbling idiots? You can't have it both ways."[132]

As Facebook began to consider more aggressive efforts, one Facebook executive declared that the proposed changes to reduce white supremacist content were "paternalistic" and that Facebook instead wanted to promote free expression and individual choice—values that happen to accord with its business model of encouraging as much engagement as possible with the platform. At times, the internal rationalization reaches the level of absurdity, with one senior executive claiming that, by deemphasizing the role of hyperusers, they could hurt a hypothetical Girl Scout troop who banded together on one account to promote the sale of cookies. Indeed, because many of the proposals to hinder white supremacist content involve decreasing the amount of salacious and provocative content, companies fear they will drive customers away and hurt their bottom lines. Indeed, one of the internal groups pushing for to reduce extremist discourse on Facebook labeled their own proposals to their superiors "antigrowth," with predictable lack of success.[133] Part of the problem is also the very nature of Facebook and other fast-growth social media companies. These companies encourage the rapid rollout of new products, pushing them to consumers before they develop appropriate protections.[134] Facebook has regularly dragged its feet or taken cosmetic measures. For example, in its often hate-filled "Groups" feature, Facebook has relied on self-selected moderators to maintain its terms of service, in part to avoid taking directly responsibility itself. These moderators, however, are often themselves part of the problem and have have often encouraged group members to break the rules and even intimidated those who threatened to report hateful content.[135]

White supremacists are also more about networks and individuals than groups, complicating the challenge. Indeed, the United States does not designate domestic white supremacist groups, even violent ones, as terrorist organizations, leaving the companies without government guidance. As a result, the companies' efforts have been "miserable failures," as one technology official told me.[136] They often focus on removing content (e.g., a post promoting violence) or even taking down members of a banned group, such as ISIS. However, taking down those who believe in white supremacy with its many facets is too tall an order. This is especially complex in that the debates and associated offensive terms change constantly, making it harder for the companies to keep up.[137]

Facebook, Twitter, and other companies at least try fitfully, but some companies have remained resistant to even limited steps. For years, Telegram mocked the idea of deplatforming users. Following the 2015 ISIS attacks in Paris, for instance, the founder of Telegram posted the flippant response "I propose banning words. There's evidence that they're being used by terrorists to communicate."[138] Indeed, the platform prided itself on its encryption, features like automatic account self-destruction, and other privacy measures. As Telegram grew, however, it began to face more political pressure to act, especially as dense networks of white supremacists began to use its platform—"Terrorgram," one expert labeled it.[139] In response to mounting pressure, Telegram did eventually carry out a major crackdown on the white supremacist presence in 2020 and 2021. However, Telegram remains more permissive for white supremacists than platforms like Facebook and Twitter and has tended to try to restrict their channels from view or otherwise limit access to them rather than blocking them outright.[140] This allows white supremacists to "go dark" rather than truly disrupting their networks. As one technology executive told me, the companies are "always dragged to the right answer" and "never initiate on their own."[141]

Companies could also work together more effectively against white supremacy. Just as they did with jihadists, they could "hash" images to prevent them from appearing on one site after being removed from another. They could also limit transitions between platforms by preventing radical commentators from embedding links in comments.[142] Most important, big companies could help smaller companies that do not have the staff and expertise to handle a sudden influx of radicals when they are deplatformed from a site like Facebook or YouTube.

Technically, Facebook, YouTube, and other companies need to "train" their artificial intelligence algorithms on a large amount of data in order to identify videos like the Christchurch shooting automatically. Once the algorithms have "learned" how to identify them, they take down such content even as it is being posted. Given the scale of what is posted to the internet, most removal of dangerous content must be done by algorithms: humans cannot keep up. However, the amount of training data the algorithms require to learn properly is massive—a problem that, Facebook claims, is exacerbated by the huge number of legitimate first-person-shooter video game clips that individual players post on the internet. In addition, Facebook uses "accelerated view" to prioritize potential suicide videos, hoping to alert first responders and otherwise act quickly.[143] Mass shootings, especially from terrorists, are, by comparison, rare and thus receive less immediate attention. Despite these barriers, Facebook's overall response time after the Christchurch shooting was relatively brief, and the blocking of a million uploads was an impressive technical feat. Indeed, Facebook had made considerable progress by the time of the Christchurch shooting: in 2017, when a man in Thailand had murdered his infant daughter and posted the video on Facebook, it had remained there for 24 hours.[144] It's a sad fact that we cannot rely on users to flag disturbing content in a timely or systematic way.

Takedown numbers, however, can also be misleading. Facebook, for example, regularly reports about the vast amounts of hateful content it removes from its platform. However, Facebook does not provide information on false positives or the overall volume of hateful comments as a percentage of overall content. So it is hard to know how precise Facebook is and whether its efforts are simply a drop in the ocean. Nor does Facebook report as to which groups suffer the most from hate speech.[145] And Facebook is easy to pick on because it provides some data—other companies report even less information.

Dangerous content is often hard to specify. White supremacists use "420" to represent Hitler's birthday; it is also a popular way to refer to smoking marijuana.[146] Similarly, white supremacists rely heavily on memes, such as Pepe the Frog, a cartoon frog that became a symbol for the movement even though its creator vehemently rejects racism and any association with white supremacists. Banning "frog images" seems absurd, but, seen in a proper context, these memes are clearly white supremacist imagery.[147]

More broadly, Facebook and other companies are not sufficiently resourcing the problem. At first glance, this criticism may seem unfair, especially for Facebook. As of July 2020, the company employed more than 350 terrorism and other dangerous organization analysts in-house and contracted with over 15,000 content moderators worldwide.[148] Both numbers are far greater than those of any other social media company. Yet even these major efforts are not commensurate with the scale of the problem. Facebook content moderation numbers are big, but so too is the number of Facebook users: over 3 billion. Moderating the accounts and content of over one-third of humanity requires the expertise needed to distinguish between terrorist and dissident groups worldwide. In turn, that requires a large team of analysts with both an in-depth knowledge of terrorism and a wide array of local and regional expertise to set globally consistent policies about which groups and content around the world qualify as terrorist or hateful. Even more, this challenge also requires moderators with the linguistic, cultural, and analytical skills necessary to apply those policies as quickly and accurately as possible—one expert noted that extreme content is far more likely to be removed if it is in English than in minor European languages.[149] The current moderators are either too low-skilled or too few in number to address the problem sufficiently.[150] And that is just Facebook, which has devoted far more resources to this problem than most platforms. If the problem is to be solved industry-wide, other companies will need to expend more resources of their own or gain greater access to shared expertise and knowledge.

There is hope, as well as frustration, as these companies have had considerable success in taking down ISIS videos and other jihadist content. From a moral point of view, white supremacist images and content are no different from their jihadist counterparts—if social media companies block one, they should block the other. They developed the tools to fight ISIS in response to pressure from lawmakers and regulators, but similar pressure on white supremacists from lawmakers is, so far, lacking.[151]

Search engines like Google also deserve more attention. For at least several months, white supremacists gamed the search algorithm so that searches for Martin Luther King, Jr., resulted in hits linked to white supremacist sites— an outcome Google was slow to fix.[152] Although companies will respond to requests from law enforcement with a warrant, they resist efforts to remove even dangerous items like bomb manuals from search results. Part of the reason for this is a culture that emphasizes free speech, and part of it is a desire to keep the search function as efficient as possible—companies like Google are loath to tweak their search engines, fearing that if they do it in one case of hateful content they will be inundated with constant demands to alter it to reflect an array of causes.

The story does not end even when companies succeed in removing content. Some extremists have turned to using small alternative platforms or hijacking other platforms, such as gaming communication channels, which are unprepared for their presence. These invaded platforms are often cesspools where the most offensive users congregate to, at best, demean and trash talk and, at worst, plan violence. Often, these platforms have no rules, do not require logins, and otherwise emphasize the freedom to act without consequences. Matthew Prince, the CEO of the web security firm Cloudflare, described them as "lawless by design."[153] Some of these platforms, like 8chan, were created, in part, because mainstream platforms kicked off extreme users. Gab, a sorta hybrid of Twitter and Reddit, declared its goal as seeking "to make speech free again and say FUCK YOU Silicon Valley elitist trash."[154] Gab had attracted almost half a million users by the end of 2018, and the Pittsburgh synagogue shooter, Robert Bowers, used it before his attack, posting conspiracy theories about white genocide and migrant caravans.[155]

Alternative platforms like Gab have become dangerous mixes of hostile voices where conspiracy theorists, antiimmigrant zealots, and others create their own reality. They often mix with more mainstream conservatives, and hashtags like #maga, #trump, and #fakenews are popular.[156] On 8chan, where Tarrant and the shooters he inspired in El Paso and in Poway, California, hung out, he was praised for his "high score," referring to a video game–like mindset for killing people.[157] Others there spend time "siegeposting": constantly putting up the writings of American neo-Nazi James Mason, the author of *Siege,* and discussing how to acquire explosives and artillery for the inevitable race war.[158]

When white supremacists and other radicals cluster on 8chan and similar platforms, there can be "petri dish" and "echo chamber" effects, whereby dangerous behavior grows rapidly in a fertile environment. Registered users of Stormfront have been linked to around 100 murders.[159] In addition, when they move from a mainstream site like Facebook to a site like Telegram, white supremacists may gain more access to encryption, which makes it harder for law enforcement officials to track them. Squire points out, however, that many of these groups and individuals have been deplatformed because they were already engaging in bad behavior—the lawless platforms did not make them worse; rather, they sought out sites like Stormfront because they were already violent.[160] In addition, some of the alternative platforms are not financially viable and go out of business quickly.[161] Nevertheless, at least some research suggests that when a toxic community is deplatformed, the more hardcore members may move to another platform where they become more active and, at times, more toxic.[162] In addition, on encrypted or small platforms, users' ability to do mass outreach is limited. However, it is nevertheless possible that the removal of the limits of mainstream platforms can make groups and individuals like Tarrant even more extreme.

Technology companies try to work together against radicals, often via the Global Internet Forum to Counter Terrorism, which brings together many large companies to share data on terrorism. The database, however, only has content from Al Qaeda and ISIS, not from white supremacists and other nonjihadist groups. This organization, moreover, is voluntary, and smaller platforms do not participate because they lack the necessary resources.

In general, companies do a bad job of pooling their data. Facebook might have information on a white supremacist Facebook group, but it is not cross-referenced with information from Google about the group's members searching, say, for how to build a bomb.[163] The companies have different policies regarding what type of hateful content is allowable.

Small companies are a particularly difficult challenge. Often, they are just starting up and do not have the institutional or financial capacity to moderate content or police their membership, leaving them vulnerable. The communications app Zello, for example, which was used to help coordinate the January 6, 2021, assault on the U.S. Capitol, has little ability to control content on its own platform.[164] The smaller companies also often have lax security or don't police their own activities carefully, often not making changes because, so far, they haven't had a problem: "they didn't have a Cambridge Analytica happen to them," notes Squire, referring to the scandal in which private data from millions of Facebook accounts ended up being sold, which in turn forced Facebook to better monitor the ways its platform and its data were being used.[165]

What Can Governments Do?

So why can the U.S. or other governments not step in?

New Zealand made it illegal to possess a copy of Tarrant's manifesto or video, and Germany polices hate speech, even arresting individuals who post hateful content online and taking away their phones and computers.[166] Similar restrictions violate the First Amendment in the United States, which provides broad protection of what can be said on platforms, including speech that promotes hate, violence, or illegal conduct, unless it is likely to incite "imminent lawless action."[167] Companies, however, as private entities, can still kick off users if they violate their (quite broad and vague) terms of service. Their platforms, despite white supremacists' complaints, are not public spaces, and thus First Amendment protections do not kick in as they would if a government tried to block a rally in a park. But the companies, if they choose (as they historically have) not to kick off users, enjoy considerable legal protection. Section 230 of the Communications Decency Act states that service providers, such as social media platforms, are "distributors," not "publishers," of content. Therefore, they are not legally liable for the content on their sites, a designation that remains even if they take voluntary steps to restrict content.[168] As a result, social media companies cannot face legal action in response to content on their platforms even if, as is often the case, they underfilter or even encourage illegality like revenge porn.[169] Nevertheless, even though these are global companies and Americans are only a small percentage of overall users today, their genesis in the United States meant their policies and cultures were heavily shaped by U.S. ideals of free speech.[170]

The bigger problem is political, especially in the United States. In America, a disproportionate number of hyperactive users are conservative. (The reverse is true in other countries.) Thus, Facebook, Twitter, and other companies fear that reducing white supremacist content on their platforms will indirectly reduce content from conservative publishers and users, leading to charges of bias.[171] Similarly, European political leaders who whip up anti-Semitic and anti-LGBTQ+ sentiment call for social media companies not to take down hate speech.[172] False positives that remove accounts of Muslims by accident are one thing; removing accounts of powerful white men is another. Technology companies, which are businesses after all, do not want to offend. Indeed, they are likely to face blowback from mainstream right-wing voices if they block white supremacist content.[173] As one former technology company official told me, "no one wants to be the first to pull the Trump trigger."[174] The official went on to note that the same pressures would be true for other leaders, particular those of other democracies. Twitter, for example, has proven reluctant to ban many white supremacists from its platform, and, in internal discussions, its leadership has explicitly cited the political risk of doing so. As Berger notes, "cracking down on white nationalists will therefore involve removing a lot of people who identify to a greater or lesser extent as Trump supporters, and some people in Trump circles and pro-Trump media will certainly seize on this to complain they are being persecuted."[175]

Indeed, politicians themselves enjoy a loophole. Facebook's policy, as of January 2021, was to exempt politicians from fact-checking and treat their speech as newsworthy unless there was a clear risk of real-world violence.[176] Some politicians, of course, are part of the problem, as their rhetoric can normalize hatred of minorities and signal that violence is acceptable. Representative Marjorie Taylor Greene, for example, "liked" a comment that "a bullet to the head would be quicker" to remove House Speaker Nancy Pelosi and other posts calling for executing FBI agents who were supposedly part of an anti-Trump "deep state."[177]

At times, it is worth keeping bad users on social media platforms, for when governments are looking for them, the internet can become a tremendous vulnerability, revealing networks as well as specific plans. Extremists remain highly vulnerable to infiltration online. For propaganda to be effective, they must reach new members. These new members can be would-be terrorists—but they can also be private researchers or FBI agents and police officers.

Even as Beam and others used dial-in services in the 1980s, the FBI was there. The Bureau tapped into an Aryan Nations bulletin board and discovered death threats against civil rights and political leaders that it later used as evidence.[178] As social media has become a standard way to communicate, the government has stepped up its efforts. Google has given to law enforcement detailed personal information—including real names and credit card numbers—of white supremacists using its platform to threaten others.[179] Even encrypted platforms are vulnerable, as informants may pass information to government. German intelligence, for example, was able to monitor WhatsApp despite white supremacist groups believing its encryption protected them.[180] White supremacist leader Ben Daley warned his followers: "I would be mindful of saying anything that could be misconstrued as a call to violence. I know people who literally have feds show up at there [*sic*] door over posts."[181]

Even when white supremacists use encryption or other useful forms of operational security, they remain vulnerable. "End-to-end" encryption protects data as it goes back and forth, but the humans and the devices on both ends remain vulnerable. "You need only one dumb person," notes Squire. If he talks out of turn—and many of them love to boast in open chatrooms or other public online venues—it attracts the attention of the FBI, putting the whole network at risk.[182] Following the January 6, 2021, Capitol insurrection, government investigators used a wide range of sources, many from social media postings bragging about the attacks, to identify participants. As one police expert noted, "if the event happened 20 years ago, it would have been 100 times harder to identify these people. But today it's almost impossible not to leave your footprints somewhere."[183]

Setting standards is an important role of government. Indeed, without a government push, the companies' profit motive will keep them from taking dramatic steps. "It's like asking the meatpacking industry in 1903 about severed fingers," complained one government official who had pushed for change.[184] The big companies are often reluctant to be first-movers in deplatforming or setting higher content standards, fearing the criticism that will result. If the government sets standards, it protects companies from criticism and spurs them to action. At times, however, governing bodies work at cross-purposes. The European Union, for example, has passed regulations disallowing proactive scanning of content on privacy grounds but, at the same time, encouraged proactive scanning and more content removal in another regulation designed to fight various forms of terrorism.[185] Similarly, the government can require companies to build content moderation into their business models from the start.[186]

More transparency would also help. It is difficult to learn how big the white supremacist presence is online, who they are targeting, the effectiveness of various responses, and other important counterterrorism questions. Equally important, it is difficult to learn the cost of counterterrorism measures: How many people are unjustly denied access to internet platforms by mistake?

All these solutions require a mindset shift in counterterrorism practice. For issues like propaganda and recruitment, private company policies, not government action, are often the most important factor today. In addition, because of the global nature of these companies, no country alone can tackle this problem, even within its own borders. The situation requires cooperation—between companies, and between the government and the private sector—that, so far, has been limited.

6

Strategies of White Supremacy and the Weaknesses of the Cause

When Patrick Crusius murdered 23 people in his shooting spree at an El Paso Walmart in 2019, he claimed he was responding to a "Hispanic invasion" and that the killings would provide an "incentive" for Latinos to leave the United States. In his manifesto, "An Inconvenient Truth," he contended that migration needed to be reversed to "remove the threat" that "they" posed to the white majority.[1] Crusius's attack quickly became fodder for a broader political debate over immigration in the United States, with critics of President Trump using it to blast him for inflaming sentiment against migrants.[2]

Crusius's attack came on the heels of the killing of 11 worshipers at the 2018 Tree of Life synagogue in Pittsburgh by Robert Bowers and Dylann Roof's murder of nine worshipers at a Black church in Charleston, South Carolina, only a few years earlier. These three individuals are responsible for the deadliest white supremacist attacks in years, but none was a member of a particular group. Rather, they were steeped in a culture of hate and white supremacy, often online. This extreme decentralization made it harder to detect, and stop, these killers, but it is also indicative of the many problems the movement faces.

White supremacists such as Crusius regularly kill people, but does their violence work? To answer this question, it is useful to flip perspectives, focusing on what Crusius and like-minded extremists have wanted to accomplish. They did not just kill people for the sake of killing them. Rather, the shooters had goals, however far-fetched, that they hoped to achieve, and they believed violence would serve those ends. Breivik, Tarrant, and other killers had ambitions similar to those of groups past and present such as the KKK, The Order, Aryan Nations, and the Atomwaffen Division. However, they often differed in their tactical and operational objectives, as well as in their broader influence on the movement as a whole.

As was true for Klan groups in the past, white supremacists can use violence in conjunction with participation in broader political movements.

However, in contrast to the Klan of yore, the opposite is usually true: they turn to violence because they see the political system writ large as failing them and because they are too weak politically to counter this. Some groups and violent individuals seek to topple governments. Others want to frighten minorities and other groups, forcing them to leave the country or become second-class citizens. Still others have given up on wide-scale political change and seek to establish whites-only enclaves. For many, the steps between the act(s) of violence and their eventual victory are hazy: they kill with no real logic. Despite this confusion, it is possible to determine and assess an array of strategies these groups and individuals are pursuing.

Groups and individuals often embrace "leaderless resistance," an idea promulgated decades ago by American white supremacist ideologue and leader Louis Beam that has become popular around the world. Although this approach is often portrayed as the ultimate nightmare for counterterrorism, it is really a strategy of the weak, even by the standards of terrorists. Leaderless groups and networked individuals still kill people, but it is far harder for them to achieve any of their political goals. Indeed, in many ways, it is not really a strategy, as it is unclear even to many of its perpetrators what they hope to accomplish beyond killing people.

Organizational necessity often drives action more than strategy. Groups and the movement as a whole must attract recruits, raise money, buy weapons, propagandize, and otherwise grow, or at least survive. Often, the imperatives of the organization dominate the day-to-day actions of its members: the purpose of the group becomes sustaining itself, not fomenting a white power revolution. Indeed, much of the reason for the movement's decentralization today is that past groups could not sustain themselves in the face of public opprobrium and government pressure.

This chapter first discusses the relationship between white supremacist violence and broader electoral politics. It then identifies the different strategies white supremacists use and how they try to recruit and organize themselves. Finally, this chapter assesses these strategies and the common problems white supremacists face when they try to implement them.

Elections and Respectability

Some groups with extreme views favor using the instruments of democracy to achieve an undemocratic result—radical politics, not terrorism, if they do not also use violence. By winning elections, groups can pass legislation and use the power of the executive branch to ban immigration from nonwhite countries, expel nonwhite immigrants, restrict the activities of religious minorities, ban gay and interracial marriage, and otherwise achieve their agenda. This is effectively what many American racists did for many decades before the civil rights era, supporting elected leaders and working with local governments to terrorize and intimidate the Black community.

Today, elections and political success can still whip up violence, but there can also be an inverse relationship with political success. Attacks and hate crimes in the United States grew in 2008 and 2009, the same period when America elected and then inaugurated its first Black president. Eight years later, racist incidents surged again after the election of Donald Trump, with zealots often invoking the president's name as they assaulted minorities.[3] Europe, where many countries have parliamentary systems that allow smaller party representation, saw parties with antiimmigrant and anti-Muslim agendas like Jobbik in Hungary, Golden Dawn in Greece, Alternative für Deutschland in Germany, Lega Nord in Italy, and the National Front in France, among others, win significant numbers of seats in their parliaments and, in some cases, join the governments.

There is no simple relationship between political parties sympathetic to white supremacy, violent white supremacists, and the overall political process. Peaceful politics, however, can inhibit violence, as even those with extreme views reject it because it alienates voters whose support they need to win. In addition, politics can create an outlet for ideas, even hateful ones, and thus a safety valve.

Politics, however, can also normalize extreme ideas and serve to mobilize potentially violent communities. Partial success, or even failure, at the polls also has its advantages for extremists. Electing a white supremacist to a position of power gives a leader and the cause as a whole visibility and legitimacy. Depending on the number of those elected and their electoral power, the movement also gains some influence over a country's laws and institutions. In the 1920s, American Klan groups were an important force in passing laws restricting immigration and supporting eugenics. If the group draws a significant number of votes, other parties may move in its direction to siphon off the group's support, giving it an indirect political victory. Even the process of campaigning helps, as it puts the group's ideas into the public realm. In Europe, antiimmigrant parties surged in elections in Germany and other countries after 2015, but other parties, even when their support ebbed, had embraced more critical rhetoric against immigrants and favored less-welcoming policies.

White supremacist violence can surge during election years when racial and immigration issues are in the headlines. In part, this is because citizens are bombarded with messages to act. Some conservative politicians stressed that civil rights legislation in the 1960s, and then gun legislation in the 1990s, were truly existential threats. With such rhetoric in mind, the most extreme are inspired to use violence. In addition, in their eyes, violence separates the truly committed from those who just talk.[4]

Open white supremacists themselves have had, at best, mixed results in U.S. elections in the post–civil rights era. George Lincoln Rockwell, who headed the American Nazi Party until his murder in 1967, labored to create a mass movement. Rockwell held provocative, but peaceful, rallies in controversial places to create backlash and gain greater publicity. His party had ranks and uniforms, clearly denoting hierarchy and membership. Yet he never gathered more than a couple of hundred supporters. David Duke, the telegenic neo-Nazi and Klan leader, won a place in Louisiana's House of Representatives in 1989 and came close to winning a Senate seat and then the governorship in 1990 and 1991, respectively. Though he lost both races, he won a majority of the white vote. Race played a major role in his campaign. His campaign manager later recalled his push to focus on Black Americans: "the Jews just aren't a big issue in Louisiana. We keep telling David, stick to attacking the blacks. There's no point in going after the Jews, you just piss them off and nobody here cares about them anyway."[5]

Duke tried to make white supremacy palatable, moving away from hoods and cross burnings to business suits and public relations campaigns. Instead of emphasizing white power, he emphasized white grievances. During the contention in Boston over school busing, as a Klan leader, he organized "Freedom Rides North" for Klansmen to aid the cause of white protestors. Stunts like this, which capitalized on broader white racial discontent but did not involve overt violence, garnered him considerable attention—and he later tried to mainstream the movement further through his campaigns for elected office. Although some European parties and movements resort to violence (Golden Dawn's rallies in Greece, for instance, often include assaults on immigrants and vandalism), others combine politics with similar stunts or extralegal actions, but not terrorism, against their preferred targets. French Identitarians holding a feast with pork to exclude Muslims is a peaceful example.

As these tactics suggest, many of the ideas of white supremacists have echoes in legitimate mainstream opinion. White supremacists loathe the idea of preferential treatment for minorities, but it is also unpopular among many Americans. Gun rights, not an inherently white supremacist issue but one of concern to many, is another issue that has considerable popular support.[6] When Klan members went after Vietnamese fishers in the 1970s, they pushed the (false) idea that the refugees were welfare cheats and otherwise played to the New Right's hostility to government programs that helped minorities.[7] These plays to mainstream opinion make it harder to crack down on white supremacist groups and leaders, allowing them to garner sympathy from at least some mainstream voters.

The influence goes both ways, and more mainstream voices are also echoing propaganda themes found in the white supremacist world. Trump's 2016 campaign regularly warned of an "invasion" of immigrants from Mexico in their advertisements. Representative Matt Gaetz (R-FL), a vehement Trump supporter, claimed that the left wants to "replace" America and that Black Lives Matter seeks "cultural genocide." Commentators on Fox News declared that Ilhan Omar (D-MI), a Muslim, has religious beliefs that were "antithetical" to the Constitution and warned that Democratic elites are trying to replace so-called real Americans with immigrants. Andrew Anglin, who runs the *Daily Stormer,* calls Tucker Carlson's show "Daily Stormer TV."[8] More broadly, President Trump repeated the social Darwinist rhetoric of many white supremacists, dividing the world into winners and losers, often by the way people look or their countries of origin.[9]

The relationship between the white supremacist community and President Trump and his administration was disturbing but complex. He appointed individuals with strong anti-Muslim and antiimmigrant views, though he was more careful about avowed racists and anti-Semites. We see a correlation between support for Trump and antiimmigrant sentiment, racism, sexism, and other beliefs common to white supremacists. In addition, studies show that exposure to Trump's rhetoric made prejudiced views more likely.[10] Many white supremacists saw Trump as like-minded, and they favored those of his policies that separated Latin American migrant families, increased deportations, and ended protections for children of illegal immigrants brought to the United States.[11] When he won the 2016 election and assumed office, violence against minorities surged. This may have been because white supremacists assumed that his election would bring more toleration of, and support for, their ideas and felt emboldened by his and his supporters' rhetoric.[12] Many white supremacists also saw his election as the beginning of a new era. The alt-right, a clean-cut and articulate, but racist and xenophobic, movement that has tried to reshape the mainstream conservative movement, initially saw Trump as an opportunity to "red pill" followers.

Various leaders and their groups came together in the Unite the Right rally in Charlottesville in 2017, ostensibly to protest the planned removal of the statue of Confederate general Robert E. Lee but really as a show of strength. As discussed earlier, the rally turned violent, and Heather Heyer, a ocounterprotester, was killed when a white supremacist drove a car through a crowd. A similar annual march in Poland, which grew from several hundred to tens of thousands and brought together different strands of the movement—anti-Semitic, antirefugee, anti-LGBTQ+—inspired the organizers. Indeed, a political bloc inspired by the street demonstrations eventually took 11 seats in the Polish parliament and, incredibly, used the Confederate flag as one of their symbols.[13] Charlottesville, however, was a public relations disaster—and public relations was what the march was all about. The images of neo-Nazis with torches stripped away the alt-right's claim to be simply mild-mannered traditionalists. "The veil was removed after Charlottesville," notes Southern Poverty Law Center expert Cassie Miller. In addition to the fallout from the death of Heyer, march organizers became entangled with long-standing lawsuits.[14]

As the Trump administration went on, many of the most extreme white supremacists' attitudes became more nihilistic and antipolitical, with a goal of dismantling the entire political system. The most extreme in the white supremacist community, moreover, were often not Trump allies. They saw most Trump supporters as insufficiently committed to white supremacy and as couch warriors, even though their hearts were in the right place. Trump failed to make good on their most extreme hopes about subordinating Black people, and his Jewish son-in-law and the prominent role several Jews played in senior positions in his administration were proof to many that Trump, too, was part of the problem. There is historical precedent for this phenomenon of disillusionment. Although President Reagan, for instance, campaigned in opposition to affirmative action, gun control, and other hot-button white supremacist issues, he also squarely rejected white supremacists and worked through conventional politics rather than opposing "The System" (inevitably capitalized) as a whole.[15]

In both cases, white supremacists quickly saw these administrations as proof that the very idea of politics and The System itself were both irredeemable because they made electoral victories impossible. Thus, they thought, efforts by David Duke and others to make a difference through politics were doomed to failure.[16] *Siege* author James Mason notes that when it comes to politicians who betray their people, one does not vote against them, "one KILLS THEM."[17] The extremists are right that the system is stacked against them. Although racist politicians regularly win office, the most extreme do not. Indeed, they are rarely able to turn out large crowds—dozens, not thousands, are a common number.[18]

Strategies and Concepts for Violence

If peaceful politics only gets you so far, what is left? The strategies of violent white supremacist groups and the goals of individual attackers vary considerably, but few achieve the adherents' ambitious goals. Many groups and individuals simply act, with their ultimate goals unclear beyond hurting or killing someone from a community they dislike. Groups often favor multiple strategies, some of which contradict each other in practice. Some of the strategies listed here overlap or represent different phases of a similar game plan, with white supremacists disagreeing about where the movement and society are currently positioned. These strategies should thus be considered rough guides to action for the white supremacist movement, not concrete plans.

Bring On the Race War

The most extreme groups and individuals reject any role for peaceful politics. Combining racist and religious elements, some white supremacists believe in a violent clash where whites battle Jews and other minorities, culminating in Aryan rule. As Beam declared, "we intend to purge this entire land of Every non-White person, gene, idea and influence."[19] America, or the world as a whole, is enmeshed in a "race war," an important concept that shapes several strategies. Indeed, "RAHOWA," an acronym for "racial holy war," is a common slogan for white supremacist social media and graffiti. For some white supremacists today, RAHOWA is already happening, and they are warriors in a cosmic battle. Because the race war is ongoing or imminent, violence is framed as defensive: They are merely "fighting back" against oppression.

Fears of a race war have popped up throughout American history, often linked to broader conspiracies and paranoia. Before the Civil War, southern whites repeatedly invoked the specter of a slave rebellion to justify brutal repression and created patrols to catch "runaway" enslaved people—forerunners of Klan groups and other organizations that worked with the state to preserve racial supremacy. In the war's immediate aftermath, false rumors of a "Christmas insurrection" led to violence against the formerly enslaved, as well as the passage of repressive laws, the infamous Black Codes, to ensure the subordination of Black citizens.[20] During the Cold War, Beam and others believed that a U.S.-Soviet nuclear war was likely. In the resulting chaos, there would be a race war for which whites needed to prepare immediately. Beam sought to organize 600 cells around the country in an attempt to do so. Decentralization was necessary, as each would be 100 miles away from the others and safe should the likely nuclear strike devastate other cells.[21]

These ideas spread beyond the United States. Blood & Honour, an international racist skinhead group with chapters in multiple countries, sought a race war to purify the country. Feuerkrieg Division, which split off from Atomwaffen Division, is a small neo-Nazi group that seeks to foment a race war and largely organizes itself online. Feuerkrieg has chapters throughout Europe, as well as in the United States and Russia, seeks a "whites-only ethnostate" via a race war, and has sought to attack the Black community, Jews, and other enemies to bring one about.[22] The Base, too, sought to spark a race war and through it to create "a white ethno-state."[23]

Spark for the Masses

To win the race war, the movement needs soldiers. If there are not enough warriors to win the race war today, then perhaps a few dedicated souls can be the spark that lights a broader conflagration. The hope, common to terrorist groups of every stripe, is that "the masses" are truly on their side and just need to be awakened. Violence is thus a form of propaganda. It will attract attention to the white supremacist cause through media coverage (and now amplification by the groups themselves on social media) and bring in recruits, money, and other support, enabling further attacks. Perhaps more important, it will inspire those afraid of The System, giving them courage that it can be challenged—and beaten.

"There is no such thing as Jewish domination, only white submissiveness," Beam claimed.[24]

Sparks, however, often fail to light. James Mason, in his influential series of essays in the journal *Siege*, notes that in the 1970s and 1980s, violent groups like The Order lit many sparks, but the masses never rose. Mason praises the "superhuman" efforts of The Order but laments that The System replaces the lost parts after attacks, with erstwhile white supporters doing nothing. All the masses want, according to Mason, is to pursue pleasure.[25] In the 1990s, white supremacists complained that they could not inspire whites to seize the government because "the American people was too complacent, lazy, and undisciplined."[26] Even the election of Donald Trump, perceived by many white supremacists as a promising sign, has not altered this issue. A series of leaked Twitter chats from The Base has one member hoping the "MAGA folks" will play a role but admitting: "i doubt they have it in em."[27]

Nevertheless, the hope persists. In 2016, members of the Crusaders, a small white supremacist Kansas group who held anti-Muslim views, sought to blow up an apartment complex in Garden City, Kansas, where many Somali American Muslims lived—the first of several planned attacks. Blaming "the Orlando thing" (the 2016 massacre of 49 people at Pulse, a nightclub in Orlando, Florida, by a self-proclaimed ISIS member), the group sought to inspire others to attack Muslims and end immigration from Muslim countries. The Crusaders also sought to "wake people up" through the attack. As with so many white supremacist attacks, conspiracies played a role. Group members blamed "that cunt bitch Hillary and that nigger [then President Obama]" for the immigration of Muslims and believed local sheriffs, mayors, and others were also in on the plot.[28]

The attraction of this idea is that small group action is meaningful, even in the face of broader hostility or apathy. The harder, and perhaps impossible, task of creating a political movement or broader insurgency thus is not necessary.

Accelerationism and Polarization

If the flames of the race war cannot be sparked, then perhaps the masses will join the fight due to fear. A strongly held belief among a minority of white supremacists worldwide today is the idea of "accelerationism." This term, first coined by science fiction writer Roger Zelazny, describes a belief that technological change and capitalism are moving unstoppably fast and will upend the current social and political system—and that this rapid change is a good thing and should be further accelerated.[29] The idea enjoyed some popularity among philosophers, and white supremacists have embraced some of its tenets too. The System cannot—and, more important, should not—be saved, according to this concept. Rapid technological change, environmental degradation, and other kinds of transformation are all stressing The System. Indeed, the current order is doomed: social divisions are exacerbating tensions in every white country and moving the world inexorably toward a race war.

White supremacists, for example members of the modern groups The Base and Atomwaffen, or simply motivated individuals, hope to "accelerate" this process through violence and propaganda, hurrying the supposed day of reckoning. Atomwaffen emerged in 2016 out of the online forum Iron March and was active several years before the FBI effectively shut the group down in 2019 and 2020.

Mason, the ideologue and *Siege* author whose work inspired these groups, has pointed out that The Order's efforts to inspire the masses failed and argues that the goal is not simply to kill Black people but rather "to FAN THE FLAMES!" and make whites feel uncomfortable.[30] Members of The Base, in their own internal chats, noted: "successful acceleration entails increasing civil disorder enough that it strains System resources & therefore ability to contain it sufficiently."[31]

False-flag operations are employed too. Before a 2020 gun rally in Richmond, Virginia, the FBI arrested three members of The Base, accusing them of planning to shoot into a crowd to cause fear and outrage in the hope that attendees would naturally blame political leftists.[32] In Belgium, Blood, Soil, Honor, and Faith (Bloed, Bodem, Eer en Trouw) embraced accelerationism in 2006 and sought to bring about a race war.[33] They plotted to murder far-right leader Felip Dewinter, hoping the public would blame Muslims for the attack. The group would then kill Dyab Abou Janjah, a Belgian politician of Lebanese origin, believing that this back-and-forth would polarize the country.[34] In Germany, members of the white supremacist group Hard Core sought to livestream attacks on mosques and kill politicians, believing that these attacks would foster a civil war.[35]

Capitalizing on, or even creating, polarization is not a new strategy. During the 1960s and 1970s, as the Cold War raged, right-wing (but not white supremacist) terrorists initiated a "strategy of tension" to destabilize public order in Italy. Right-wing groups conducted dozens of attacks, several quite bloody, to sow fear and panic. They hoped to repeat history, as this approach, in a nutshell, was the way Mussolini had risen to power; he had declared: "during times of crisis, violence should be employed to arouse and polarize the public."[36] As order collapsed, Mussolini believed that ordinary people would demand an end to the chaos and thus support an authoritarian regime. The second time around, however, the strategy of tension backfired in Italy. Public order indeed suffered, but communist and socialist parties stepped into the void far more effectively than authoritarian groups did.[37]

During the Trump administration, societal polarization increased in the United States; it also increased in many European countries, with divisions in attitudes on race becoming more pronounced. More often now, citizens see those whose opinions oppose theirs as close-minded, unpatriotic, and immoral. This is still far from the world white supremacists imagine is ready for racial war, but in their eyes it is moving in the right direction.[38]

What to do after accelerating the race war is a source of disagreement. Some believe that whites will again rule, having purged or subordinated all minorities and repressed deviant behavior. Atomwaffen Division members, in contrast, believe they can carve out an all-white homeland in the U.S. Northwest once the federal government collapses.[39]

Overwhelming The System

Strategists like Mason recognize that law enforcement, the courts, civil society, the media, and other American institutions are firmly against them. If they act in small numbers, The System can easily suppress them—it will take more than a spark to succeed. However, because they believe The System is unpopular and controlled by a small group of conspirators, they contend that it cannot handle a broad revolt.

Mason argues that small groups and individuals attacking the U.S. economy and targeting influential leaders, Jews, and race traitors can overwhelm The System. Constant attack is best, with the attackers not worrying about capture but instead fighting to the end. "I firmly believe that enough of it, aimed correctly and within a short enough time-frame, would force the situation out of the doldrums and into a state of revolution."[40] A member of The Base in a confidential chat with other members similarly argues: "the goal is to destabilize the system and cut it up while it is down."[41] Important works like *The Turner Diaries* imagine large numbers of small bands who, together, overwhelm law enforcement, even as the white supremacists themselves suffer during the process.

Even with this approach, smarter leaders recognize the weakness of the white supremacist movement. As Mason points out, "we simply cannot stand to take on the full weight of the System's Pigs, now or in the foreseeable future." Some members must go deep underground and prepare for a harsh System backlash.[42]

The movement, because of this weakness, must capitalize on other developments instead, such as a race riot, that might polarize the situation.[43] In other words, they need to prepare and be opportunistic, waiting for The System to show its weakness before trying to strike. Here, this approach meshes well with accelerationism, which contends that white supremacists can speed up the overall weakening of The System.

Social Intimidation

Some organizations focus their efforts locally rather than on the grandiose world of racial holy war and its variations. They try to shape their towns and neighborhoods, often by using violence against their neighbors.

The civil rights–era KKK always had a state and local focus, with various chapters pursuing different aspects of a shared but broad agenda, frequently in competition with other so-called Klaverns. In the post–civil rights era, what remained of various KKK chapters usually focused on local intimidation, with various chapters calling for measures such as boycotting Jewish businesses. Defense, not offense, is still their rhetoric today. One modern Klan group patrolled local schools "to protect white students from black violence in integrated classrooms" and made similar claims of protecting white voters by donning combat fatigues.[44]

Intimidation makes life miserable for local communities and can profoundly shape local demographics, as families stay away, or move away, from the threat of violence. The Knights of the Ku Klux Klan's campaign against Vietnamese fishers in the 1970s, which sent a message by parading armed men in Klan robes on a fishing boat and hanging a Vietnamese fisherman in effigy, terrified the new immigrant community. Intimidation is easier when the white supremacists have the sympathy of local law enforcement and the local community, making it hard to prosecute those involved.

In Europe, groups often employ an intimidation strategy against immigrants, harassing them in their daily lives and employing a vigilante-style justice if they suspect their prey of committing crimes.[45] The Soldiers of Odin have patrolled Finland against supposed migrant crime, walking with large dogs through areas where Muslim migrants have settled.[46] Members of National Action, a British neo-Nazi group that emerged in 2013, initiated an anti-Semitic Twitter campaign against several members of Parliament, marched in "White Man" demonstrations, and ran a "Miss Hitler" pageant in 2016 to intimidate Jews and other opponents.[47] Golden Dawn has regularly assaulted minorities and with the use and threat of violence has forced many minorities to flee their homes.[48]

Overall, however, local intimidation has declined as an effective strategy, although propaganda efforts like passing out racist flyers are still common. Groups like the Klan have fallen in influence and membership: as the Southern Poverty Law Center has pointed out, "younger extremists prefer Fred Perry polo shirts and khakis to Klan robes."[49] As racial attitudes have (mostly) changed, and as local violence gains more attention, it is harder for groups to maintain dominance in a local area without being prose-cuted or otherwise disrupted by local law enforcement. In the past, white supremacists enjoyed broad sympathy among law enforcement officers in some locales, and this problem, while it persists, is not comparable with what it was in the pre–civil rights era, when local police and Klan groups worked hand in hand.

At times, social intimidation blends into the idea of violence just for the sake of violence. Skinheads, for example, like to drink beer and fight, and they often beat up minorities, vandalize synagogues and mosques, and oth-erwise use violence. Rarely, however, have they sought any broader political change through the use of violence.

A Home of Their Own

Rather than changing or defeating The System in the United States or an-other country, another option white supremacists think they have is to create a homeland where true believers can live and build their strength in the ra-cially pure world they seek. Although superficially nonviolent, in practice, this would require forced deportations of minorities and revoking citizenship for nonwhites. David Duke had a plan to partition America into different racial groups.[50] David Lane, The Order member whose iconic "14 words" have helped define modern white supremacy, wrote from prison to encourage whites to relocate to remote parts of the country. There they could control the political system, creating a haven where they could breed Aryan children. The founder of Aryan Nations, Richard Butler, sought a whites-only homeland in the Pacific Northwest (a favorite area of white supremacists given the low nonwhite population), claiming parts of Idaho, Washington, Oregon, Montana, and Wyoming—the so-called Northwestern Territorial Imperative. The area has a history of hostility toward Black residents and immigrants, and several groups have had a heavy presence in this area.[51] Groups also advocated a white homeland in the "Carolina Free State" or the "Mid-America Survival Area." These ideas of local autonomy free from federal control often overlap with those of militias or other antigovernment groups.

Advocates of separation—who call themselves racialists, not racists—claim that whenever different races must share the same territory, there will be conflict and, even worse in their eyes, interracial dating and marriage, which dilutes supposedly pure Aryan blood. Tom Metzger, the former KKK grand dragon who founded WAR, feared that "races which live in the same proximity no matter what the prevailing standards will eventually mix."[52] So separation is best for all races, not just white people. Pierce, however, was more honest. He noted that separatism is for white supremacists "who have abandoned hope of bringing back racial segregation and white dominance of American society." Similarly, Jeff Berry of the American Knights of the Ku Klux Klan said that he uses the term "white separatism" because "they'll put us on the list of terrorists" for using the label "white supremacist."[53]

The good news is that few welcome an influx of white supremacists to their communities. In addition, white supremacists lack the money to buy large tracts of land or the numbers to influence local elections. Their actions, when they do relocate, often run afoul of the law, particularly when they overlap with militias or other antigovernment groups, as many refuse to recognize the authority of local and federal law enforcement, making them vulnerable to arrest, fines, and other forms of disruption.

White supremacists have, however, made the federal government chary of direct confrontations. The federal law enforcement disasters in the 1990s in Waco and Ruby Ridge, both of which led to the deaths of innocents (including children), generated tremendous media and political criticism of federal agencies. Fearing the political fallout of a confrontation, especially one that goes awry, federal and state officials often tolerate groups that flout local laws and engage in low-level intimidation of their neighbors. In January 2016, when antigovernment militants occupied the Malheur National Wildlife Refuge in Oregon, federal authorities closely monitored the situation but refrained from seizing the refuge or otherwise directly confronting the militants. Instead, they negotiated for weeks, allowing militants to come and go. The FBI arrested several leaders, who departed, and eventually negotiated a surrender, but not before killing one of the militants who refused to surrender and reached for a gun during a standoff.

Leaderless Resistance and Its Limits

One of the most famous concepts white supremacists embrace, leaderless resistance—the idea that like-minded individuals working in isolated, small groups can overthrow The System—originated from anticommunist conspiracies, as self-proclaimed patriots pondered how to combat the impending Soviet occupation of America and decided that small cells working autonomously would be best. Louis Beam—a fixture in the white supremacist constellation, who started with the KKK before moving to Aryan Nations and who also had ties to The Order—first promulgated the idea in the white supremacist world in 1983 and then published a revised version in 1992. Beam's timing was good: he wrote just before the clashes at Ruby Ridge and Waco.[54]

Beam pointed out that the white supremacist movement does not have funding from the top or outside support. Moreover, as the 1988 Fort Smith trial and other trials had proven, a hierarchical movement is vulnerable to infiltration and disruption. Various Klan chapters and other white supremacist groups had suffered repeatedly when federal authorities arrested a top leader, leading to arrests of many of his followers, the bankruptcy of the group due to legal fees or successful lawsuits, and other disasters. To prevent this, like-minded activists must act alone or in small groups so the arrest of one individual would not doom the movement as a whole. "Any one cell can be infiltrated, exposed and destroyed, but this will have no effect on the others," Beam contended. When the FBI broke up The Order in the 1980s, some leaders of the movement were not indicted, as the government could not show that they had direct ties to the violence.[55]

Leaderless resistance has tremendous advantages in operational security. Beam is worth quoting at length here:

> this scheme of organization, the pyramid, is however, not only useless, but extremely dangerous for the participants when it is utilized in a resistance movement against state tyranny. Especially is this so in technologically advanced societies where electronic surveillance can often penetrate the structure revealing its chain of command. Experience has revealed over and over again that anti-state, political organizations utilizing this method of command and control are easy prey for government infiltration, entrapment, and destruction of the personnel involved. This has been seen repeatedly in the United States where pro-government infiltrators or agent provocateurs weasel their way into patriotic groups and destroy them from within.[56]

As Beam's essay makes clear, leaderless resistance is a response to state strength and the fear of government penetration. It also recognizes the movement's political weakness. This is not an approach the movement would take if it had more freedom to operate. Indeed, the movement at the time was still reeling from the federal government's use of infiltrators to take down several leading white supremacist groups, and Beam and others were learning from past prosecutions.[57] Leaderless resistance depends on numbers, and the concept assumes broad public support for the white supremacist movement. The government, Beam wrote, would face an "intelligence nightmare" with "a thousand phantom cells" flitting in and out and overwhelming its capabilities.[58]

Leaderless resistance seemed to reach its apogee, in terms of violence at least, in the United States, in 1995 with Timothy McVeigh's bombing of the federal building in Oklahoma City. Although initial reports suggested that McVeigh largely acted alone, and the government only prosecuted a small group of people, McVeigh communicated regularly with different figures in the white supremacist movement.[59] It was a success for the concept: high impact, with only a few of the guilty convicted. In Europe, Breivik showed what an individual could do, and a later independent investigation chastised the government for underestimating the danger of one person acting alone.[60]

Numerous white supremacist groups and leaders today have embraced leaderless resistance, urging their supporters to act as "lone wolves" rather than members of a formal group. Indeed, both in the United States and around the world, the deadliest white supremacist attacks have been carried out by individuals and informal cells, not organized groups.[61] Britain's Combat 18, Germany's Freie Kameradschaften, and others have found this concept inspiring, and Sweden's Security Service reports that leaderless resistance has gained ground there, with individuals sharing a digital hate culture.[62] A self-proclaimed splinter group of the Atomwaffen Division issued a pamphlet telling potential recruits that lone-wolf attacks can be highly effective. "Don't join a cell. Create a cell," the pamphlet exhorts, noting: "remember, there is only one leader of the AWD [Atomwaffen Division]. And that leader is you."[63] Some of the most lethal white supremacist attacks, like the Christchurch, El Paso, and Tree of Life synagogue attacks, as well as Breivik's in Norway, qualify as lone-wolf attacks.

Law enforcement and intelligence officers regularly warn of how dangerous leaderless resistance can be. Nicholas Rasmussen, who headed the National Counterterrorism Center, warned in 2017 of the lone-wolf threat and that "lone actors are harder to detect and identify because—by definition—they are acting alone and hiding what they are doing, even from the people closest to them."[64]

Part of the fear of the lone wolf, as Berger notes, arises because the media, and often the government, downplay the actual connections between individuals, making the "lone wolf" seem more alone than he actually is.[65] White supremacists, like all people, are often close to friends, families, and neighbors and thus have numerous social ties. These ties are often part of the radicalization process, as comrades embolden one another and can work together outside a formal organizational structure. The individuals are rarely truly "alone" and thus can be detected and disrupted through these relationships.[66] As the historian Belew contends, "white power violence has too often been described as the disconnected acts of lone wolves or madmen, and this is precisely because people—the public, prosecutors, jurors, the government—haven't understood it as a connected and coherent social movement."[67]

Because of the networked nature of the movement, even the formal dissolution of a group often matters little. Atomwaffen Division has claimed to have disbanded, but individuals tied to it continue to disseminate propaganda that is gobbled up by its affiliates in other countries.[68]

Leaderless resistance's greatest strength, decentralization, is also its greatest weakness, as white supremacists themselves have acknowledged.[69] Too decentralized a process means that believers all go in different directions, reducing their overall impact, and the actions of one undisciplined member, freed from the guidance and security strictures mandated by group leaders, can lead to government crackdowns. As one white supremacist tied to Atomwaffen Division noted in private texts, "decentralized as much as possible would obviously be necessary but if it's too decentralized it loses effectiveness so it's a conundrum."[70] In addition, decentralization reduces the ability to conduct complex attacks, such as those against well-guarded targets. This may explain the dearth of attacks on government targets since Oklahoma City, as many government facilities have had better security since then.

Furthermore, despite all the big talk of ideas and elaborate strategies, when white supremacists attack, they often do so with little purpose in mind, lashing out at local targets, with no enduring impact. Mason condemned using violence in "stunts" against supposed "expendables" like African Americans. Worse, from his point of view, he complained that the attackers often ran away without a plan for follow-up. He contended that it took discipline for a terrorist group not to lash out in anger and conduct revenge attacks, which groups often plot after the arrest of a member.[71] Members of The Base, a group heavily influenced by Mason, complained after the Tree of Life synagogue massacre in Pittsburgh that they had not had a significant impact and losing "one of our guys" in exchange for "eleven elderly heebs" was not worth it.[72]

As these complaints suggest, most white supremacists are unable to prioritize. Frazier Glenn Miller, Jr., the former Klansman and neo-Nazi who attacked a Kansas City synagogue in 2014, tried to come up with a point system in the 1980s: killing African Americans was worth one point, while "white race traitors" and Jews merited ten. Judges were worth fifty, and Morris Dees—the SPLC leader whose lawsuits had devastated so many white supremacist groups, was worth 888 (an inevitable Hitler reference). Miller's own attack on the synagogue was amateurish. After he was arrested, he asked: "how many fucking Jews did I kill?" (He killed none—the three victims were not Jewish.)[73] Miller's point system never caught on, and white supremacists tend to find a local target or are motivated by a mix of personal, as well as ideological, grievances rather than tailoring their targeting to their overall strategy.

Nor does leaderless resistance ensure harmony in the broader movement. Individual cells rarely work well together without coordination, and frictions arise when cells vie for recruits, money, and power, often trying to subsume each other.[74] Group ambitions are often matched only by the size of their leaders' egos, and fighting over who is in charge is a near-constant for many organizations. If a group does not have a hierarchy, it can easily divide over ideas, tactics, leadership, and the appropriate level of violence to use. For example, one U.S. chapter of Blood & Honour split over the question of whether to promote white power through music or to use terrorism and assassination.

The advent of the internet, and especially social media, seemed to answer white supremacists' prayers with regard to leaderless resistance. Now they have a way of easily, and cheaply, disseminating messages and overall strategic guidance to their followers.[75] In addition, models of how to attack, like Breivik's, could spread rapidly to all corners of the earth and, as others followed an attacker's lead, become a common script for isolated white supremacists to follow. However, the decentralization of white supremacist messaging and splits within the movement have hindered a vital element of the leaderless resistance concept: an overarching strategy. The movement has many different paths to victory, at least in its own eyes, and the choice of which approach a cell or individual should take is not clear. As one member of The Base noted, in private correspondence later made public: "yeah you may have a lot of lone wolf attacks but realistically those don't really achieve shit aside from scaring people which isn't the goal."[76] The ability of social media companies and government authorities to monitor the internet also makes it far easier to detect potential attackers, who often boast about their plans online.

Not surprisingly given all these problems, some white supremacist leaders have opposed leaderless resistance. They contend that leaderless resistance keeps an already divided movement further divided, leads to ill-conceived acts of violence that backfire, and when militants do want to act, prevents them from drawing on others for support. These leaders also note that employing leaderless resistance denies the movement the benefits of acting as an aboveground peaceful (if extreme) social and political movement. Pierce, for example, has argued that the concept reflects "blatant ineptitude and rank incompetence."[77]

There is still reason to be wary. Whereas group leaders are often more cautious—recognizing, for instance, that the mass killing of innocents can backfire politically and lead to a law enforcement crackdown—individuals are less restrained.[78] Often, individuals in a social media network egg one another on, encouraging "high scores" or other kinds of mass killings.[79]

But the many strategic problems white supremacists face indicate their broader dilemma: they remain dangerous but are nowhere near successful on their own terms. No longer do groups like the Klan intimidate the Black community and their white neighbors on a mass scale to ensure white supremacy. A shooter like Crusius is lethal, but his attack did little to stop immigration to the United States and may have even backfired, creating outrage against white supremacists. Instead, violent white supremacists have only a range of far-fetched strategic goals they are not close to achieving.

7

The (D)evolution of White Supremacist Violence and the Mismeasurement of Terrorism

In the years preceding the civil rights struggle and in the movement's early days, Ku Klux Klan organizations inflicted constant misery on the Black population of the American South. Some Klan members worked with state officials, while other white supremacists were even part of the state itself: it was state troopers, not the Klan, who attacked John Lewis and other civil rights marchers in Selma, Alabama, in 1965. Klan organizations conformed with the societal values and segregationist policies of state and local governments and tried to shore up the existing (racist) system. The groups were status quo actors—albeit extralegal, nonstate ones, in many ways. For many years, this violence enabled white supremacists to ensure white dominance, enforce Jim Crow laws and racist social mores, and deny Black Americans even a semblance of social justice.

Today, white supremacists exert less social control, and the movement is fragmented and often strategically incoherent. Although racism remains prevalent, public attitudes have changed substantially, and both the law and the government now oppose white supremacy. However, the white power movement today is more global and often more deadly, and it has a longer list of enemies, including the U.S. government, as opposed to Klan groups in the early 1960s, who saw themselves as patriots. The post-1960s collapse of larger, more coherent groups like various Klan organizations has also occasionally led to more high-profile violence as extreme individuals go off on their own. Today's movement overlaps with other extreme right-wing political causes, magnifying its influence. Making the picture more complex, some of this movement's views of Muslims and immigrants have moved to the mainstream, increasing the political influence of their cause, though not the power of the most violent adherents. In 2021, U.S. intelligence agencies have warned that white supremacists and other right-wing extremists are a top terrorism threat.[1]

Too often the threat is judged by easily quantifiable measures such as lives lost and plots attempted. Although these are important, other metrics should include political impact, organizational strength, strategic plausibility, and political and social concessions given to the movement as a whole. Counterterrorism's success also depends heavily on politics, both to delegitimate terrorists and to ensure necessary backing for aggressive government action.

The Nature of Violence Today

Although the Walmart and Tree of Life type of massacres grab the headlines, they are outliers. Most white supremacist attacks kill few people: In the post-9/11 period, the average hovered around one person killed for every two attacks.[2] Frightening, but nonlethal, acts of vandalism and intimidation like cross burnings remain common.

Religious and racial minorities, immigrants, and the LGBTQ+ community are common targets of white supremacist terrorism today. According to the Anti-Defamation League, anti-Semitic actions carried out by white supremacists in the United States soared in 2017 and continued to rise in the years that followed.[3] Often the preferred target reflects the fears of the moment. Attacks against Muslims and mosques spiked after 9/11, and then again after 2014 as anti-Muslim fears grew and rhetoric heated up, particularly with the emergence of ISIS and the immigration crisis in Europe. In the United States, September and October 2001 saw more reports of anti-Muslim and anti-Arab hate crimes than in the previous 10 years combined.[4] Spikes of violence continued, often linked to events overseas such as ISIS beheadings or manufactured crises in the United States such as the controversy over the "9/11 mosque" in New York City, when Muslims planned to build a mosque near the location of the destroyed World Trade Center buildings. When COVID-19 spread in 2020 and 2021, with President Trump and others labeling it the "Chinese virus," attacks on Asian Americans surged. Since Oklahoma City, attacks on government targets on the other hand have been quite rare and, in contrast to Europe, the left has been less of a target.[5]

In addition to looking at figures for terrorism, it is also useful to consider hate crimes—defined by Congress as "crimes that manifest evidence of prejudice based on race, gender, or ethnic identity, religion, disability, sexual orientation, or ethnicity."[6] Hate crimes can include terrorism, but many perpetrators of hate crimes, unlike terrorism, are not seeking a broader psychological and political effect, for example when a Black man is assaulted because of his skin color but the attacker is not trying to create a broader impact on community and society. The FBI's report *Hate Crimes Statistics, 2019* clearly indicated, notwithstanding the many problems with its data, that hate crimes were at their highest level in more than a decade. Black people were the biggest victims of hate crimes, but Latinos were becoming a larger share of the overall pool, with Jews, Muslims, and the LGBTQ+ community also representing a large share of the victims.[7] As a pastor of a Black church targeted by white supremacists noted, "trauma is a way of life for us. So we grieve, but we keep pushing forward."[8]

Roughly half the attacks in the United States since 1994 have involved the use of explosives, often Molotov cocktails or small bombs, at immigrant or religious facilities, as a way to intimidate people. The federal government has gotten better at tracking explosive material since Oklahoma City, making it harder to make massive bombs like McVeigh's truck bomb. Guns have been used in over a quarter of attacks—and gun use has grown dramatically since 2016.[9] More important, guns have been the most common weapon used in the attacks that have actually killed people.[10] In the United States, firearms are relatively easy to access, while getting guns is a bigger challenge for radical individuals in Europe, where you often need to be a member of a shooting club, pass a background check, or otherwise face restrictions and government scrutiny.[11] Not surprisingly, in 2019, most of the severe attacks in Europe involved knives and blunt instruments or beating and kicking victims, though gun attacks have risen in risen years.[12] Using cars to run over pedestrians, as in Charlottesville, is another technique that is increasingly used—one analysis found 43 malicious cases, with 39 drivers charged.[13] More rarely, white supremacists use cutting-edge technologies. The Halle synagogue attacker used a 3D printer to make parts for weapons he used in his attack. Livestreamed video of the attack shows the weapons jamming, but the precedent is unnerving.[14]

There is no simple demographic profile of white supremacists today, but there are some commonalities. In general, white supremacist movements are more working-class than elite.[15] In the United States, participants are more likely to be students, employed at low-end jobs, or unemployed. Moreover, they live in areas whose populations are poorer and less educated.

Strikingly, many have criminal backgrounds unrelated to their involvement in white supremacist activity. Data compiled by scholar Arie Perliger indicate that over 70 percent of those who have engaged in white supremacist violence have had a prior arrest.[16] In the United States, the majority of homicides by individuals linked to white supremacist causes have been committed for personal, not ideological, reasons.[17] European counterterrorism authorities report that a similarly large number of white supremacists also have criminal records.[18] In 2018, 70 percent of the members of Finland's Soldiers of Odin and Nordic Resistance chapters had criminal records, most for violent crimes.[19]

As Pete Simi, an expert on white supremacy, has written, many individuals are violent before they become associated with an ideological white supremacist movement.[20] Nor should we assume that those who embrace violent ideas will necessarily act on them. Simi notes that "ideas are poor predictors of behavior" and that "fortunately, there is far more violent talk than violent acts."[21] However, Simi also told me that white supremacists' ideas stress the notion that the world out there is a dog-eat-dog one: whites and nonwhites cannot coexist peacefully. This brutal view ensures that there is a movement.[22]

With all these changes, white supremacists have become highly decentralized yet densely networked, adhering to what the U.S. intelligence community describes as a "diverse" set of ideas.[23] This decentralization began in the 1960s and 1970s after the decline of the Klan and mass-action-oriented groups such as the American Nazi Party and gained speed as the government took apart small, clandestine groups such as The Order in the 1980s. Movements like the skinheads never had any overarching organization, and most local skinhead groups would quickly rise and fall. Today, in both the United States and Europe, the problem is networks, not groups. White supremacists cluster around different individual leaders and at times join formal organizations, but they regularly desert one and join another due to leadership changes, the emergence of a new grievance, and other common changes. Few groups survive more than a few years, but many of their members simply join another organization or continue their involvement via online activity.[24] In both the United States and Europe, there are tens of thousands of white supremacists who are part of broader extremist networks,[25] and that number is far higher if a broader definition of support for the white supremacist cause is used.

Radicalized individuals, for example Crusius and Bowers, who are part of the network and consume propaganda on social media but are not members of a group, carry out much of the violence today. Perliger's data indicate that 58 percent of the violence is committed by a single person, and 18 percent by only two: less than a quarter of it is perpetrated by a group as a whole. In addition, many attacks are spontaneous. These attacks, often carried out by younger supporters, are common, particularly against mixed-race couples.[26] Perliger's findings follow trends in white supremacist violence in the post–civil rights era: Bowers, Crusius, and Roof acted alone, and even The Order, a larger group, used only four members to kill Berg. Groups like Atomwaffen and The Base still exist and even have limited transnational ties, but they are small compared with past Klan organizations, lack the Klan's former social status and community role, and are themselves highly decentralized and networked.[27]

White supremacists are regularly engaged in more mundane violence that is usually not recorded as terrorism. Unlike jihadists attacks in the United States and Europe, much of the white supremacist violence is not an attempt to create a broader psychological effect, and some of it is not linked to politics. Data from the Anti-Defamation League also show that, aside from high-profile acts of terror, white supremacists are involved in murders of minorities and others as well as criminal and other nonpolitical violence, often against one another. The ADL reports over 200 lower-profile killings from 2011 to 2020, commenting that "for every person killed by an extremist, many more are wounded or injured in attempted murders and assaults."[28]

Some individuals have flitted in and out of groups while staying part of the overall movement. Wade Michael Page, a former paratrooper, was discharged from the Army in 1995 for his links to the neo-Nazi National Alliance and later played in white supremacist punk and metal bands with names like Blue Eyed Devils, a name that comes from the teachings of Elijah Muhammad, the Black supremacist leader of the Nation of Islam. Largely on his own, Page attacked a Sikh temple in 2012.[29] Frazier Glenn Miller, Jr., who attacked a Kansas City synagogue in 2014, had been a member of the neo-Nazi National Socialist Party and the Carolina Knights of the Ku Klux Klan, but he was not an active member of any group when he carried out his attack.[30]

Some groups still exist, of course. Atomwaffen Division has been linked to five murders in the United States, as well as attacks in Europe. Law enforcement was slow to take the group seriously but, as the scope of its violent ambitions became clearer, eventually acted. The group claimed in 2020 to have dissolved after a series of arrests, but it has linkages to groups or sup-posed affiliates in Germany, the Baltic states, Ukraine, Russia, Germany, and the United Kingdom. Yet even these formal groups show how networked the movement as a whole is and how non–group members influence it. Atomwaffen emerged from a neo-Nazi message board, Iron March, linked to an Uzbek national living in Moscow, and members later organized them-selves on Discord. In their propaganda, they idolized Breivik and Tarrant, as well as Americans like McVeigh and Roof, and regularly read *Siege,* claiming that it changed their lives—"Siegepilling," they called it.[31] Some of them were also members of The Base. Both these groups were small compared with groups like the Klan in the past, and The Base was more quickly disrupted once law enforcement became aware of the threat of Atomwaffen.[32] As the sociologist and white supremacist expert Cynthia Miller-Idriss argues, it is best to see these groups "as a spectrum or as a cluster of overlapping ideolo-gies and practices."[33] Similarly, Berger argues that it is better to think of these and similar groups as part of a "*Siege* culture" movement rather than focusing too much on any one organization.[34]

The convergence of different movements and ideologies that began after the civil rights era continues. Many in the militia movement became fer-vently anti-Muslim after 9/11, plotting to attack mosques and other Muslim targets.[35] The number of hate groups in the United States surged after the election of President Obama.[36] For some, the reality of a Black man as America's leader was simply unacceptable. Others feared his administration would take their guns and implement socialism. Groups like The Base had ties to militia movements that had an antigovernment—but not always (or even often) white supremacist—ideology, like the Boogaloos.[37] This often makes it hard to tease out what is white supremacist extremism, what is better classified as antigovernment violence, and what falls under conspiracy theories like QAnon. Events like the storming of the U.S. Capitol on January 6, 2021, involved elements of all these movements.

For a movement that, in the past, was highly nationalistic, the intellec-tual globalization today is quite striking. The skinhead movement and Identitarian ideas came to the United States from Europe, as did the inspira-tion for the Unite the Right rally in Charlottesville. White genocide and even the symbols of the Confederacy all spread to Europe from the United States.

Jigsaw's Beth Goldberg notes that 15 years ago, many extremist commu-nities were stovepiped and rarely talked to one another (with the notable exception of Stormfront). Indeed, some Identitarian white supremacist groups have prided themselves on not appearing as overtly racist as neo-Nazi groups. In the last few years, however, different groups and movements have converged, resulting in a bewildering array of hybrids, such as white supremacists who follow QAnon or antivaccine white supremacists. Many are drawn not just to the ideas of other causes but also to their online communities, seeking a sense of belonging.[38] When they use violence, they are often showing off or otherwise speaking to other members of these communities.[39]

The movement is also global in much of its rhetoric and connections, though transnational cooperation is still limited at best. The Great Replacement, white genocide, and other ideas are now shared among white supremacists around the world, and an attack like Tarrant's is eagerly discussed by other white radicals. However, the groups themselves do relatively little together, in part because of distance, distinct agendas, and relatively few personal connections. As Matthew Heimbach, who helped organize the 2017 Unite the Right rally in Charlottesville, noted, "American members of the far right and white nationalist groups have been trying to get Europe to return their calls for a decade now."[40]

In addition, the movement still has links to the political system, albeit far less so than in the past. Police violence against communities of color, in particular, remains a problem. At times, this manifests in direct attacks on Black citizens and other minorities, but often its effects are more indirect, ranging from ignoring or downplaying violence against these communities to not sufficiently resourcing the problem, with too few investigations of violence and a lack of protection for the community.

Data Limits

We have only snapshots of the white supremacist threat because the data we have are limited and uneven. In the United States, Congress tried to rectify this problem in 1990 with the Hate Crime Statistics Act, which made the FBI responsible for collecting data based on state and local reporting. The goal was both to get an accurate picture of the problem and, by following up with prosecutions of hate crimes, to reassure vulnerable communities. However, for the act to work in practice, the community must trust the police in general and believe that its reports will produce action. Then, state and local officials must convey the reports to federal authorities, who compile the data. Usually, all of these steps are lacking. As a result, many parts of the country have reported no hate crimes over multiple years, including larger cities with histories of racial problems, for example Birmingham and Baton Rouge.[41] Some states have no hate crimes laws at all, making it hard to determine the scope of the problem. Even when they do have laws on the books, what constitutes a hate crime varies by state. In New Jersey, a victim only has to perceive that there was a bias motivation; in other states, more proof is needed, for example a symbol of white supremacist membership.

Europe, too, has this problem. Ravndal notes that most countries in northern Europe have watchdog organizations and aggressive media that cover white supremacist violence. In Greece, Italy, and Spain, however, reporting is far worse, and attacks go undercounted.[42] Rafal Pankowski of Poland's Never Again Foundation notes ironically that "the bigger the number of hate crimes, the better"—if a country has many hate crimes, it shows it is monitoring the problem and trying to stop it, while many countries claim low numbers and that is because they are not even trying. The United Kingdom, for example, has large numbers by European standards, but that is in part because they gather data seriously.[43]

Only around one-third of hate crimes are reported to the police, meaning the police are unaware of two-thirds, and of that one-third only a fraction are reported to the federal level. The 2020 FBI hate crimes report had data from 2,172 law enforcement agencies out of a total of more than 15,000.[44] Over 70 cities with populations of over 100,000 did not report a single hate crime.[45] Police departments often do not track hate crimes or label them as such if they occur. Most hate crimes are low-level (think graffiti at a mosque): they are upsetting for local communities but often get little outside attention. In addition, hate crimes are low on the FBI priority list, and federal officials usually defer any reports to the state and local level, even though they know most locals will not act. Few local officials want the notoriety that comes with hate crimes, fearing that investigating them would damage their community's reputation, so they limit potential hate crime charges to vandalism or assault, both of which carry less shame.

In addition, hate crimes are, by their very nature, more likely to affect the Black community, Jews, Latinos, the LGBTQ+ community, and other common white supremacist targets. Some of these communities have poor relations with law enforcement and suffer more unsolved crimes than those who have good relations, increasing the likelihood that some political violence is undercounted.[46] Skewing numbers further, as one official involved in the data evaluation told me, some of these communities, with differing attitudes toward the police, are more likely than others to report crimes, making it difficult to track trends.[47] Finally, FBI data are published incredibly late—almost a year after the filing of the initial reports.[48] As a result, it is difficult to shift resources in response to a surge until the problem is well developed.

Even when hate crimes are reported, prosecutors often need a high standard of evidence to prove them in court. They have to prove intent and, as one prosecutor complained, "crawl into someone's head." As a result, prosecutors prefer other, more easily provable charges. In some states, a crime classified as a hate crime does not involve additional punishment, decreasing the incentives to collect the information necessary to prove that one occurred. In Texas, of the almost 1,000 hate crimes cases reported to police from 2010 to 2015, there were only five convictions.[49] The federal government is most likely to go after hate crimes symbolically in major cases, like that of Charleston shooter Dylann Roof, who already faced multiple murder charges, rather than focus on cases that have not been addressed.[50]

The FBI itself does not offer useful information for understanding the threat. The FBI often refers to "domestic terrorism" investigations (basically all nonjihadist ones), but this covers a host of ideologies, including ecoterrorism and antigovernment violence. In addition, the FBI uses this term to refer to assessments and preliminary operations as well as full operations the FBI is conducting, and all these situations differ. This makes it difficult for the public to understand the threat and for Congress to oversee and resource the response appropriately.[51] The FBI also frequently fails to incorporate information from other parts of the government. One official involved in data gathering and evaluation for another agency told me that they rarely brief police or the FBI on their findings; so reports and data may not be linked to policy.[52]

Some sense of the picture—and the missing pieces—can be gleaned by comparing the FBI's annual report, the Uniform Crime Reporting system, with an occasional survey done by the U.S. Bureau of Justice Statistics.[53] The FBI reports around 6,000 to 10,000 hate crimes annually, drawing on incidents reported to police and then conveyed to the FBI. However, the Bureau of Justice Statistics report, which surveys households and follows up aggressively to get a high response rate rather than relying on official reporting, has concluded that the true figure is around 260,000—that is, the official FBI numbers are undercounted fortyfold. Mark Potok, who tracked white supremacist groups for the SPLC for many years, has noted: "you cannot tell if hate crimes are going up year over year from the FBI reports."[54] Making the numbers more complex, there is some good news: the percentage of hate crimes being reported is going up. However, this means that the numbers can often look higher when they are just due to better reporting, not more hate crimes.

The consequences of these statistics are profound. If an act is classified as terrorism, the likelihood of investigation and prosecution is far greater than if it is "merely" a hate crime (and, of course, even more than if it is not classified at all). Federal prosecutors and investigators, in addition to avoiding bringing terrorism charges and usually referring investigations to the state and local level, keep the scope narrow: it is usually easier to prosecute white supremacists based on gun or assault charges than on more nebulous hate crime or terrorism claims, which can involve messy free speech arguments.[55] A terrorism investigation, in contrast, would be better resourced and conducted with an eye toward disrupting future attacks and focusing on the network as a whole.

A World of Conspiracy

The white supremacist world is awash in conspiracy theories, and it is impossible to keep up as new ones emerge daily. During the civil rights era, many Klan members came to believe that Jews and communists controlled the media, while key figures like William Luther Pierce emerged out of the John Birch Society, which believed that a cabal of bankers and corrupt politicians secretly controlled world events and that communists had penetrated the U.S. government (and that President Eisenhower himself was compromised). Pierce later argued that democracy itself was a Jewish plot, as Jews' supposed control over the media enabled them to brainwash non-Jews.[56] Christian Identity, with its theology depicting Jews as the children of Satan and extolling a race war, was another bizarre set of ideas influencing the movement.

Here are some other recent examples of conspiracy theories that are common in the broader far-right extremist ecosystem and that many white supremacists have embraced:

- The Federal Emergency Management Agency is building camps to imprison patriots who resist the government. These are disguised as camps for victims of disaster relief.[57]
- United Nations troops are hiding in national parks, waiting to seize power in America.[58]
- The militarization of police is proof that they are becoming an instrument of world government.[59]
- European neo-Nazis claim there is a "Kalergi plan" to destroy white people. This refers to the Austrian philosopher and politician Richard Nikolaus Graf von Coudenhove-Kalergi, who saw racial integration as part of Europe's future but whose ideas have been misrepresented as endorsement of a Jewish-dominated order that would destroy white people through migration.[60]
- The COVID-19 pandemic was unleashed by some combination of the New World Order, Agenda 21 (a UN economic development plan), Jewish financier George Soros, and the Chinese government—each of whom has a vested interest in eradicating the white race.[61]
- George Soros—a Jewish philanthropist and Holocaust survivor—is also supposedly encouraging Central American migration to the United States in order to drive white "Western civilization" to extinction.[62]
- The "Eurabia" narrative: European elites—originally led by former French president Charles de Gaulle—purportedly conspired with elites from the Arab world to "Islamize" white European culture in exchange for access to Middle Eastern oil.[63]
- The public outcry following George Floyd's May 2020 murder at the hands of white police officers was a "total hoax" designed to give cover to Black people who want to attack white people.[64]
- A "large scale killing" of white South African farmers was carried out, presumably by nonwhite politicians seeking to execute "white genocide" in the country.[65]
- Similar to the "birther" conspiracies directed against President Obama, Vice President Kamala Harris is not be eligible to serve because her parents purportedly were not naturalized citizens at the time she was born.[66]

Beliefs often overlap with more mainstream conspiracies. The idea that President Obama is a secret Muslim is, for instance, widely shared among much of the public and was promoted by President Trump—but it is dogma for many white supremacists.[67] During his presidency, Trump also played up conspiracies about migrant caravans coming up from Latin America funded by George Soros. As pitiful and frightening as these individual conspiracies are, even more worrisome is the finding that nearly everyone who believes one conspiracy theory also believes in others: these peculiar ideas join and multiply in dangerous and unpredictable ways.[68] The internet facilitates this, enabling conspirators to find one another and expose others to their fantastical ideas. The internet also facilitates individuals' repeated exposure to a conspiracy theory, which makes them more likely to believe it.

At times, groups go from standard white supremacy tropes to the bizarre. In the 1970s, the Order of Nine Angles emerged in the United Kingdom, revering both Hitler and Satan. David Myatt, one of its founders, was a former leader of the neo-Nazi National Socialist Movement, but in 2006 he converted to an extreme form of Islam and supported killing Muslim apostates. The Order of Nine Angles also reportedly infiltrated Atomwaffen Division, with "normal" Atomwaffen members leaving the group as it embraced Satanism.[69]

Ideas, and the conspiracies that go with them, now easily cross borders. David Duke's book *Jewish Supremacism* has been published in Germany, Poland, Russia, and other countries, and Duke even lived in Russia for several years.[70] American white supremacists embrace the "Kalergi plan" and other claims that Jews and leftists are orchestrating the Great Replacement.

Some individuals act on these conspiracies. Bowers, for example, believed Jews were behind Muslim immigration to the United States, which is why he attacked a synagogue. One extremist group tried to attack U.S. military bases, because they believed Chinese troops were being trained there, and even sold their homes and businesses to raise money for operations.[71] In 2019, the FBI warned that conspiracy theories "very likely encourage the targeting of specific people, places, and organizations, thereby increasing the likelihood of violence against these targets."[72]

Organizational Dilemmas

White supremacists have crazy ideas, and extremists in their ranks regularly kill people, but the most violent members of the movement are handicapped because their organizations are weak. White supremacists must recruit, raise money, procure weapons, train their people, and otherwise be able to sustain and grow their organizations. They must do so while carrying out attacks and trying to avoid being caught and jailed. Most fail. Others survive but do not prosper, spending most of their time treading water, unable to carry out their ambitious plans. The cause itself often gets lost in the daily demands of fund-raising, recruiting, propagandizing, and fighting.

Recruitment Problems

White supremacists try to reach a wide range of audiences to recruit, using white power music, events like the Unite the Right rally, books like *The Turner Diaries*, essays like those in *Siege*, and other forms of enter-tainment and propaganda to reach new members. Some leaders have even tried to promote sex as a reward for recruits, emphasizing the ea-gerness of white women to pair up with their defenders. Richard Butler, who headed Aryan Nations, promised David Lane: "there will be many wives waiting for Brother Lane when he walks out of ZOG's prison."[73] (Lane would die in prison.) The KKK, in contrast, emphasized rituals and titles, making its members feel they were part of a secret world and special community. Unlike Klan organizations in the past or groups like Hezbollah and Hamas today, today's white supremacists do not offer community services or have large social wings to complement military activity. Today, the most common approach is to use social media, pro-moting grievances, conspiracy theories, and duty to the white race as inducements for joining.

The quality of personnel is poor—a particular problem, as many strategies call for an elite vanguard to lead the country into revolution through their skill and dedication. Many group members have histories of criminality, do-mestic violence, drug use, and other problems.[74] One member of the neo-Nazi group Vanguard America, for instance, texted another, with a touch of irony: "there's nothing more Aryan than entheogenic drug use."[75]

Uncommitted members plague the movement. George Lincoln Rockwell complained that the American Nazi Party was ruined by "hobbyists" attracted to Nazi symbols but unwilling to dedicate themselves to the cause.[76] Decades later, Pierce, who founded and headed the neo-Nazi National Alliance, rejected uneducated recruits like skinheads and favored strict rules for mem-bership.[77] "We want CPAs, high school teachers, engineers," he said, rather than stereotypical racists, who were "400-pound women and guys who are missing teeth at a Klan rally."[78] White supremacists today often lament the keyboard warriors who are active on social media and talk big but do little.

Because of the porous and networked nature of the movement, many groups have welcomed volunteers of various sorts without significant vetting. The results can be disastrous. The cohesion of Aryan Nations declined as skinheads and neo-Nazis began attending this group's congresses in the late 1980s, bringing drug and alcohol abuse with them.[79] In general, though many groups prohibit drugs, their use is as common as is alcohol abuse. Some members focused first and foremost on feeding their addiction, and in general, substance abuse made members less skilled and more likely to be caught. The neo-Nazi Free German Workers' Party, active in the 1980s and early 1990s, found that random violence done in its name decreased its popularity; it blamed attacks on immigrants on "irresponsible skinheads," but the party declined anyway.[80]

White supremacist leaders recognize that their followers are, at best, raw material. Many are not sufficiently indoctrinated, participating merely because a friend has joined up or they like how they look in Nazi gear. Others are enthusiastic but unskilled. To remedy this, some groups offer training camps, teaching their followers how to use weapons, build explosives, and otherwise kill. Louis Beam did this in Texas and other states in the 1970s, and in the last five years, Atomwaffen did this outside Las Vegas. The Base trained followers in Georgia, and the Identitarian movement trained white Europeans from multiple nations in France.[81] Some of this is done online. The Base offered an online library replete with works on gunsmithing, bomb making, guerrilla war, counter-surveillance, and other instructions for would-be warriors.[82] Nevertheless, Squire notes that, while The Base had some skilled leaders, it also had "a lot of goofballs."[83]

An alternative to training is recruiting people with the right backgrounds. This is not new: Vietnam War veterans like Beam played an important role in many white supremacist groups in the 1970s and 1980s. Atomwaffen and The Base sought to recruit applicants who had served in the military or who knew how to use explosives.[84] As noted in chapter 4, investigations in Germany in 2020 revealed that violent white supremacist groups have made significant inroads into the military.[85]

Leaders, too, are often of poor quality. Some are purists who excommunicate those who do not meet their standards. Others foster personality cults. The Covenant, Sword, and Arm of the Lord, a once-vibrant movement, fractured when its leader declared himself the divinely ordained King of the

Ozarks and took a second wife—and then became a government witness against other white supremacists in the Fort Smith trial.[86]

Money and Its Discontents

Groups need money to buy weapons, pay their operatives, post bail for those jailed, and cover legal defenses for arrested members. When groups cannot help their people financially, they become more vulnerable to law enforcement pressure: without a salary, a poor group member may turn on his comrades and become a government informant to earn reward money. Prosecutors can offer a reduced sentence to an arrested white supremacist who feels his group has abandoned him.

For many groups, violence, including violence related to fundraising, is meant to have a moral basis. "Plundering the Philistines" was one doctrine for groups in the 1980s that justified robbing those who did not share the supposedly true Christian faith and white race of some groups.[87] White supremacists justified robbing pornography stores, as they supposedly degraded white women, and banks, as they were supposedly Jewish controlled. Counterfeiting was also acceptable, even desirable, as it was a way of undermining the conspiratorial Federal Reserve.[88]

Money, however, is a constant problem, as white supremacist ranks tend to skew poor. The KKK relied on dues from its members, but not all groups have that advantage. The Order, for example, committed crimes such as robbing armored bank cars to fund a race war, and associates also engaged in counterfeiting. Networked individuals, for their part, do not even have these limited group benefits. Mason, a key ideologue for groups like Atomwaffen, lived in public housing and ate at soup kitchens.[89] For some members, getting married, and especially having kids, has given them a sense of financial responsibility (and increased their fear of going to prison), leading them to drop out. Moreover, if the group could not pay them, they often had less time to hang out and instead focused on the world outside their comrades.[90]

Making the financial pressure worse, lawsuits by the government and civil society groups like the SPLC are a constant financial drain. The more visible groups and individuals are often denied credit cards from banks and access to financial transaction sites like PayPal, making this financial stress worse today. Some groups have tried to shift to cryptocurrency to offset this, but, despite the buzz this generates, many of these currencies are hard to access and vulnerable to theft or other problems.[91]

Money problems often lead to infighting. Aryan Nations could not afford to pay staff as it lost money, destabilizing the group and weakening the position of its leader.[92] Combat 18 members fought with one another and rival groups to control the white power music scene.[93]

Because of crime, misbehavior, or bungling, white supremacist groups are also often on the radar screen of law enforcement. Some white supremacists accidentally detonate their bombs while building them, injuring themselves and drawing law enforcement attention. Others deal drugs, abuse their girlfriends, or otherwise draw the attention of police.[94] The FBI was able to target and dismantle The Order, for example, because a member used counterfeit money to buy a lottery ticket and was detected. Fearing death at the hands of The Order for his mistake, he became a government informant.[95] Sweden's WAR carried out several bank robberies, leading to the jailing of several of their leaders.[96]

The Dilemma of Decentralization

The shift away from organized groups like the American Nazi Party and The Order and toward networks with no clear leadership has benefits in terms of avoiding arrest but comes with a heavy price. On balance, attacks by groups who have more resources and can specialize their personnel are more effective and result in more fatalities and injuries than those carried out by individuals.[97]

Because they are not institutionalized and thus lack a succession plan, the various networks and small groups are highly vulnerable to the arrest of their leaders. German police devastated the neo-Nazi group Feuerkrieg when it arrested several leaders. Other groups, too, have split over leader behavior. The Free German Workers' Party, for example, divided into factions over internal fights about the homosexuality of their leader Michael Kuhnen.[98]

Often the infighting is violent. France's White Wolves Klan assaulted members who tried to leave, leading to unwanted attention from police. More than 10 percent of skinhead attacks were against other skinheads— and those were just the ones that got reported.[99] Leadership rivalries can be bloody, too. A former Nazi thrown out of the American Nazi Party assassinated George Lincoln Rockwell, the group's longtime head, and infighting plagued successor fragments. One of Rockwell's successors, Joseph Tommasi, was also later murdered by a fellow neo-Nazi. In 2017, Vanguard Alliance saw a leadership coup, and the loser was locked out of the group's Discord server.[100] This lack of cohesion can be devastating for the cause: a study of successful groups found that internal cohesion was an especially important factor in their success.[101]

The problem is acute among nonviolent extremists as well. The Traditionalist Workers Party collapsed into chaos when its leader had an affair with the wife of the group's cofounder (and his father-in-law). After the 2017 Unite the Right rally in Charlottesville and the killing of Heather Heyer, different groups began finger-pointing, with some disavowing white supremacy and others rejecting violence—and some branding those who tried to appeal to the mainstream as craven "cucks": a term derived from pornography and "cuckolds" that white supremacists use to refer to more mainstream and peaceful figures.[102]

Pressure from Law Enforcement

Since the civil rights era, the police, the FBI, and other security agencies have targeted white supremacist groups. Often the pressure has been weak or fitful, with violent white supremacists in many countries, including the United States, enjoying far more toleration than domestic jihadists or violent Black groups. Nevertheless, even that limited pressure has proven devastating. The FBI crushed the Klan in the late 1960s and early 1970s, dismantled The Order in the 1980s, and still regularly arrests and otherwise disrupts individuals seeking to kill in the name of the "white race." Europe, Canada, New Zealand, and Australia have also seen ups and downs, but in all these countries, white supremacists risk arrest and the criminalization of their groups. White supremacists have had to adapt to this pressure, but that adaptation is often incomplete and almost always costly for them. As Ravndal contends, "it is almost impossible to run a terrorist group in a competent Western democracy."[103]

Like most terrorist and underground movements, violent white supremacist groups need to balance security with recruitment and running an effective organization. Groups that are open and seek out new members quickly learn that any discussion of criminal activity is likely to be detected, with the result that the entire group is arrested. The Base used a cell structure to maintain operational security, limiting knowledge of its membership and operations so that the arrest of one individual did not jeopardize the entire organization. The Base also tried to vet potential recruits in its online recruitment and, to ensure security, allowed them to use pseudonyms and otherwise hide their true identities.[104] This supposed protection, however, also allowed law enforcement and civil society groups like the SPLC to monitor their activities more easily by pretending to be group members and joining online discussions.[105]

The movement today lacks a haven or even areas where it is highly concentrated or enjoys the toleration of law enforcement. The Deep South is no longer a hotspot for violence; Mississippi and Alabama are in the lower half of U.S. states when it comes to attacks.[106] In Europe, there is no one state or region where white supremacists have free rein, although their presence in Ukraine is concerning. This lack of geographic concentration hinders white supremacists' efforts to win political power, as they lack a critical mass in any locality, dilutes resources for recruiting and training, and makes them more vulnerable to arrest: although white supremacist sympathizers have penetrated the police in a few locales, this is not something the broader movement can count on.

Through shrewdness or by default, groups learn to modulate their violence based on government officials' sensitivity. The German group Community of the New Front feared that targeting government officials would lead them to be banned, as had happened to previous groups who had gone to war with the state. Instead, the group focused on targeting minorities and others who were not law enforcement priorities, enabling the group to be active for several years.[107] Low-level violence against immigrants and minorities is less likely to grab political and law enforcement attention, as these are communities that, in the United States and Europe, often have poor, or at least weaker, relationships with the police—enabling groups to continue attacks with less interference.

Limited Popular Support

A great many of the problems violent white supremacists face are tied to a lack of broad popular support. As a result, it is hard to recruit and fundraise. In addition, when they commit crimes or try to hide from authorities, today's public is willing, often eager, to turn them in. This stands in sharp contrast to the pre–civil rights era, when the Klan and other groups operated with a degree of impunity, in part because they enjoyed significant popular support.

The movement's violence also often backfires, leading to more public pressure for a crackdown. In addition, the more open racism of the extreme groups can delegitimate the cause as a whole.[108] The violence and Nazi imagery associated with the 2017 Unite the Right rally in Charlottesville generated a backlash, including among conservatives whom the marchers hoped to woo, discrediting figures like Richard Spencer, who, like David Duke before him, hoped to mainstream the movement. As Matthew Heimbach, one of the organizers of the rally, put it, "besides, violence doesn't work. We know this. Violence doesn't create converts; it just makes you an asshole."[109]

In part because of this negative reaction to violence, some white supremacists active on the internet are trying to mainstream their ideas, with immigration, in particular, being an issue around which they are trying to unite with a broader community. Indeed, the movement has successfully mainstreamed itself to some degree, with many of its ideas appearing within the Trump administration and the broad political movement he built. Trump's "Build the Wall" slogan was a theme of David Duke, and the vehement anti-Muslim sentiment of Trump administration figures like Michael Flynn meshes with many white supremacist ideas.[110] Unfortunately, part of the base of the Republican Party also embraces some of the conspiracy theories and parts of the worldview of white supremacists.

How to Think about the Threat of White Supremacist Terrorism

A review of the white supremacist movement since the civil rights era suggests that, although attacks and plots are important measures of the threat, less observable metrics are equally and, at times, more valuable.[111] The political impact of violence, the movement's organizational strength, the plausibility of its strategies, the concessions received, and the counterterrorism capacity of the state all shape how dangerous the threat is.

Lives Lost and Plotted Attacks

The most obvious way to measure terrorism, and the one most frequently used, is the death toll.[112] Since 9/11 through July 2021, white supremacist violence in the United States has killed almost 100 people, according to the

New America Foundation.[113] This is roughly comparable to jihadist violence but is still relatively limited in scope—in the last 20 years, there has been no event comparable to Oklahoma City, let alone 9/11. In Europe, there have been numerous white supremacist attacks, especially on immigrants, but the death toll from jihadist groups has been far higher in the post-9/11 era. In addition, as noted, white supremacists also kill people due to personal grievances, intragroup rivalries, or in spur-of-the-moment attacks with no intention of creating a broader psychological effect—attacks that are not terrorism but nevertheless increase the death toll.

Not all, or even most, attacks kill people, but they still instill fear. Data from Jigsaw indicate that there were fewer than 10 white supremacist attacks annually in the United States from 2008 to 2011. The numbers spiked briefly to 16 in 2012 but then returned to below 10 annual attacks for the following years. Starting in 2015, however, the number again reached 16, as it did in 2016, before climbing to 31, 40, and 33 for the next three years. Germany saw almost no reported attacks until 2014, but attacks surged in 2015 in particular, with 53 (most on refugee camps), before settling down in subsequent years. The United Kingdom also saw significant increases after 2010, with zero reported attacks that year but rising numbers in the years that followed, peaking at 12 in 2017.[114] (We should be careful, however, in assuming too much precision in these figures, as data issues and uneven law enforcement undoubtedly skew these numbers, as well as other data on white supremacist violence.)

Yet this approach has faults. A more dangerous potential threat can, and should, lead to more law enforcement attention, which stops some plots before they succeed—diminishing the number of attacks but not the potential threat. As the white supremacist threat grew, so did the number of FBI arrests related to potential terrorist attacks, although accurate numbers are lacking, as many arrests were made using state-level charges related to violence, not terrorism.[115] This threat and response dynamic makes it hard to know whether the white supremacist threat was high but was mostly disrupted by law enforcement or was low to begin with and no action was truly needed.

FBI director Christopher Wray testified that the FBI made around 100 domestic terrorism arrests in the fiscal year 2019, most of which involved white supremacists—a number that was close to that for international terrorism–related arrests.[116] This number actually represents a decrease: in 2017 it was around 150, and it fell to 120 in 2018. European officials' outlook is more grim. Jürgen Stock, the secretary general of Interpol, warns that white supremacist violence is rising dramatically: "things are getting worse." British police saw their case load double in 2019: one-quarter of all their arrests and one-third of the plots to kill they monitored were driven by white supremacists.

In addition, it is useful to distinguish higher-level, bloodier attacks from lower-level ones. In Europe in particular, neo-Nazi skinheads were responsible for large numbers of attacks in the 2000s, but many of these were not political and involved assault and vandalism, not mass murder. The decline of the skinhead movement led to a decline in the overall number of white supremacist attacks, but many people focus, often appropriately, on killings and more spectacular attacks.[117]

Measuring plots is another way to consider potential lives lost. Figures 7.1 and 7.2 show both the dead and wounded from white supremacist attacks in the United States from 2010 to 2019 and the ratio of foiled to successful plots, respectively. As these figures make clear, both the scale and scope of white supremacist violence increased in these years. Looking at successful as well as unsuccessful attacks helps to isolate at least some of the effects of counterterrorism, enabling observers to ask, "What if?" with regard to the scope of true danger. However, the United States does not keep a database of aborted terrorist plots; figures 7.1 and 7.2 include those prominent enough to make the news but almost certainly fail to include many that are not. Moreover, effective counterterrorism has a deterrent effect, such that would-be terrorists, fearing arrests, simply do not consider some plots that would otherwise have occured.[118]

As always, there is a data problem. Part of this is due to the heavy overlap between white supremacists and criminality, where many of their crimes, for example robbery or drug trafficking, are apolitical. Many of those arrested as part of terrorism investigations are charged with gun, drug, or other nonterrorism offenses, as these are often easier to prove. In addition, the media do not cover many investigations, and others are not widely known, making it difficult to determine how many plots there truly are.[119]

Political and Psychological Impact

Terrorism's death toll may be low, but it differs from COVID-19, car accidents, and other forms of death because it is meant to have a political

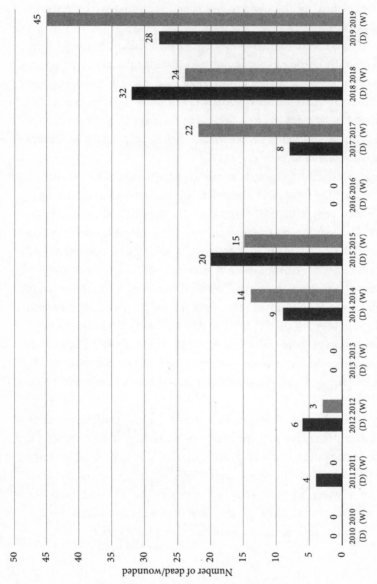

Figure 7.1 Dead (D) and wounded (W) totals in white supremacist plots, 2010–2019). *Sources:* Data for 2010–2018 from Southern Poverty Law Center, "Terror from the Right" archives. Data for 2019 from University of Maryland, START, Global Terrorism Database, which uses a different methodology from the SPLC and is included for comparative purposes only.

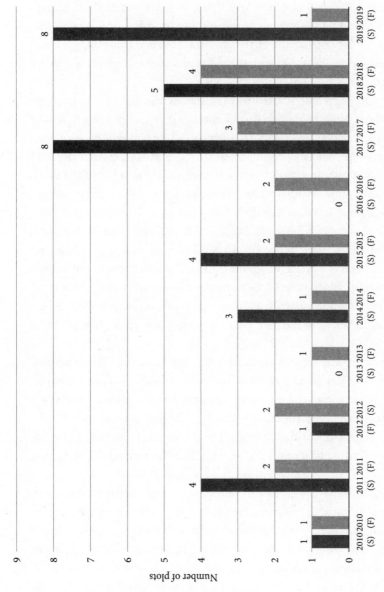

Figure 7.2 Successful (S) and foiled (F) white supremacist plots, 2010–2019. *Sources:* Data for 2010–2018 from Southern Poverty Law Center, "Terror from the Right" archives. Data for 2019 from University of Maryland, START, Global Terrorism Database, which uses a different methodology from the SPLC and is included for comparative purposes only.

and psychological impact. As an IRA terrorist once commented, "you don't bloody well kill people for the sake of killing them."[120] The economic and political effects of terrorism can be vast, ranging from shaping travel and consumption patterns—as people fear flying or going out to shop, respectively—to dissuading individuals from running for office or otherwise engaging in civic life. Before the civil rights era, violence from the Klan and like-minded groups helped ensure the political and social subordination of the Black community, especially in the South.

Today, white supremacist terrorism remains deadly, but the political impact of violent white supremacists is diminished. Violence even hurts the white supremacist cause as it increases fears of white nationalism, and nonviolent white supremacists oppose violence for this reason.[121] After the 2017 Unite the Right rally in Charlottesville turned violent and led to the death of one counterprotester, law enforcement pressure grew, media became more critical, and subsequent rallies fizzled, even as narratives and rhetoric remained strong.[122] Similarly, Black politicians have made tremendous strides: In addition to electing a Black president for two terms in 2008 and 2012, in 2020 voters elected record numbers of women of color and a Black vice president.[123] Black voters were registered in numbers roughly comparable to those of white voters in 2020, and in some southern states the percentage was higher.[124] In the past, violence would have made such advances unthinkable.[125]

The psychological impact remains keen. Much of the white supremacist violence is low-level and does not meet the definition of terrorism because it is often focused on individuals rather than seeking a broader political and psychological effect—but it is dangerous nonetheless. The psychological impact of daily violence and continued racism is considerable, contributing to mental and physical health problems for minority communities.[126]

The political impact is greater in Europe, especially when it mixes with mainstream politics. In France, Germany, and other countries, racist politicians tone down their rhetoric as they seek election, but their antiMuslim and antiimmigrant agendas remain. In Poland, some individuals who have headed small radical street movements are now in parliament.[127] Similarly, in the United States, white supremacists have been better able to advance their cause when they have mixed with more mainstream voices, as occurred during the Trump era, when the administration hired many antiimmigrant and anti-Muslim figures who would have once been anathema.

Organizational Strength

Examining organizational and movement strength is another way to measure the potential danger. Many terrorist organizations only use limited violence but have the potential to use far more. Lebanese Hezbollah, for example, is a highly skilled terrorist organization, but its international terrorist attacks in recent years have been relatively few in number and largely calibrated to its overall goals regarding Israel. To judge Hezbollah's danger to the United States or Israel by the current level of attacks would miss much of its latent capacity.

The number of white nationalist groups has soared in recent years, increasing by more than 50 percent between 2017 and 2019—an increase often cited as an indication of a greater danger. This surge occurred even as traditional neo-Nazi and Klan groups declined, with Identitarian and similar movements growing in their place. This topped a recent peak in 2011, when hate against America's first Black president was high.[128] Looking at the number of groups, however, is an odd way to assess a threat. If a local Klan chapter splits due to a personal rivalry, it is probably weaker, not more dangerous. Indeed, focusing on the number of groups ignores the far bigger danger of networked individuals who have little or no relationship to overall groups.

At the same time, however, the white supremacy movement as a whole suffers from numerous problems. It is internally divided and thus is less than the sum of its parts. Its recruits are often uneducated criminals or otherwise of poor quality. In addition, the conspiracy theories that plague the movement further reduce its effectiveness.

Both individual groups and the movement as a whole should be examined. The organizational strength of current groups such as Atomwaffen is a fraction of that of the Klan at its peak, and many groups quickly come and go. Yet, even as group after group is crushed, the movement endures. Part of this endurance is the popularity of many of its causes, ranging from opposition to immigration to racism and anti-Semitism to misogyny and other grievances.[129] Another part of this endurance is that individuals are highly networked and have access to guns, increasing individual lethality. As a result, it is easy to create new groups or radicalized individuals de novo or out of the remnants of old ones. In addition, as the movement splinters, many of the fragments become more violent, and some target a broader set of enemies. The Klan, for all its horrors, was more restrained than Atomwaffen.

Strategic Plausibility

A question related to organizational strength is whether the movement has a compelling strategy for victory—an issue discussed in detail in Chapter 6. The Klan in 1960 could hope to repeat the successes of the Klan after Reconstruction and the political impact of the Klan in the 1920s. However, from the 1970s onward, various strategies of victory clearly had little chance of success: David Duke failed to build a large political movement, The Order failed to incite the masses, and Timothy McVeigh failed to spark a revolution. Although social polarization in the United States is high, today's white supremacists' efforts to accelerate the collapse of government appear to have little hope of succeeding.

During Trump's time in office, because his administration and he himself seemed to tolerate white supremacism, fears of such violence increased. Trump played down police violence against the Black community, declared that Mexican immigrants were "rapists," and proclaimed that COVID-19 was a "Chinese virus," among many other remarks. When violence flared, as happened during the 2017 Unite the Right rally in Charlottesville, Trump claimed that the white supremacists' ranks included "very fine people."[130] Not surprisingly, a 2019 poll found that half of Americans saw Trump as a racist.[131] This spilled over into government, with senior Homeland Security officials playing down intelligence warnings of white supremacist violence.[132] This overlap has allowed radical voices a chance to shape the United States' broader political agenda: the result does not fulfill white supremacists' racist dreams, but strains of their argument affect a broader part of the body politic now.

Also of concern is the overlap between white supremacy and other forms of right-wing terrorism, notably antigovernment extremism. Claims of government illegitimacy and election fraud in the United States, even if unfounded, are widely believed.[133] These claims provide additional grievances and expand the possible range of targets for groups and individuals with white supremacist beliefs who also share other antigovernment views and conspiracies.

Counterterrorism Capacity

To understand the strength of white supremacist and other forms of violence, it is necessary to understand what is arrayed against it. The U.S. government has a strong (some would say alarming) counterterrorism capacity, and other actors, ranging from the SPLC to social media companies that deplatform white supremacists, also play a role.

Chapter 8 examines how counterterrorism might change to better manage the threat of white supremacist terrorism.

8

Fighting White Supremacy

In the summer of 2019, a white supremacist terrorist attack did not occur.

On August 8, 2019, the FBI searched the home of Conor Climo in Las Vegas, finding bomb-making materials, an AR-15 rifle, and schematics for building improvised explosives. Climo had first come to the attention of law enforcement several years before, when he did a television interview while "patrolling" his neighborhood in combat gear, carrying an assault rifle and high-capacity ammunition magazines. He later confessed that he had plotted online with members of the neo-Nazi Feuerkrieg Division to firebomb a Las Vegas synagogue or a bar that catered to the LGBTQ+ community. In an online chat, he had admitted his murderous designs to an FBI under-cover officer, as well as an informant, and prosecutors used this information to bring him to justice. Technically, he was not convicted of terrorism, or even of attempted arson. Instead, he pled guilty to possessing an unregistered firearm. He went to prison for two years for his plotting, and he would be supervised and would receive mental health treatment upon his release.[1]

Climo's case is unexceptional, but it captures many key elements of the white supremacy challenge today and demonstrates how the grinding gears of the U.S. government counterterrorism apparatus combat white supremacy. Climo, who was not a member of an organized group, made himself vulnerable to detection when trying to communicate with like-minded extremists on social media—an increasing vulnerability for members of the movement. The law offered numerous ways to charge Climo, but, in the end, he was not prosecuted with charges related to terrorism, despite the terroristic nature of his plans.

When Does White Supremacy Thrive? A Quick Review

To understand when and how counterterrorism works best, it is useful to briefly review the conditions under which white supremacists thrive or stumble.

White supremacists thrive when they have access to power. At their peak before the civil rights era, they partnered with state and local government officials; although today open support is thankfully rare, in many countries and localities they still enjoy the toleration of those in power. This gives them the freedom to organize, recruit, fundraise, and otherwise make their organizations stronger while plotting attacks. Even without a link to government, white supremacists benefit when significant parts of society sympathize with them. This not only aids recruiting but also makes it harder for law enforcement and intelligence services to learn about white supremacists' activities: informants are considered snitches, not citizens doing their civic duty. White supremacist groups, like all organizations, also do better when they are unified and can focus on their enemies, not on their rivals. Finally, white supremacists benefit when they have access to skilled personnel, whether by recruiting them directly from the military or police or by sending recruits to training camps and otherwise making them more dangerous.

Conversely, the white supremacist cause suffers when it is hunted by law enforcement and when society rejects it, as members then spend their time hiding, not acting. In addition, when there are barriers to fundraising and communications, the groups' propaganda and operational reach decline. If the skill level of their members falls, so too does the danger the group poses and its ability to attract recruits—after all, no one wants to join a group of losers and incompetents. White supremacists also suffer when their movement is divided, with groups fighting each other as much as their supposed enemies.

For much of the post-9/11 period, white supremacists have been ignored or treated as a sideshow, especially when compared with jihadist organizations like ISIS. As Daniel Benjamin, a former senior U.S. counterterrorism official, notes, "the U.S. government has a complete inability to do two things at once."[2] The jihadist groups, however, are largely focused on changing U.S. and European foreign policy, and most of their ambitions are alien to the countries and cultures of the West. White supremacists, in contrast, are often tapping into broader political and cultural demands, presenting themselves as heirs to a glorious past as well as offering a model for the future. As a result, their violence is often more politically consequential even as it is politically more difficult to confront them. White supremacist violence can impede social progress, undermine confidence in government, worsen divisions between communities, and warp political institutions. As online extremism expert Maura Conway notes, "attitudes toward white supremacists are different because *they are us*," rather than a group like ISIS that is alien to the bulk of citizens in Western countries.[3]

Dimensions of Counterterrorism

Counterterrorism works best when it fosters problems for white supremacist groups that make them less popular and less capable. Some of these steps are obvious and have direct results, for example arresting white supremacists who are planning to use violence; others are difficult to measure (but no less important), for example inhibiting fundraising and trying to turn public opinion against white supremacism.

The Government Mindset

The previous chapters have shown three basic government positions toward white supremacists: complicity, toleration, and hostility. Even when the government is not actively supporting white supremacists, government officials have tolerated white supremacists, allowing them to preserve a foothold and, at times, act without significant interference. The U.S. and European governments have also underresourced the white supremacist threat, especially in comparison with the resources they have devoted to fighting jihadist violence. Perhaps most important, politicians at times embrace aspects of the white supremacist cause, and even when elected officials reject violence, their use of extreme rhetoric and white supremacist talking points heartens the broader movement.

Governments often are less aggressive in targeting white supremacist violence than jihadist violence because of a key difference between the two.[4] Jihadist attacks like 9/11 or the 2015 ISIS attacks in Paris are perceived as striking at "us"—all in a society, regardless of race or religion, feel at risk. Because white supremacists, in contrast, usually target immigrants, the LGBTQ+ community, Jews, Muslims, Black people, or other minorities, if you are part of the white, Christian majority, you do not feel directly threatened. Even in well-integrated societies, such attacks are often considered attacks on "them" and do not always evoke the same horror and political pressure.[5]

Ensuring that we really treat "them" as "us" is vital. Leaders can set the tone for the country and ensure that aggressive counterterrorism is not made a political football, and the FBI and police can act without the fear that one set of politicians will undercut their efforts. Under President Trump, homeland security officials felt pressure to downplay the threat of white supremacists, while Trump made himself a spokesman for aggrieved white males, with many of his supporters continuing his rhetoric even after he lost power in 2021. Indeed, some law enforcement officials feared that Trump's rhetoric would be viewed as giving "mentally unwell, violence-prone individuals as permission to engage in acts of violence."[6]

Politicians must also reassure minority communities, which often have a poor relationship with the police. Although only a tiny minority of police are linked to white supremacist groups, the impact of those who are is considerable. One investigation has found connections between white supremacists and police in Alabama, California, Connecticut, Florida, Illinois, Louisiana, Michigan, Nebraska, Oklahoma, Oregon, Texas, Virginia, Washington, West Virginia, and elsewhere in the last 20 years.[7] Existing hate crimes laws designed to protect minority communities are not regularly invoked. As law professor Frank Pezzella has observed, "the same people that these laws are designed to protect are the ones with the most strained relationships with the police—Black residents, LGBT people, undocumented aliens."[8] Police violence against minority communities also poses a particular problem for gaining public trust in police departments' ability or will to fight white supremacist terrorism.

Ensuring that minority communities see the government as an ally is vital. After the Christchurch attack, New Zealand's prime minister, Jacinda Ardern, issued a statement in Arabic, as well as one in English, declaring solidarity with the victims of the attack. A husband of one of the Christchurch shooting victims told reporters that terrorists "want to incite between one group with another. Maybe they were hoping that if they target some Muslims, then maybe Muslims will retaliate. But we Muslim leaders are saying that's not gonna happen."[9] For this noble response to become reality in other countries, communities must believe that their government will protect them.

Politics, law, social change, and effective counterterrorism all go hand in hand. Social change can force politicians to pass new laws and enforce existing ones: the laws that helped shut down the Klan had been on the books for 10010 years but simply had not been enforced. Hate crimes laws do not necessarily deter crime, but they do increase resources for fighting racial violence and attract community attention to the problem.[10] This attention and resources, in turn, make it easier for the police to fight white supremacist violence. Focusing on hate crimes can also prod local officials to take the problem more seriously and help identify individuals who might be relevant for more extensive terrorism investigations.[11]

Community Programs

The strength of white supremacists, like all terrorists, depends heavily on their relationship with the broader communities where they live and that they claim to represent. Sympathetic communities, as in the American South before the civil rights era, will not cooperate with law enforcement, and the authorities at the local level are riddled with sympathizers or even outright members of the white supremacist groups. Obtaining evidence, leveling criminal charges, and securing a conviction become almost impossible. Once a community turns against white supremacists, its members are far more likely to report suspicious behavior to the police and cooperate with investigations.

After the Christchurch killings, the official inquiry into the attack emphasized the need for community engagement, recognizing that not all citizens were affected equally by the murders. The report even began with acknowledgments to the victims, referring to them as "the 51 shuhada." The use of the Arabic word for martyrs was a gesture of respect, as was the prominent call for the government, including intelligence agencies, to prioritize engaging Muslim communities as part of counterterrorism. The report notes that Muslim communities in New Zealand fear being treated as terrorists, and thus it is hard for them to work with security agencies to help the government prevent terror attacks targeting Muslim Kiwis. This is a sentiment also felt by groups in the United States and Europe—Muslims, the Black community, and others—who are the targets of white supremacist violence but often have historical reasons for distrusting police and intelligence services. Having security services whose members are diverse and can engage effectively with minority communities is vital.[12]

Programs like those used to counter violent extremism, many of which were created to woo Muslims away from radical Islam in the wake of 9/11, should be developed or expanded to counter white supremacism as well, with a recognition of the many differences between these dangers. Social workers, clergy, health professionals, and others can all play a role. In Germany, the program Exit-Deutschland has been used to help neo-Nazis reintegrate into society. Similarly, the British government has stepped up the use of its program Prevent, originally designed to counter jihadists, against white supremacists.[13] Social media companies might also try to develop programs to counter white supremacist ideas, though these often fail or even backfire if the targeted radicals do not trust the messenger, as is usually the case. For now, at least, the evidence is not there to say that these programs to counter white supremacist ideas work, according to several experts I spoke with.[14]

In general, counterterrorism officials should always try to make it easy to exit a white supremacist group, particularly for lower-level members who are not as involved in violence.[15] Groups constantly fight over priorities, money, group disciplinary policies, and who will lead. Those who leave may be angry and may need protection, both of which can push them into the arms of law enforcement. These disaffected members are valuable information sources and can testify against their former comrades. In addition, they are often the most persuasive voices to convince other movement members to renounce their views or at least move away from active participation.

The United States should also focus on its prison population. White supremacists aggressively recruit in prison, and, in general, a prison population is full of violent young men who are attractive potential recruits.

Law

Much of the day-to-day effort against violent white supremacists involves monitoring their activities and then successfully prosecuting them: the jobs of police, prosecutors, and domestic security agencies. When group leaders are in jail, it is harder for them to orchestrate violence on the outside, inspire their followers, and build their movements. When leaders are arrested, groups may collapse or fall into infighting over succession.[16] Even the arrest of smaller fish can help, as they may work with law enforcement against more senior extremists to avoid going to jail. In addition, the threat of jail time serves as a deterrent, helping keep groups away from violence for fear of punishment. Law enforcement raids can also serve to gather intelligence. The story of the demise of groups like the Klan, WAR, The Order, and others involves the arrest and jailing of key leaders.

Early interventions are particularly effective. As part of their mindset, white supremacists disdain weakness, and if they are not quickly condemned and prosecuted, they are often emboldened.[17] Charging them as terrorists also has symbolic value, showing Americans in general and minority communities in particular that the U.S. government sees the threat as serious. It also helps probation officers and others manage the individual better after he is released from jail by helping to ensure that he stays away from other extremists and otherwise putting appropriate conditions on his release.[18]

One of the most powerful U.S. legal tools is a charge of conspiracy, often called the "prosecutors' darling," which enables the government to target leaders for the crimes of their followers and to target a group as a whole even when only a few members may have committed a particular attack. Conspiracy charges can be brought if a crime is intended but does not occur. This is especially important for going after key nodes in white supremacist networks; by targeting leaders and organizers, a conspiracy charge can disrupt significant portions of the movement as a whole. The Department of Justice went after the prison gang the Aryan Brotherhood, the Aryan Circle, and other groups with statutes originally designed to fight organized crime.[19] Neo-Nazi ideologue James Mason warns that he avoids even using the word "conspiracy" and that confidential informants will try to foster conspiracies to entrap group members.[20]

Charging white supremacists as terrorists, however, is difficult. A study by Michael German and Emmanuel Mauleón found that in U.S. law there are 51 "federal crimes of terrorism," plus an additional crime that prohibits "material support" for them. Many of these crimes, however, are obscure and have definitions that do not apply to most white supremacist violent acts. Hate crimes laws offer additional firepower for prosecutors, as do laws that enable prosecutors to go after groups as if they were organized crime syndicates. Yet prosecutors often do not use federal charges even when the actions meet the statutory definition of domestic terrorism, as happened, for example, when an Atomwaffen member killed a gay Jewish man in California in 2018. Instead, as already discussed, prosecutors prefer more easily provable charges involving illegal gun possession, drug trafficking, and assault. As one retired senior government official put it, "federal firearms laws are the Achilles heel of white supremacists."[21] In Germany, many white supremacist attacks are not labeled as terrorism because there is no clear connection to a specific organization—a legal requirement that ignores the network-based nature of much of the white supremacist movement today.[22]

Given the highly politicized nature of the term "terrorism," to enact a federal domestic terrorism law in the United States would be risky. In theory,
such a law could reassure minority communities that the government was
taking violence against them seriously and make the government more likely
to devote resources to fighting white supremacist violence. However, such a
law would be unlikely to change actual operations in any significant way. In
part, this is a limit of the First Amendment: the United States can take action
against jihadists or other non-Americans with hostile viewpoints abroad,
but when it comes to Americans at home, it cannot put penalties on a group
just because it is hateful. In addition, many of the most powerful laws, like
murder charges, and much of the manpower operate at the state, not federal,
level.[23] The risk of abuse is also high. Under President Trump, for example,
the Department of Justice might have used such a statute to target part of
the Black Lives Matter movement or political opponents more than white
supremacists or other true threats.

The seditious conspiracy charge the government has tried to use against
various white supremacists has often failed because juries find it hard to believe that the conspirators represent a credible threat to overthrow the government, even if the intent is there.[24] Prosecutors usually try to fill that void
by stretching laws to cover threats as they evolve. For example, in a conspiracy
involving three members of The Base who sought to murder a couple they
believed was with Antifa, prosecutors added charges for "stealing and killing
a ram," as the plotters planned to use it for a Norse pagan ritual sacrifice.
For the former Coast Guard lieutenant Christopher Hasson, who sought to
emulate Breivik, they added drug and firearms charges but issued no charge
linked to terrorism.[25] The Klan's intimidation of Vietnamese fishers was
halted in part due to a Texas law that banned unauthorized "military companies."[26] The FBI worked with local prosecutors in Seattle to remove guns
from an individual they feared would conduct an attack; while they had no
federal authority to do so, Washington State has a "red flag" law that allows
such a temporary removal for dangerous individuals.[27] As these examples
suggest, it is often a mix of local ordinances, state law, and federal law that
provides the best way to target white supremacists.

Although terrorism-related charges are often difficult to use, law enforcement still has many opportunities to act because so many white supremacists
are involved in other crimes, including theft, domestic abuse, and narcotics
trafficking. This is at both the upper and lower levels: David Duke went to
jail for tax and mail fraud, fleecing his followers by using their donations for

gambling trips and other personal expenses. One expert has described most white supremacists as "career criminals who hate Black people."[28] Indeed, police often learn about a violent white supremacist through such crimes. The so-called Crusaders' plot to bomb a Somali American apartment complex was foiled after one of the plotter's girlfriends contacted the police to report domestic violence.[29] Swedish police learned about a Nordic Resistance Movement plot after arriving at one of the plotter's homes to tell him that his firearms license had expired. When entering the home, they discovered far more weapons, as well as a contraption for firing a shotgun from inside a bag. They then notified Swedish intelligence, leading to a computer search and the discovery of more plots.[30] Jonathan Leman, an expert on violent Swedish groups, found that almost half of those who had become involved in the Swedish far right linked to violence had previous arrests, often on violence or weapons charges.[31] The more national-level intelligence and security agencies can work with local-level police, the more this criminal behavior can be exploited. In the United States, the Department of Justice's Civil Rights Division can coordinate investigations with the Criminal Division, using criminal charges to disrupt the movement as a whole.[32]

The U.S. government can also go after white supremacist groups on firearms charges. Law professor Mary McCord notes that all 50 states have some provision prohibiting private paramilitary activity; though the Second Amendment protects one's right to bear arms to protect oneself and one's property, it does not protect one's right to band together with others to form a self-proclaimed police force.[33]

European countries are far more restrictive of gun ownership, and they often have legal tools the United States lacks. Countries with more recent experiences of tyranny, like Greece and Spain, accept that democracy can be precarious and are therefore more willing to ban political groups they feel threaten the political order. In Italy, a racist group can be banned simply for distributing propaganda, and in the Netherlands it only takes a judge's order to prohibit a racist political party. The United Kingdom—one of the more liberal European countries when it comes to free speech—banned National Action because it praised the murder of Jo Cox, a member of Parliament; such a move would not be possible in the United States due to First Amendment protections.[34] In contrast, the United States and Australia do not ban self-proclaimed racist groups and otherwise tolerate all groups that do not openly endorse violence, even if their goals are antidemocratic.

When law enforcement cracked down on right-wing violence in Germany after an attack or outrage, the less-committed members often dropped out, fearing jail time or other penalties. In addition, increased law enforcement led to greater distrust and divisions within the more violent movements, diverting energy and making it harder for them to attract new recruits. As their problems mounted, the lack of success itself became a problem, further reducing recruitment and creating tensions between those who favored violence and those who pushed for electoral politics.[35] Similarly, in Greece, the broad legal action against Golden Dawn and its supporters highlighted the party's violence, leading to its decline in electoral success, as well as scaring away many members from violent activities, contributing to a decline in attacks as well.[36] Some group members, however, go elsewhere. After the German government banned the National Socialist Action Front in the early 1980s, the Free German Workers' Party became far more extreme as members of the banned group simply migrated to the group that remained legal.

United States law enforcement learned at Ruby Ridge and Waco that aggressive confrontations can backfire, fostering an image of an oppressive government and rallying disparate right-wing elements against supposed tyranny. Indeed, U.S. agencies found that deescalation, rather than confrontation, often works: stretching out negotiations and trying to isolate groups after a confrontation. Over time, the headlines and outrage fade, and those who might rally to the cause go back to their jobs and families.[37] The government, moreover, has the luxury of time. This can be frustrating, as the white supremacists may be in violation of the law and as law enforcement attracts action-oriented people; however, an overreaction can be costly, not only in immediate lives lost but also in confidence in government.[38]

In the United States, civil society groups have proven to be key partners in bringing white supremacists to court. Lawsuits from the SPLC devastated the White Patriot Party, the Confederate Knights of the Ku Klux Klan, and other groups. The SPLC focuses on leaders and on organizations as a whole rather than lower-level group members, believing (correctly) that they will have a greater impact this way. Indeed, the SPLC successfully sued white supremacist leader Tom Metzger, who had promoted leaderless resistance and otherwise tried to escape responsibility for the actions of white supremacists he inspired and trained. The SPLC also monitors information on the internet, which the FBI cannot do unless it has an open case. The SPLC is thus able to find considerable incriminating information and suspicious material that are later important for law enforcement.[39]

Intelligence

For law enforcement to work, prosecutors and police must know whom to target. This, in turn, requires monitoring, penetrating, and otherwise gathering information on white supremacist groups; all of these actions are within the purview of intelligence agencies. In addition, intelligence agencies can manipulate white supremacist organizations to weaken and divide them. For example, the FBI's covert campaign against various Klan organizations in the 1960s and 1970s shattered them, and white supremacist groups never regained the levels of organization and public presence the various Klan groups enjoyed.

Intelligence is often more easily obtained after an attack, when the public both horrified by the violence and sensitized to the danger, and when the killer himself has left a trail to follow. After the Christchurch killings, tips to New Zealand's intelligence services about possible white supremacist activity spiked.[40] The challenge, of course, is that intelligence agencies seek information before an attack in order to prevent it, and successfully identifying a shooter or a bomber after many people are dead is a hollow victory.

Confidential informants, wiretaps, and other intelligence means are used again and again against white supremacists, albeit far less aggressively than was done against the Klan in the 1960s and 1970s or is done today against suspected jihadists.[41] The FBI has regularly inserted undercover agents and recruited informants when it learned that a white supremacist group might use violence. United States government informants have attended large white supremacist gatherings, like the 1984 Aryan National World Congress at Hayden Lake, Idaho, giving the government a sense of who is who in the movement as a whole.[42] The Order was dismantled in part by FBI special agent Wayne Manis, who went undercover with the group. By infiltrating The Order, Manis was able to identify and locate the group's leader, determine the group's guiding principles and strategy, demonstrate the group's responsibility for a series of crimes, and ultimately arrest and convict a significant number of members.[43] In Europe, informants contributed to the demise or weakening of groups including Combat 18, Feuerkrieg Division, The Hard Corp, National Action, Avanguardia Ordinovista, and others.

Governments often dangle supposedly interested newcomers with expertise in areas like explosives in front of groups to entice them to recruit informants.[44] This tactic is particularly effective against white supremacist groups, as many have grandiose ambitions but lack people who can build bombs or are otherwise highly skilled.

Fortunately for governments, the groups themselves are usually poorly trained in operational security. Most groups are desperate for recruits and thus easy to penetrate.[45] Many members are eager to boast to their fellows and often do not know when they are incriminating themselves and others. As neo-Nazi ideologue James Mason wrote, "stupid people are more dangerous than any time bomb."[46] He constantly warned against informers and agents provocateurs, publicly telling his followers not to do anything illegal but slyly noting that if they did, "they should do it alone and in secrecy."[47] Despite constant warnings, though, the movement remains highly vulnerable. As one former senior counterterrorism official told me, "they will quickly rat out their buddies."[48]

Some white supremacist groups are aware of government monitoring and try to police themselves. The Aryan Nations, for example, kicked people off its website when they called for violence or asked for advice on how to convert a semiautomatic weapon into an automatic one, which is a federal crime.[49]

Much of the law enforcement action is at the state or even county level, which is where white supremacists act and live on a daily basis. A key task of agencies like the Department of Homeland Security and especially the FBI is to work with local officials, ensuring they have the necessary information to act against violent extremists.[50]

Civil society groups can also perform an important intelligence function. In 2017, British authorities thwarted the plot of Jack Renshaw, a member of National Action, to kill the Labour member of Parliament Rosie Cooper. The antiracism group Hope Not Hate had an informant inside National Action, and the informant told the police, who were already watching Renshaw because of his involvement in sex crimes against teenage boys, about the plot.[51] Community Security Trust, an antihate organization focused on "protecting Britain's Jewish community," tries to act as "eyes and ears" for the police.[52] Information from civil society groups can also further divide white supremacists. When the SPLC published tapes of the neo-Nazi William Pierce calling skinheads and other white supremacists "freaks" and "weaklings," it embittered skinheads and furthered divisions within the movement.[53]

Social media posts and activity are often a significant source of intelligence. In 2017, Ethan Stables planned to attack a gay pride parade in the United

Kingdom with a machete. He researched firearms and how to make bombs on the internet; on Facebook he posted a picture of a machete, claiming that he was "going to war" and would conduct a "slaughter." HeHe then started a Facebook group, and a person who was mistakenly added to it informed the police about Stables's intentions.[54] Similarly, the FBI inserted an undercover agent into The Base after he was supposedly vetted online, which made it easier for the government to concoct a plausible backstory and cover for him. The agent then met and trained with Base members for months, helping the FBI overcome the group's encrypted communications and eventually arrest group members.[55] As Berger has wryly noted, "it takes the government about 10 minutes to associate a Telegram account with a white supremacist's location."[56]

In addition to the aforementioned bias that FBI and local officials have in favor of successful prosecution, which makes them more likely to focus on charges that are easy to prove rather than those that might show a broader conspiracy, part of the challengePart of the problem for governments seeking to prosecute white supremacists is the same one that plagues the white supremacist movement: many are talkers, not doers—a particular problem with regard to social media. After an attack, it is common to note that the attacker "declared" his intentions. However, as one informant noted, "you have talkers and doers out there, and 99 percent of the people are talkers." [57] Often, it is only in hindsight that we can separate the signal from the noise.

That said, when the government makes a concerted effort, the effect is often devastating. The FBI has developed a successful playbook for undercover operations when going after suspected American jihadists—making contact, providing them with explosives or other aid to ostensibly help them commit violence, and then arresting them—and is now using it with white supremacists.[58] Law enforcement personnel are also more comfortable with the world of white supremacy, where they do not face the language and cultural barriers involved in targeting jihadists. As one expert has noted, "there are a lot of Bubba FBI agents and police."[59] Another has pointed out that "U.S. law enforcement is optimized for penetrating groups of pudgy white guys."[60] Indeed, the government at times has been too aggressive in the use of undercover operatives and confidential informants, with informants in particular often providing dubious intelligence or egging on extremists, helping to convert them from big talkers to actual terrorists.[61]

Atomwaffen disbanded in the United States after five of its members were arrested. The charges ranged from "swatting" journalists to sharing child pornography, none of which are strictly tied to terrorism. As James Mason, Atomwaffen's primary ideologue, declared, "the level and degree of federal infiltration and the numerous arrests stemming from that have so severely hampered the group's ability to function as a group that it would be pointless to even pretend that anything resembling organizational activity could continue."[62] Similarly, the United Kingdom "decimated" National Action due to a sustained campaign against the group.[63] Even when groups do not succumb directly, the indirect effect can be tremendous. Before their arrests, Atomwaffen members admitted that they spent so much time on operational security that they found it hard to conduct new attacks.[64] Mason later distanced himself from Atomwaffen, fearing arrest for its activities.

Intelligence is also vital for tracking, and hopefully disrupting, the global connections of white supremacists. In prosecuting a leader of The Base who had entered the United States from Canada, the government used "Google location data, cell phone location data, [and] recorded telephone calls," along with the postarrest statement of another member, to reconstruct the leader's entry onto U.S. soil.[65] Similarly, the Department of Homeland Security should track and share the travels of Americans and others who go to and from Ukraine who may be working with white supremacists there.[66]

Disrupting Ties to the Security Forces and Police

Historically, white supremacists have worked with, recruited from, and otherwise benefited from a relationship with military and police forces, and this problem persists in the United States and various European countries. Some white supremacists also intentionally target the military and police for recruitment, adding to this concern, although in many countries such targeting is often more talk than action.[67] Similarly, Immigration and Customs Enforcement and Customs and Border Protection have many members who express antiimmigrant views.[68] This problem grew during the Trump administration, when the increased aggressiveness of these two agencies' personnel created the perception that they were antiimmigrant, not just seeking to secure America's borders.[69]

Investigations in 2019 in the United States revealed 3,500 social media accounts linked to current and former law enforcement officers who were posting racist and anti-Semitic comments. Audits of car camera recordings, random photographs, and other evidence revealed officers affiliated with Klan and other racist imagery, conversations about shooting Black men and women, and other disturbing connections between law enforcement and the white supremacy movement. A group of sheriff's deputies in Los Angeles County known as the Lynwood Vikings allegedly shot and killed minorities, trashed houses, and otherwise brutalized locals. In Sacramento, California, the police even worked with neo-Nazis to charge antiracism activists, treating local neo-Nazis who perpetrated violence as victims and then seeking their cooperation to investigate and arrest counterprotesters who were present at white supremacist and far-right rallies.[70] Although courts have ruled that individuals in public sector jobs, including law enforcement, do not have First Amendment protections that preserve one's employment if one uses racist speech, few police departments explicitly prohibit ties to white supremacist groups, and when individuals are uncovered, the response is often a mild reprimand. Some officersofficer who has been terminated for white supremacist activities are hired by other departments.[71] The FBI itself is so concerned about this problem that it often warns its own people to put white supremacist suspects on "silent" watchlists only, so that their identities will not become known to local police, who might tip them off—an approach that limits the utility of a watchlist, which is designed, in part, to warn local officials that someone might be dangerous.[72]

Police bias has numerous dangerous effects. First, it can lead to the direct abuse of the Black and Latino communities and other minorities by racist police. Second, police may fail to respond to violence in a timely way. Third, they might jeopardize an investigation by not following up on leads or by deliberately interfering with evidence. Even if police have no direct ties to a white supremacist group, those with such beliefs are more likely to trivialize white supremacist violence, exaggerate the threat of movements like Antifa or Black Lives Matter, or otherwise not show the proper concern and duty regarding the danger—for example, law enforcement in Huntington Beach, California, claimed a lack of resources in failing to investigate assaults against a journalist by the violent white supremacist Rise Above Movement but did prosecute an antifascist protester who tried to defend the journalist against the group.[73] Furthermore, biased police can undermine public trust, making communities less likely to provide information to law enforcement.[74]

With more than half a million active police officers in the United States, it is inevitable that at least a few will have white supremacist leanings. Investigating police departments is vital—it is hard to imagine similar federal inaction if police had ties to ISIS or a similar foreign group. Indeed, the FBI and Department of Justice have a responsibility to protect citizens' civil rights but have not made ensuring white supremacists are not active in police ranks a priority even though this can lead to grave civil rights issues .[75] Similarly, police unions should take a stand and instead of defending bigots from termination should try to purge them from the force. Police departments, however, often lack even basic tools, for example tattoo databases, for finding out if a white supremacist is applying for a job.

Going after Logistics

Terrorist groups do not exist in isolation. Their leaders need to raise money, communicate with members, issue propaganda, acquire weapons and explosives, and otherwise maintain and grow their organizations. Each of these necessities is a potential vulnerability. Too often, attention focuses on the shooters, but if the organizations and networks that support them can be destroyed or degraded, the individuals in question are often easy to identify and less dangerous. In addition, the groups themselves often exist within a broader ecosystem of radical organizations and criminal networks that also have their own vulnerabilities.

European counterterrorism officials enjoy a tremendous advantage compared with their American counterparts in one key area: guns. In Europe, it is often difficult to acquire guns, and when groups do, it is usually illegal. Several European groups have been broken up when they have begun to stockpile guns.[76] More restrictive gun laws and better tracking of weapons purchases would make white supremacists less dangerous and offer more opportunities to disrupt them.

Civil society organizations and businesses like social media companies are also vital for stopping logistics. Successful lawsuits against Aryan Nations, WAR, and various Klan chapters effectively bankrupted these groups. When groups are short on money, they cannot pay members or acquire weapons. Deplatforming and depriving groups of access to financial services or to streaming services like Spotify can prevent white supremacists from reaching larger audiences and otherwise weaken them.

Acting Abroad to Stop Violence at Home

Because of white supremacists' global connections, stopping them at home often means fighting them abroad. Groups and individuals share ideas from one country to another, and propaganda and recruitment networks increasingly cross borders. Groups in Europe, Australia, and elsewhere live on social media platforms based in the United States, while Russian companies play an important role in helping white supremacists stay online when groups and individuals are deplatformed from companies like Facebook. As white supremacist expert Heidi Beirich has told me, "you can't fight white supremacy only at a domestic level."[77] White supremacists do not rely on foreign havens as do jihadists and are otherwise less networked internationally. Nevertheless, U.S. intelligence cooperation with European countries has scored major successes against jihadists, and similar cooperation could weaken white supremacist groups and movements, with investigations in one country revealing clues about networks in another.[78]

For the United States, an international connection—and designation—changes the rules for intelligence and law enforcement. If a group is formally designated as a Foreign Terrorist Organization or if individuals or entities are labeled as Specially Designated Global Terrorists, as the Russian Imperial Movement was in 2020, then supporting these groups at home is illegal, as is true for designated jihadist groups like ISIS and Al Qaeda. As a result, anyone who assists in fundraising, recruitment, and other forms of support—not just violence—risks prosecution under tough laws related to material support for terrorism. However, formal white supremacist groups are far smaller, and their global networks are more limited than their jihadist equivalents.[79]

The United States, however, in contrast to the way it handles jihadist groups, has done little on the white supremacist front internationally. As former counterterrorism official Eric Rosand notes, "we're totally about brown men, not white men, when it comes to international cooperation."[80] Part of the problem is the lack of a legal framework, both at home and abroad, for pursuing and prosecuting domestic groups comparable to what is in place for groups like ISIS. The U.S. government is also, understandably, more reluctant to share information on its own nationals, even if they are white supremacists, than on foreign jihadists.[81] In addition, the long years of U.S. inaction have diminished America's credibility on these issues. European intelligence officials have long expressed frustration that their

U.S. counterparts have not answered their requests for legal assistance and information.[82]

The United States should designate more foreign white supremacists and groups as Foreign Terrorist Organizations or Specially Designated Global Terrorists, thus greatly increasing the risk for those at home who aid them. This would also incentivize social media companies and financial institutions to shun these groups. In addition, the United States should start more initiatives, lessons learned studies, and other steps short of formal laws and treaties to build momentum as it moves toward greater cooperation.[83]

Politics as Necessary for Counterterrorism

A bright line should be drawn between peaceful political activity, even if racist, and terrorism. A range of groups, movements, and political leaders oppose immigration, favor "tough on crime" policies that disadvantage minorities, and otherwise overlap with the white supremacist agenda. A far smaller number endorse, or at least flirt with, openly hateful policies and rhetoric that denigrate entire communities. Political leaders with such agendas can bolster existing racists and bigots and attract new ones, making it seem more permissible for them to express their views and attract recruits.

Stifling all hateful voices, however, can be counterproductive. In Sweden, for example, even legitimate debates over questions such as the economic impact of a high immigration rate were dismissed as racist. This stigmatized immigration critics and, in so doing, moved those worried about immigration out of more mainstream parties and into radical ones that opposed the system in general.[84]

Indeed, fighting against white supremacy depends heavily on legitimate political groups who care about gun rights, limits to migration, and other hot-button issues but reject violence and are open in their condemnation of racism and other aspects of white supremacy. Such groups are credible messengers on these issues and can delegitimize the use of violence in a way that less conservative voices cannot. In addition, they often have inside knowledge and know who the extremists are within the movement.

An example of this power is when leading Republicans rejected David Duke's attempt to win political office as a Republican in the 1990 gubernatorial election in Louisiana and then run for U.S. Senate in 1991. Then-president George H. W. Bush declared: "when someone has a long record, an ugly record, of racism and bigotry, that record simply cannot be erased by the glib rhetoric of a political campaign. So I believe David Duke is an insincere char-latan. I believe he's attempting to hoodwink the voters of Louisiana. I believe he should be rejected for what he is and what he stands for." Mitt Romney, the 2012 Republican presidential candidate, similarly distanced himself from Kansas politician Kris Kobach because of Kobach's extreme hostility to immigrants.[85] Kobach would later play an important role working with President Trump.[86]

The future of the pro-Trump movement is an important question mark in this regard.[87] The movement is hard to define, as it includes ordinary Americans motivated by a strong sense of perceived nationalism, along with white supremacists, antigovernment extremists, and conspiracy theorists. Indeed, part of Trump's magic was to bring together a range of groups who normally hated, or at least competed with, one another.[88] Trump mobilized huge numbers of supporters, at least some of whom could be motivated to-ward violence, particularly if they felt the political system was corrupt and thwarting them, as happened on January 6, 2021, when a Trump-inspired mob stormed the U.S. Capitol. As this event shows, mainstream Americans can interact with, and be further radicalized by, white supremacists and others with an extreme and violent agenda. The spread of conspiracy the-ories, racialized grievance narratives, and other aspects of the movement to more mainstream political and media figures is an important win for the cause, even if the growth of these ideas falls short of terrorism. White supremacists do not gain outright victory from the fracturing of society, but it makes government action against them harder, renders recruitment easier, and is dangerous for the health of democracy.

The white supremacist movement is highly opportunistic, and components of it will try to exploit the Trump wave for their own purposes.[89]

Because of this risk, the effort against white supremacist and other vio-lent groups should not neglect politics. For organizations such as Al Qaeda, which has almost no support in either the American Muslim community or the country at large, the politics is assured. Against white supremacists, in contrast, counterterrorism success requires U.S. counterterrorism agencies to navigate sensitive political issues such as gun control, federal versus state power, free speech rights on social media, and other contentious issues. Too often, these issues only come to the fore during a crisis, and the counterter-rorism agencies face pressure to either underreact or overreact based on the political winds rather than the threat profile.

A political consensus is thus vital for ensuring the availability of the necessary resources for intelligence and directing security agencies to focus on white supremacy. As one government expert has noted, "we have enough tools, but we need the political will and resources."[90] In the 1960s, repugnance over white supremacist attacks on civil rights workers created political pressure, which in turn led President Johnson to push the FBI to crack down. In contrast, beginning in 2009, the Department of Homeland Security cut research on white supremacist extremism and canceled briefings on it to state and local officials, fearing controversy if it was perceived as labeling "right-wing" groups as terrorists, no matter how extreme their beliefs.[91] In Europe, attacks on immigrants and other minority communities often receive little or only belated attention.

The absence or presence of a political consensus often has indirect effects, shaping how social media and financial companies act. During the Trump administration, the president and his allies regularly blasted social media companies as biased (even though, in reality, their algorithms were more likely to recommend conservative voices), making these companies fearful of blocking white supremacist content.[92] In contrast, when leaders have united over issues ranging from child sexual exploitation to the presence of ISIS online, companies have been quick to respond. It is no accident that social media companies became more aggressive against white supremacists (and against President Trump himself) *after* President Biden won the 2020 election.

Conclusion

Effective counterterrorism can be thought of as part of a cycle each step of which makes the groups and the movement as a whole weaker. By changing community attitudes, the recruitment pool is made smaller, and groups have less space in which to maneuver freely. By changing government policies, groups will be under more pressure, and any slip-up could prove fatal to the group. Community programs can also further reduce recruitment, encourage defections, and make more information available to law enforcement. The police and intelligence services, acting at home and abroad, can put constant pressure on groups and detect freelancing individuals, making it harder for them to plot and carry out successful attacks.

Success, however, does not mean perfection. All of the steps in the cycle can greatly reduce the danger of white supremacist terrorism, but they will not eliminate it. Breivik and Tarrant illustrated what one highly motivated person acting alone can do; knowing this, it is difficult to prepare for every eventuality. Failure to prevent violence, too, should be seen as both a tragedy and an opportunity. Government and civil society actors can use the carnage to remind society of the danger white supremacists pose, creating more support for a tough response and thereby making it more likely that they prevent the next attack.

Notes

Introduction

1. "New Zealand Mosque Shooter Names His 'Idols' on Weapons He Used in Massacre," *Daily Sabah*, March 15, 2019, https://www.dailysabah.com/asia/2019/03/15/new-zealand-mosque-shooter-names-his-idols-on-weapons-he-used-in-massacre.
2. "Shitposting, Inspirational Terrorism, and the Christchurch Mosque Massacre," *Bellingcat*, March 15, 2019, https://www.bellingcat.com/news/rest-of-world/2019/03/15/shitposting-inspirational-terrorism-and-the-christchurch-mosque-massacre.
3. Åsne Seierstad, *One of Us: The Story of Anders Breivik and the Massacre in Norway* (London: Macmillan, 2015), 359.
4. Seth Stephens-Davidowitz, "The Data of Hate," *New York Times,* July 12, 2014, https://www.nytimes.com/2014/07/13/opinion/sunday/seth-stephens-davidowitz-the-data-of-hate.html.
5. Devlin Barret, "Hate Crimes Rose 17 Percent Last Year," *Washington Post,* November 13, 2018, https://www.washingtonpost.com/world/national-security/hate-crimes-rose-17-percent-last-year-according-to-new-fbi-data/2018/11/13/e0dcf13e-e754-11e8-b8dc-66cca409c180_story.html.
6. Paige Cunningham, "Trump Blamed Mental Illness for Mass Shootings," *Washington Post,* August 6, 2019, https://www.washingtonpost.com/news/powerpost/paloma/the-health-202/2019/08/06/the-health-202-trump-blamed-mental-illness-for-mass-shootings-the-reality-is-more-complicated/5d48657e88e0fa1454f80177/.
7. Erin M. Kearns, Allison Betus, and Anthony Lemieux, "Why Do Some Terrorist Attacks Receive More Media Attention Than Others?," *Justice Quarterly* 36 (January 2019): 985–1022, https://www.tandfonline.com/doi/abs/10.1080/07418825.2018.1524507.
8. Interview with Ta-Nehisi Coates, *Daily Show,* July 23, 2015, http://www.cc.com/video-clips/s8kuhf/the-daily-show-with-jon-stewart-exclusive---ta-nehisi-coates-extended-interview-pt--1.
9. Interview with Benjamin Wittes, February 6, 2021.
10. Jade Gailberger, "Spy Agency Wants Terror Laws Extended," *News.com.au*, September 23, 2020, https://www.news.com.au/world/middle-east/spy-agency-wants-terror-laws-extended/news-story/cd83bc9574642bf7a6be61693eacf7cf; Department of Homeland Security, "Homeland Threat Assessment," October 2020, https://www.dhs.gov/sites/default/files/publications/2020_10_06_homeland-threat-assessment.pdf.
11. Kathleen Belew, *Bring the War Home: The White Power Movement and Paramilitary America* (Cambridge, MA: Harvard University Press, 2018), ix–17.

12. Cas Mudde, "Right-wing Extremism Analyzed: A Comparative Analysis of the Ideologies of Three Alleged Right-wing Extremist Parties (NPD, NDP, CP '86)," *European Journal of Political Research* 27, no. 2 (1995): 203–224.

13. Ruud Koopmans, "The Dynamics of Protest Waves: West Germany, 1965 to 1989," *American Sociological Review* 58 (October 1993): 637, https://www.jstor.org/stable/2096279.

14. Sidney Tarrow, *Power in Movement: Social Movements, Collective Action and Politics* (Cambridge: Cambridge University Press, 1994), 2.

15. Federal Bureau of Investigation (FBI), "State of the Domestic White Nationalist Extremist Movement in the United States," December 13, 2006, 3.

16. Jakob Aasland Ravndal, "Thugs or Terrorists? A Typology of Right-Wing Terrorism in Western Europe," *Journal for Deradicalization* 3 (Summer 2015): 15, https://journals.sfu.ca/jd/index.php/jd/article/viewFile/16/16.

17. "Assessing the Threat from Accelerationists and Militia Extremists, Subcommittee on Intelligence and Counterterrorism of the Committee on Homeland Security," Before the Committee on Homeland Security, 116 Congress, testimony of J. J. MacNab, Fellow with the Program on Extremism, George Washington University, July 16, 2020, https://docs.house.gov/Committee/Calendar/ByEvent.aspx?EventID=110911.

18. Sam Jackson, *Oath Keepers: Patriotism and the Edge of Violence in a Right-Wing Antigovernment Group* (New York: Columbia University Press, 2020). Jane Coaston, "The 'Boogaloo' 'Movement,' Explained," *Vox.com,* June 8, 2020, https://www.vox.com/2020/6/8/21276911/boogaloo-explained-civil-war-protests; Samantha Kutner, "Swiping Right: The Allure of Hyper Masculinity and Cryptofascism for Men Who Join the Proud Boys," International Centre for Counter-Terrorism, May 26, 2020, https://icct.nl/publication/swiping-right-the-allure-of-hyper-masculinity-and-cryptofascism-for-men-who-join-the-proud-boys/; Will Carless, "They Joined the Wisconsin Proud Boys Looking for Brotherhood. They Found Racism, Bullying and Antisemitism," *USA Today,* June 21, 2021, https://www.usatoday.com/story/news/nation/2021/06/21/proud-boys-recruitment-targets-men-looking-community/7452805002/.

Chapter 1

1. "On This Day in Alabama History: Mother's Day Was Born," *Alabama NewsCenter,* May 10, 2018, https://www.alabamanewscenter.com/2018/05/10/day-alabama-history-alabama-representative-helps-creating-mothers-day/.

2. Horace Mann Bond, *Negro Education in Alabama: A Study in Cotton and Steel* (Tuscaloosa: University of Alabama Press, 1994), 173.

3. Douglas A. Blackmon, *Slavery by Another Name: The Re-enslavement of Black Americans from the Civil War to World War II* (New York: Anchor Books, 2008), 122, 222, 225, 232.

4. Blair L. M. Kelley, *Right to Ride: Streetcar Boycotts and African American Citizenship in the Era of Plessy v. Ferguson* (Chapel Hill: University of North Carolina Press, 2010), 160; "Heflin on Rampage," *Los Angeles Times*, March 28, 1908.

5. Glenn Feldman, *Politics, Society, and the Klan in Alabama, 1915–1949* (Tuscaloosa: University of Alabama Press, 1999), 80–84.

6. Feldman, *Politics, Society, and the Klan in Alabama*, 92;

7. Elbert L. Watson, "J. Thomas Heflin," in *Encyclopedia of Alabama*, May 26, 2017, http://www.encyclopediaofalabama.org/article/h-2952?printable=true.

8. Allen W. Trelease, *White Terror: The Ku Klux Klan Conspiracy and Southern Reconstruction* (London: Secker & Warburg, 1972).

9. This figure is from the end of Reconstruction (1877) to 1950, and thus includes the second Klan era of the 1920s. Equal Justice Institute, "Lynching in America: Confronting the Legacy of Racial Terror," 3rd ed., Equal Justice Initiative, 2017, https://lynchinginamerica.eji.org/report/, and Charles Seguin and David Rigby, "National Crimes: A New National Data Set of Lynchings in the United States, 1883 to 1941," *Socius: Sociological Research for a Dynamic World* 5 (January 2019): 1–9, https://doi.org/10.1177%2F2378023119841780.

10. Philip Jenkins, "'It Can't Happen Here': Fascism and Right-Wing Extremism in Pennsylvania, 1933–1943," *Pennsylvania History* 62, no. 1 (Winter 1995): 33.

11. Linda Gordon, *The Second Coming of the KKK: The Ku Klux Klan of the 1920s and the American Political Tradition* (New York: Liveright, 2017), 164.

12. As quoted in Greg Grandin, *The End of the Myth* (New York: Metropolitan Books, 2019), 161.

13. As quoted in Grandin, *The End of the Myth*, 162.

14. Arie Perliger, *American Zealots: Inside Right-Wing Domestic Terrorism* (New York: Columbia University Press, 2020), 33.

15. Grandin, The End of the Myth, 165.

16. Robyn Pennacchia, "America's Wholesome Square Dancing Tradition Is a Tool of White Supremacy," *Quartz*, December 12, 2017, https://qz.com/1153516/americas-wholesome-square-dancing-tradition-is-a-tool-of-white-supremacy/.

17. As quoted in Jenkins, "'It Can't Happen Here,'" 45.

18. Leonard Dinnerstein, *Anti-Semitism in America* (New York: Oxford University Press, 1994); Pamela S. Nadell, "Anti-Semitism in the US Today Is a Variation on an Old Theme," *Conversation*, November 6, 2019, https://theconversation.com/anti-semitism-in-the-us-today-is-a-variation-on-an-old-theme-123250; Bradley W. Hart, "America's Dark History of Organized Anti-Semitism Re-emerges in Today's Far-Right Groups," *Conversation*, November 29, 2018, https://theconversation.com/americas-dark-history-of-organized-anti-semitism-re-emerges-in-todays-far-right-groups-106292; Pamela S. Nadell, "Why We Were Overdue for a Fierce Debate about Anti-Semitism in America," *Washington Post*, March 7, 2019, https://www.washingtonpost.com/outlook/2019/03/07/why-we-were-overdue-fierce-debate-about-anti-semitism-america/;. Michael N. Dobkowski, "American Anti-Semitism: A Reinterpretation," *American Quarterly* 29, no. 2 (Summer 1977): 166–181, https://doi.org/10.2307/2712357.

19. In addition to Gordon, see also Rory McVeigh, *The Rise of the Ku Klux Klan: Right-Wing Movements and National Politics* (Minneapolis: University of Minnesota Press, 2009).

20. Perliger, *American Zealots*, 38.

21. Michael S. Rosenwald, "A Black Man Accused of Rape, a White Officer in the Klan, and a 1936 Lynching That Went Unpunished," *Washington Post*, July 19, 2020, https://www.washingtonpost.com/history/2020/07/19/atlanta-lynching-police-ku-klux-klan/.

22. Atlanta Police Department, "History of the APD," no date, https://www.atlantapd.org/about-apd/apd-history.

23. David Cunningham, *Klansville, U.S. A.: The Rise and Fall of the Civil Rights-Era Ku Klux Klan* (Oxford: Oxford University Press, 2013), 67, 101–106.

24. Cunningham, *Klansville, U.S.A.*, 96.

25. As quoted in David Cunningham, "Ambivalence and Control: State Action against the Civil Rights–Era Ku Klux Klan," *Qualitative Sociology* 32 (2009): 361.

26. As quoted in Cunningham, *Klansville, U.S.A.*, 4.

27. FBI, "Klan Organizations, Section III, 1958–1964," December 1964, 9, https://archive.org/details/foia_FBI_monograph-Klan_Organizations-Section_III_1958-1964/.

28. FBI, "FOIA: Mullins, Eustace C.-NYC-1," January 22, 1960, https://archive.org/details/foia_Mullins_Eustace_C.-NYC-1.

29. Cunningham, *Klansville, U.S.A.*, 39, 146.

30. FBI, "Klan Organizations," i.

31. Cunningham, *Klansville, U.S.A.*, 53.

32. David Chalmers, *Backfire: How the Ku Klux Klan Helped the Civil Rights Movement* (Lanham, MD: Rowman and Littlefield, 2003), 5.

33. FBI, "Klan Organizations," iv.

34. Quote is from FBI, "Klan Organizations," 71. For FBI source reporting on Shelton, see FBI, "Robert Marvin Shelton," September 29, 1966, https://archive.org/stream/RobertM.Shelton/Shelton%2C%20Robert%20M.-HQ-3_djvu.txt. See also David Cunningham, "Ambivalence and Control," 360.

35. Cunningham, *Klansville, U.S.A.*, 63, 100–133.

36. Cunningham, *Klansville, U.S.A.*, 46.

37. Scott Ellsworth, "Interview with Eddie Dawson," William Henry Chafe Oral History Program at Duke University, May 26, 1977, Volume/Box: Acc. 87/85: Box 2 c.130.

38. Cunningham, *Klansville, U.S.A.*, 62.

39. As quoted in Cunningham, *Klansville, U.S.A.*, 124.

40. Cunningham, *Klansville, U.S.A.*, 132.

41. Perliger, *American Zealots*, 44.

42. Chalmers, *Backfire*, 16–18.

43. FBI, "Klan Organizations," ii.

44. FBI, "Klan Organizations," 15.

45. FBI, "Klan Organizations," 26.

46. Southern Poverty Law Center, "Civil Rights Martyrs," no date, https://www.splcenter.org/what-we-do/civil-rights-memorial/civil-rights-martyrs.

47. Cunningham, *Klansville, U.S.A.*, 119; Department of Justice, "The Attorney General's Eighth Annual Report to Congress Pursuant to the Emmett Till Unsolved Civil Rights Crime Act of 2007 and Second Annual Report to Congress Pursuant to the Emmett Till Unsolved Civil Rights Crimes Reauthorization Act of 2016," June 2019, https://www.justice.gov/crt/page/file/1194046/download.

48. Chalmers, *Backfire*, 3.

49. Chalmers, *Backfire*, 52.

50. FBI, "Klan Organizations," 112–114.

51. FBI, "Klan Organizations," iv, 112–114.

52. "Meet the Players: Other Figures" (article), *American Experience*, n.d., https://www.pbs.org/wgbh/americanexperience/features/meet-players-other-figures/#:~:text=Eugene%20%22Bull%22%20Connor%2C%20Selma%2C%20AL&text=He%20was%20known%20as%20an,elapse%20before%20the%20police%20arrived.%22.

53. John Drabble, "From White Supremacy to White Power: The FBI, COINTELPRO-WHITE HATE, and the Nazification of the Ku Klux Klan in the 1970s," *American Studies* 48, no. 3 (Fall 2007): 58, https://journals.ku.edu/amsj/article/view/3133.

54. Cunningham, *Klansville, U.S.A.*, 9.

55. Chalmers, *Backfire*, 23.

56. Chalmers, *Backfire*, 24.

57. Kathleen Belew, *Bring the War Home: The White Power Movement and Paramilitary America* (Cambridge, MA: Harvard University Press, 2018), 61.

58. Chalmers, *Backfire*, 19–20.

59. Cunningham, *Klansville, U.S.A.*, 6.

60. As quoted in Chalmers, *Backfire*, 39.

61. Chalmers, *Backfire*, 36.

62. Department of Justice, "The Attorney General's Eighth Annual Report to Congress Pursuant to the Emmett Till Unsolved Civil Rights Crime Act of 2007 and Second Annual Report to Congress Pursuant to the Emmett Till Unsolved Civil Rights Crimes Reauthorization Act of 2016."

63. Richard Goldstein, "Edgar Ray Killen, Convicted in '64 Killings of Rights Workers, Dies at 92," *New York Times*, January 12, 2018, https://www.nytimes.com/2018/01/12/obituaries/edgar-ray-killen-convicted-in-64-killings-of-rights-worker-dies-at-92.html.

64. Cunningham, *Klansville, U.S.A.*, 203.

65. Chalmers, *Backfire*, 50.

66. Cunningham, *Klansville, U.S.A.*, 57.

67. Chalmers, *Backfire*, 89.

68. Zoom interview with David Cunningham, January 5, 2021.

69. Drabble, "From White Supremacy to White Power," 53.

70. Cunningham, *Klansville, U.S.A.*, 206.

71. Cunningham, *Klansville, U.S.A.*, 59, 188.

72. Cunningham, *Klansville, U.S.A.*, 59.

73. Cunningham, "Understanding State Responses to Left- versus Right-Wing Threats: The FBI's Repression of the New Left and the Ku Klux Klan," *Social Science History* 27, no. 3 (Fall 2003): 344.

74. Jack Anderson, "Hoover Smear Tactics Hurt Civil Rights Case," *Evening News* (Newburgh, NY), March 21, 1983, https://news.google.com/newspapers?nid=1982&dat=19830 321&id=QV1GAAAAIBAJ&sjid=zTENAAAAIBAJ&pg=2477,2441456&hl=en.

75. Drabble, "From White Supremacy to White Power," 52.

76. U.S. Congress, Senate, Select Committee to Study Governmental Operations with Respect to Intelligence, Final Report, 94th Congress, 2nd Session, Book II, *Intelligence Activities and the Rights of Americans* (Washington, DC: Government Printing Office, 1976), 87, https://www.intelligence.senate.gov/sites/default/files/94755_II.pdf; Drabble, "From White Supremacy to White Power," 52.

77. The testimony is confusing, and 6 percent is a safe estimate, though in some cases it was certainly much higher. Cunningham, "Understanding State Responses to Left- versus Right-Wing Threats"; Emma North-Best, "FBI Leadership Claimed Bureau Was 'Almost Powerless' against KKK, Despite Making Up One-Fifth of Its Membership," *MuckRock*, December 8, 2017, https://www.muckrock.com/news/archives/2017/dec/08/fbi-kkk/.

78. Cunningham, "Understanding State Responses to Left- versus Right-Wing Threats," 344–360.

79. Internal divisions were a regular subject of covert collection. See, for example, FBI, "Original Knights of the Ku Klux Klan Louisiana (1964–65)," November 16, 1963 file no. 105-71801, part 1 of 2, https://archive.org/details/foia_Original_Knights_of_KKK-HQ-2; FBI, "FOIA: National Knights KKK-22," May 13, 1968, https://archive.org/details/foia_National_Knights_KKK-22.

80. FBI, "(COINTELPRO) White Hate Groups," October 1, 1964, sub 8, section 1, 157–159, https://archive.org/details/foia_COINTELPRO-White_Hate-HQ-sub8.

81. Cunningham, *Klansville, U.S.A.*, 195–198.

82. Drabble, "From White Supremacy to White Power," 53–55.

83. Zoom interview with David Cunningham, January 5, 2021.

84. Chalmers, *Backfire*, 99.

85. Cunningham, "Understanding State Responses to Left- versus Right-Wing Threats," 336.

86. U.S. Congress, Senate, Select Committee to Study Governmental Operations with Respect to Intelligence, *Intelligence Activities and the Rights of Americans* (Washington: U.S. Government Printing Office, 1976), 216–217.

87. U.S. Congress, Senate, Select Committee to Study Governmental Operations with Respect to Intelligence, *Intelligence Activities and the Rights of Americans*.

88. Ellsworth, "Interview with Eddie Dawson," 50.

89. Drabble, "From White Supremacy to White Power," 55–56; Cunningham, "Understanding State Responses to Left- versus Right-Wing Threats," 363.

90. Drabble, "From White Supremacy to White Power," 56.

91. Cunningham, "Understanding State Responses to Left- versus Right-Wing Threats," 344–346.

92. Cunningham, *Klansville, U.S.A.*, 188.
93. See reporting under FBI, "Robert Marvin Shelton," 5.
94. Bryan Burrough, *Days of Rage: America's Radical Underground, the FBI, and the Forgotten Age of Revolutionary Violence* (New York: Penguin, 2015); ACLU, "ACLU Report Documents FBI Abuse since 9/11," September 17, 2013, https://www.aclu.org/press-releases/aclu-report-documents-fbi-abuse-911.
95. U.S. Congress, Senate, Select Committee to Study Governmental Operations with Respect to Intelligence, Final Report, 94th Congress, 2nd Session, Book III, *Supplementary Detailed Staff Reports on Intelligence Activities and the Rights of Americans* (Washington, DC: Government Printing Office, 1976), 241n58, https://www.intelligence.senate.gov/sites/default/files/94755_III.pdf; North-Best, "FBI Leadership Claimed Bureau Was 'Almost Powerless' against KKK."
96. Chalmers, *Backfire*, 59.
97. Cunningham, *Klansville, U.S.A.*, 93.
98. Cunningham, *Klansville, U.S.A.*, 94.
99. Zoom interview with Professor David Cunningham, January 5, 2021.
100. As quoted in Cunningham, "Ambivalence and Control," 367.
101. Cunningham, *Klansville, U.S.A.*, 7–15, 98, 193.
102. Cunningham, *Klansville, U.S.A.*, 208.
103. Cunningham, "Understanding State Responses to Left- versus Right-Wing Threats," 336.
104. Cunningham, "Ambivalence and Control," 368.
105. As quoted in Cunningham, "Ambivalence and Control," 371.
106. Cunningham, *Klansville, U.S.A.*, 189.
107. Cunningham, *Klansville, U.S.A.*, 198.
108. Chalmers, *Backfire*, 94, 98.
109. Cunningham, *Klansville, U.S.A.*, 200.
110. FBI, "Klan Organizations," 67.
111. FBI, "Klan Organizations," 68.
112. Chalmers, *Backfire*, 13.
113. Chalmers, *Backfire*, 150.
114. FBI, "Klan Organizations," iv.
115. Quoted in FBI, "Robert Marvin Shelton," 4.
116. Zoom interview with David Cunningham, January 5, 2021.
117. FBI, "Klan Organizations," 13–14.
118. Ellsworth, "Interview with Eddie Dawson," 22.
119. Cunningham, *Klansville, U.S.A.*, 63.
120. Zoom interview with Professor David Cunningham, January 5, 2021.
121. Chalmers, *Backfire*, 54–58.
122. Ellsworth, "Interview with Eddie Dawson," 2, 13, 20, 23.
123. Ellsworth, "Interview with Eddie Dawson," 25–27, 37, 39–40, 47, 60–62.
124. Ellsworth, "Interview with Eddie Dawson," 60–62, 72.
125. Chalmers, *Backfire*, 58.

126. United States v. U. S. Klans, Knights of Ku Klux Klan, Inc., 194 F. Supp. 897 (M.D. Ala. 1961), "Opinion," June 2, 1961, https://casetext.com/case/us-v-us-klans-knig hts-of-ku-klux-klan-inc.

127. United States v. Original Knights of the Ku Klux Klan, 250 F. Supp. 330 (E.D. La. 1965), "Opinion," December 1, 1965, https://casetext.com/case/united-states-v-original-knights-of-ku-klux-klan.

128. Dahleen Glanton, "Ex-Klan Leader Convicted of 1966 Murder," *Chicago Tribune*, August 22, 1998, https://www.chicagotribune.com/news/ct-xpm-1998-08-22-980 8220120-story.html.

129. Chalmers, *Backfire*, 94.

130. Cunningham, *Klansville, U.S.A.*, 208–211.

131. Drabble, "From White Supremacy to White Power," 53.

132. Zoom interview with David Cunningham, January 5, 2021.

133. Tim Sullivan, "Long after Murders, Black Voting Still Troubled in Miss.," October 22, 2020, Associated Press,https://apnews.com/article/election-2020-race-and-ethnic ity-mississippi-voting-rights-meridian-5128c7cd5d0f01b1bc39144452b2730c.

134. Chalmers, *Backfire*, 116.

135. Center for Constitutional Rights, "Crumsey v. Justice Knights of the Ku Klux Klan," no date, https://ccrjustice.org/home/what-we-do/our-cases/crumsey-v-justice-knights-ku-klux-klan#:~:text=Case%20Description,Klux%20Klan%20Act%20 of%201871.

136. Daniel Jackson, "Forty Years Ago, They Changed How Hate Groups Are Sued," Courthouse News Service, February 21, 2020, https://www.courthousenews.com/ forty-years-ago-they-changed-how-hate-groups-are-sued/.

137. Jesse Kornbluth, "The Woman Who Beat the Klan," *New York Times Magazine*, November 1, 1987, https://www.nytimes.com/1987/11/01/magazine/the-woman-who-beat-the-klan.html.

138. See Morris Dees and Ellen Bowden, "Courtroom Victories: Taking Hate Groups to Court," February 1995, 3–4, http://hornacek.coa.edu/dave/Teaching/Core_Cou rse.03/courtroom_victories.pdf.

139. Brett Garland and Pete Simi, "A Critique of Using Civil Litigation to Suppress White Supremacist Violence," *Criminal Justice Review* 36, no. 4 (December 2011): 500, https://doi.org/10.1177%2F0734016811417855.

140. Gary May, *The Informant: The FBI, the Ku Klux Klan, and the Murder of Viola Liuzzo* (New Haven, CT: Yale University Press, 2005), 361–363.

141. Associated Press, "Klan Member Put to Death in Race Death," *New York Times*, June 6, 1997, https://www.nytimes.com/1997/06/06/us/klan-member-put-to-death-in-race-death.html.

142. See the collection at FBI, "FOIA: FIERY CROSS-4," https://archive.org/details/foia_ FIERY_CROSS-4, for a discussion on the financial issues they faced.

143. Kornbluth, "The Woman Who Beat the Klan."

144. "Robert Shelton, 73, Leader of Big Klan Faction," *New York Times*, March 20, 2003, https://www.nytimes.com/2003/03/20/us/robert-shelton-73-leader-of-big-klan-faction.html.

145. Chalmers, *Backfire*, 148.

146. See, among others, Southern Poverty Law Center, "Brown v. Invisible Empire, Knights of the Ku Klux Klan," no date, https://www.splcenter.org/seeking-justice/case-docket/brown-v-invisible-empire-knights-ku-klux-klan; Southern Poverty Law Center, "McKinney v. Southern White Knights," no date, https://www.splcenter.org/seeking-justice/case-docket/mckinney-v-southern-white-knights; Southern Poverty Law Center, "Macedonia v. Christian Knights of the Ku Klux Klan," no date, https://www.splcenter.org/seeking-justice/case-docket/macedonia-v-christian-knights-ku-klux-klan.

147. Garland and Simi, "A Critique of Using Civil Litigation to Suppress White Supremacist Violence," 505.

Chapter 2

1. FBI, "The Covenant, the Sword, and the Arm of the Lord; Domestic Security/ Terrorism," July 2, 1987, 5, in "The Covenant, The Sword, The Arm of the Lord Part 2 of 2," FBI Vault, https://vault.fbi.gov/The%20Covenant%20The%20Sword%20The%20Arm%20of%20the%20Lord%20/The%20Covenant%20The%20Sword%20The%20Arm%20of%20the%20Lord%20Part%202%20of%202/view.

2. "Beam: 'It's Not Murder When You Kill an Enemy,'" United Press International, November 18, 1987, https://www.upi.com/Archives/1987/11/18/Beam-Its-not-murder-when-you-kill-an-enemy/3377564210000/.

3. "Jury Selection Began Today in the Trial of 14," United Press International, February 16, 1988, https://www.upi.com/Archives/1988/02/16/Jury-selection-began-today-in-the-trial-of-14/2487571986000/.

4. Southern Poverty Law Center, "David Lane," no date, https://www.splcenter.org/fighting-hate/extremist-files/individual/david-lane.

5. Bill Simmons, "Defendants All Acquitted in Sedition Trial," Associated Press, April 8, 1988, https://apnews.com/article/604c50e36bd020ac70be35445b12d059.

6. Bill Simmons, "Key Prosecution Witness Admits to Prophecies, Visions," Associated Press, February 24, 1988; Laura Smith, "Lone Wolves Connected Online: A History of Modern White Supremacy," *New York Times*, January 26, 2021, https://www.nytimes.com/2021/01/26/us/louis-beam-white-supremacy-internet.html.

7. "Judge Denies Admissibility of Government Evidence against Beam," Associated Press, February 9, 1988.

8. "Juror Falls in Love with Ex-defendant," *Oklahoman* (Oklahoma City), September 13, 1988, https://oklahoman.com/article/2238993/juror-falls-in-love-with-ex-defendant. See also Leonard Zeskind, *Blood and Politics: The History of the White Nationalist Movement from the Margins to the Mainstream* (New York: Farrar, Straus and Giroux, 2009), 169.

9. Jeff Barge, "Sedition Prosecutions Rarely Successful," *ABA Journal* 80, no. 10 (October 1994): 16–17, https://www.jstor.org/stable/27835443.

10. Smith, "Lone Wolves Connected Online."

11. "13 Supremacists Are Not Guilty of Conspiracies," *New York Times*, April 8, 1988, https://www.nytimes.com/1988/04/08/us/13-supremacists-are-not-guilty-of-consp iracies.html.

12. "Sundown Towns," *Encyclopedia of Arkansas,* no date, https://encyclopediaofarkan sas.net/entries/sundown-towns-3658/; James Loewen, "Was Your Town a Sundown Town?," *UU World*, February 18, 2008, https://www.uuworld.org/articles/was-your-town-sundown-town.

13. Seymour Martin Lipset and William Schneider, "America's Schizophrenia on Achieving Equality," *Los Angeles Times*, July 31, 1977; "Freshman Survey Finds New Trends," *New York Times*, January 11, 1976.

14. See issues from 1970–1972, available at FBI, "FOIA: FIERY CROSS-3," June 25, 1971, https://archive.org/details/foia_FIERY_CROSS-3; FBI, "FOIA: FIERY CROSS-2," June 5, 1970, https://archive.org/details/foia_FIERY_CROSS-2.

15. Both quotes from John Drabble, "From White Supremacy to White Power: The FBI, COINTELPRO-WHITE HATE, and the Nazification of the Ku Klux Klan in the 1970s," *American Studies* 48, no. 3 (Fall 2007): 49, https://journals.ku.edu/amsj/arti cle/view/3133. On the FBI campaign against the Black Panthers, see Joshua Bloom and Waldo E. Martin, Jr., *Black against Empire: The History and Politics of the Black Panther Party* (Oakland: University of California Press, 2016). For more on Pierce, see FBI files available at FBI, "William Luther Pierce," October 6, 1966, Freedom of Information Act release, https://archive.org/details/foia_Pierce_William_L.-HQ-1/ mode/2up.

16. Drabble, "From White Supremacy to White Power," 64.

17. Jeffrey Kaplan, "'Leaderless Resistance,'" *Terrorism and Political Violence* 9, no. 3 (1997): 82, https://doi.org/10.1080/09546559708427417. Capitalization from the original.

18. Drabble, "From White Supremacy to White Power," 59.

19. Kathleen Belew, *Bring the War Home: The White Power Movement and Paramilitary America* (Cambridge, MA: Harvard University Press, 2018), 3.

20. Belew, *Bring the War Home*, 31.

21. As quoted in Belew, *Bring the War Home*, 31.

22. Lucy Hornby, "Deng Xiaoping and the KKK Plot Exposed . . . 30-Plus Years Later," *Financial Times*, May 17, 2015, https://www.ft.com/content/1a4b4642-fc4d-11e4-b007-00144feabdc0.

23. Southern Poverty Law Center, *Ku Klux Klan: A History of Racism and Violence*, 6th ed. (Montgomery, AL: Southern Poverty Law Center, 2011), 49, https://www.splcen ter.org/sites/default/files/Ku-Klux-Klan-A-History-of-Racism.pdf.

24. Smith, "Lone Wolves Connected Online."

25. John Burnett, "Decades after Clashing with the Klan, a Thriving Vietnamese Community in Texas," NPR, November 25, 2018, https://www.npr.org/2018/11/25/669857481/ decades-after-clashing-with-the-klan-a-thriving-vietnamese-community-in-texfas;

Vietnamese Fishermen's Ass'n v. Knights, Etc., 543 F. Supp. 198 (S.D. Tex. 1982), "Memorandum Opinion and Order," June 9, 1982, https://casetext.com/case/vietnam ese-etc-v-knights-of-k-k-k.

26. Belew, *Bring the War Home*, 42–53. The quote is on 42. See also Southern Poverty Law Center, "A Look Back: SPLC Case Brought Justice to Vietnamese Fishermen Terrorized by Klan," July 15, 2011, https://www.splcenter.org/news/2011/07/15/look-back-splc-case-brought-justice-vietnamese-fishermen-terrorized-klan.

27. Vietnamese, Etc. v. Knights of K. K. K., 518 F. Supp. 993 (S.D. Tex. 1981), "Memorandum Opinion and Order," July 15, 1981, https://casetext.com/case/vie tnamese-fishermens-assn-v-knights.

28. Vietnamese, Etc. v. Knights of K. K. K., 518 F. Supp. 993 (S.D. Tex. 1981), "Memorandum Opinion and Order," July 15, 1981.

29. Belew, *Bring the War Home*, 33–52.

30. Vietnamese Fishermen's Ass'n v. Knights, Etc., 543 F. Supp. 198 (S.D. Tex. 1982), "Memorandum Opinion and Order," June 9, 1982, https://casetext.com/case/vietnam ese-fishermens-assn-v-knights.

31. Burnett, "Decades after Clashing with the Klan, a Thriving Vietnamese Community in Texas."

32. Belew, *Bring the War Home*, 97.

33. Belew, *Bring the War Home*, 104.

34. Arie Perliger, *American Zealots: Inside Right-Wing Domestic Terrorism* (New York: Columbia University Press, 2020), 19.

35. Perliger, *American Zealots*, 42.

36. "Guide to the James N. Mason Collection," Kenneth Spencer Research Library, University of Kansas Libraries, http://etext.ku.edu/view?docId=ksrlead/ksrl.kc.mas onjames.xml; Perliger, *American Zealots*, 42–43.

37. Andrew Macdonald (William Pierce), *The Turner Diaries* (1978; reprint, New York: Barricade Books, 1980).

38. For information on sales, see Joshua D. Freilich, Steven M. Chermak, and David Caspi, "Critical Events in the Life Trajectories of Domestic Extremist White Supremacist Groups: A Case Study Analysis of Four Violent Organizations," *Criminology & Public Policy* 8, no. 3 (August 2009): 497–530, https://doi.org/10.1111/j.174133.2009.00572.x.

39. J. M. Berger, "The Turner Legacy: The Storied Origins and Enduring Impact of White Nationalism's Deadly Bible," International Centre for Counter-Terrorism–The Hague (September 2016), https://icct.nl/app/uploads/2016/09/ICCT-Berger-The-Turner-Legacy-September2016-2.pdf.

40. Will Blythe, "The Guru of White Hate," *Rolling Stone*, June 8, 2000, https://www.rolli ngstone.com/culture/culture-features/guru-white-hate-william-pierce-timothy-mcveigh-831091/.

41. Kaplan, " 'Leaderless Resistance,' " 85.

42. Ugo Corte and Bob Edwards, "White Power Music and the Mobilization of Racist Social Movements," *Music and Arts in Action* 1, no. 1 (June 2008): 13–14,

https://www.researchgate.net/publication/26620885_White_Power_Music_and_Mobilization_of_Racist_Social_Movements.

43. Stephen Vertigans, "Beyond the Fringe? Radicalisation within the American Far-Right," *Totalitarian Movements and Political Religions* 8, no. 3–4 (2007): 650, https://doi.org/10.1080/14690760701571254; Martin Durham, "Christian Identity and the Politics of Religion," *Totalitarian Movements and Political Religions* 9, no. 1 (2008), 79–91.

44. Vertigans, "Beyond the Fringe?," 641–643.

45. George Michael, "David Lane and the Fourteen Words," *Totalitarian Movements and Political Religions* 10, no. 1 (2009): 44–45.

46. Michael, "David Lane and the Fourteen Words," 52.

47. J. M. Berger, "PATCON: The FBI's Secret War against the 'Patriot' Movement, and How Infiltration Tactics Relate to Radicalizing Influences," New America Foundation (May 2012), 11, https://archive.org/details/PatconTheFBIsSecretWarAgainstThePatriotMovement.

48. Michael, "David Lane and the Fourteen Words," 45.

49. Simmons, "Key Prosecution Witness Admits to Prophecies, Visions."

50. Michael, "David Lane and the Fourteen Words," 46.

51. Ann M. Stacey Reeser, "The Tipping Point to Terrorism: Involvement in Right-Wing Terrorist Groups in the United States" (PhD diss., University of Nebraska at Omaha, 2011), 150–151, https://digitalcommons.unomaha.edu/cgi/viewcontent.cgi?article=1034&context=studentwork.

52. Michael, "David Lane and the Fourteen Words," 45.

53. "Bombs Rock Idaho City Torn by Strife over Racists," *New York Times*, September 30, 1986, https://www.nytimes.com/1986/09/30/us/bombs-rock-idaho-city-torn-by-strife-over-racists.html.

54. "Arrested Klansman Tells of Plot to Kill Rights Lawyer," Associated Press, February 10, 1985, https://www.latimes.com/archives/la-xpm-1985-02-10-mn-3361-story.html.

55. Michael, "David Lane and the Fourteen Words," 46.

56. "Arrested Klansman Tells of Plot to Kill Rights Lawyer"; James Coates and Stephen Franklin, "Court Records Detail Neo-Nazis' Network," *Chicago Tribune*, December 27, 1987, https://www.chicagotribune.com/news/ct-xpm-1987-12-27-8704060147-story.html.

57. Robert Jimison, "How the FBI Smashed White Supremacist Group the Order," CNN, August 21, 2018, https://www.cnn.com/2017/08/17/us/fbi-spying-white-supremacists-declassified/index.html; Tim Klass, "Death of The Order," *Seattle Times*, December 11, 1994, https://archive.seattletimes.com/archive/?date=19941211&slug=1946516; Michael, "David Lane and the Fourteen Words," 47.

58. Jimison, "How the FBI Smashed White Supremacist Group The Order."

59. Michael, "David Lane and the Fourteen Words," 50, 56.

60. "Feds Say Bomb Suspect Was Target of a Plot," UPI, October 21, 1986, https://www.upi.com/Archives/1986/10/21/Feds-say-bomb-suspect-was-target-of-plot/4145530251200/.

61. Belew, *Bring the War Home*, 160.

62. As quoted in Belew, *Bring the War Home*, 115.

63. Michael, "David Lane and the Fourteen Words," 50–56.

64. Soufan Center, "White Supremacy Extremism: The Transnational Rise of the Violent White Supremacist Movement" (September 2019), https://thesoufancenter.org/resea rch/white-supremacy-extremism-the-transnational-rise-of-the-violent-white-supr emacist-movement/.

65. Jo Thomas, "Dominica Unsettled in Wake of Thwarted Invasion," *New York Times*, June 7, 1981, https://www.nytimes.com/1981/06/07/us/no-headline-147552.html.

66. Kathleen Belew, "Statement," U.S. House of Representatives, Committee on Oversight and Reform, September 20, 2019, https://docs.house.gov/meetings/GO/GO02/20190 920/109977/HHRG-116-GO02-Wstate-BelewK-20190920.pdf.

67. Drabble, "From White Supremacy to White Power," 50; Berger, "PATCON."

68. Belew, *Bring the War Home*, 204.

69. Lane Crothers, *Rage on the Right: The American Militia Movement from Ruby Ridge to Homeland Security* (Lanham, MD: Rowman and Littlefield, 2003), 34–46.

70. "The Federal Raid on Ruby Ridge, ID" Hearings before the Senate Subcommittee on Terrorism, Technology, and Government Information of the Committee on the Judiciary, 104th Congress, 1st Session, September 6, 7, 8, 12, 14, 15, 19, 20, 21, 22, 26; and October 13, 18, and 19, 1995 (Washington, DC: Government Printing Office, 1997), 21, 25, 58, https://www.google.com/books/edition/The_Federal_Ra id_on_Ruby_Ridge_ID/auKF2LMaGYkC?hl=en&gbpv=0; "Ruby Ridge," *American Experience*, PBS, February 4, 2020, https://www.pbs.org/wgbh/americanexperie nce/films/ruby-ridge/#transcript; and "Report of the Ruby Ridge Task Force to the Office of Professional Responsibility of Investigation of Allegations of Improper Governmental Conduct in the Investigation, Apprehension and Prosecution of Randall C. Weaver and Kevin L. Harris," U.S. Department of Justice, June 10, 1994, http://law2.umkc.edu/faculty/projects/ftrials/weaver/dojrubyIVB.htm.

71. "Report of the Ruby Ridge Task Force to the Office of Professional Responsibility" (for chronicling of the incident, see in particular the section "Factual Summary"); U.S. Congress, Senate, Committee on the Judiciary, Hearings, *The Federal Raid on Ruby Ridge*. Testimony from involved parties. See in particular the report included as an appendix at the very end.

72. Michael J. Sniffen, "Deputy FBI Director Censured, Agencies Criticized for Weaver Shooting," Associated Press, April 5, 1995, https://apnews.com/article/eb32ea934 696498e8d7a8d2d67c14e62.

73. "Report of the Ruby Ridge Task Force to the Office of Professional Responsibility."

74. "Report of the Ruby Ridge Task Force to the Office of Professional Responsibility"; see also U.S. Congress, Senate, Committee on the Judiciary, Hearings, *The Federal Raid on Ruby Ridge*.

75. U.S. Congress, Senate, Committee on the Judiciary, Hearings, *The Federal Raid on Ruby Ridge*.

76. Crawford Gribben, "Ruby Ridge: 25 Years since the Siege That Fired Up the US's Radical Right," *Conversation*, August 25, 2017, https://theconversation.com/ruby-ridge-25-years-since-the-siege-that-fired-up-the-uss-radical-right-82863.

77. The Weavers received $3.1 million. "U.S. Settles Final Civil Lawsuit Stemming from Ruby Ridge Siege," *New York Times*, September 23, 2000, https://www.nytimes.com/2000/09/23/us/us-settles-final-civil-lawsuit-stemming-from-ruby-ridge-siege.html.

78. George Lardner, Jr., "FBI Ex-official Gets 18 Months for Role in Ruby Ridge Coverup," *Washington Post*, October 11, 1997, https://www.washingtonpost.com/archive/politics/1997/10/11/fbi-ex-official-gets-18-months-for-role-in-ruby-ridge-coverup/a2b7b3d3-710f-4aef-838e-870b278cd87f/.

79. On the "Army for God" quote, see Ashley Fantz, "Who Was David Koresh?" *CNN. com*, April 14, 2011, http://www.cnn.com/2011/US/04/14/waco.koresh/index. html For descriptions of Waco and critiques of the government response, see U.S. Congress, House Committee on Government Reform and Oversight and Committee on the Judiciary, Report, *Investigation into the Activities of Federal Law Enforcement Agencies toward the Branch Davidians*, 104th Congress, 2nd Session, August 2, 1996 (Washington, DC: Government Printing Office, 1996), https://www.congress.gov/104/crpt/hrpt749/CRPT-104hrpt749.pdf; John C. Danforth, "Final Report to the Deputy Attorney General Concerning the 1993 Confrontation at the Mt. Carmel Complex, Waco, Texas," November 8, 2000, https://www.hsdl.org/?view&did=848007 (this document has a "Statement of Facts" summarizing Waco); "Report of the Department of the Treasury on the Bureau of Alcohol, Tobacco, and Firearms Investigation of Vernon Wayne Howell, Also Known as David Koresh," U.S. Department of the Treasury, September 1993, https://babel.hathitrust.org/cgi/pt?id=mdp.39015033104830&view=1up&seq=1; Berger, "PATCON," 17; Mark England and Darlene McCormick, "The Sinful Messiah: Part Four—An Incident Involving Howell, a Young Girl," *Waco Tribune-Herald*, February 27, 1993, https://wacotrib.com/news/branch_davidians/sinful-messiah/the-sinful-messiah-part-four-an-incident-involving-howell-a-young-girl/article_79bcb8d5-24fd-5cd2-a399-2688d37f9828.html; U.S. Department of Justice, "Report to the Deputy Attorney General on the Events at Waco, Texas, February 28 to April 19, 1993," October 8, 1993, https://www.justice.gov/archives/publications/waco/report-deputy-attorney-general-events-waco-texas-child-abuse; Waco History, "Army of God"; Ashley Yeaman, "The Branch Davidian Siege," https://wacohistory.org/items/show/177; Rissa Shaw, "Sides of the Siege: Lessons Learned 25 Years after Tragic Standoff," KWTX, April 20, 2018, https://www.kwtx.com/content/news/Sides-of-the-Siege-Views-and-lessons-learned-25-years-after-infamous-standoff-480339903.html.

80. U.S. Congress, House, Committee on Government Reform and Oversight and Committee on the Judiciary, Report, *Investigation into the Activities of Federal Law Enforcement Agencies toward the Branch Davidians*; Mark England, "17 Bodies of Cult Members Unclaimed," *Waco Tribune-Herald*, February 1, 1994, https://wacotrib.com/news/branch_davidians/17-bodies-of-cult-members-unclaimed/article_b0176880-4484-5793-bc61-f6676b57cbd1.html. On the initial raid, see "Report of the Department of the Treasury on the Bureau of Alcohol, Tobacco, and Firearms Investigation of Vernon Wayne Howell, Also Known as David Koresh," 81–107. For evidence that the Davidians started the fire, including wiretaps and observations,

see Danforth, "Final Report to the Deputy Attorney General." Jonathan Tilove, "A Quarter-Century Later, 'Dark Theories' Still Hover over Waco Siege," *Statesman,* September 25, 2018, https://www.statesman.com/news/20180415/a-quarter-cent ury-later-dark-theories-still-hover-over-waco-siege.

81. Berger, "PATCON," 17; Danforth, "Final Report to the Deputy Attorney General."
82. Michael Barkun, "Appropriated Martyrs: The Branch Davidians and the Radical Right," *Terrorism and Political Violence* 19, no. 1 (2007): 117–124, https://doi.org/ 10.1080/09546550601054956; Mark Pitcavage, "Camouflage and Conspiracy: The Militia Movement from Ruby Ridge to Y2K," *American Behavioral Scientist* 44, no. 6 (February 2001): 958–961, https://doi.org/10.1177%2F00027640121956610.
83. Danforth, "Final Report to the Deputy Attorney General," 46–108.
84. "Bulldozing at Burned Cult Compound Triggers Protest by Lawyer," *Tulsa World,* May 13, 1993, https://tulsaworld.com/archive/bulldozing-at-burned-cult-compound-triggers-protest-by-lawyer/article_5b2108af-7e5f-5911-9630-f5565fd11817.html.
85. Tilove, "A Quarter-Century Later, 'Dark Theories' Still Hover over Waco Siege."
86. Zoom interview with J. M. Berger, February 5, 2021.
87. Roper Center for Public Opinion Research, Cornell University, "Waco, Branch Davidians, and Changing Perceptions," April 18, 2018, https://ropercenter.cornell. edu/blog/waco-branch-davidians-and-changing-perceptions.
88. Clyde Haberman, "Memories of Waco Siege Continue to Fuel Far-Right Groups," *New York Times,* July 12, 2015, https://www.nytimes.com/2015/07/13/us/memor ies-of-waco-siege-continue-to-fuel-far-right-groups.html; Richard Lacayo and Patrick Dawson, "State of Siege," *Time,* April 8, 1996.
89. Southern Poverty Law Center, "War in the West: A Report" (2014), https://www.splcen ter.org/sites/default/files/downloads/publication/war_in_the_west_report.pdf.
90. Pitcavage, "Camouflage and Conspiracy," 961.
91. Patricia Fernández-Kelly and Douglas S. Massey, "Borders for Whom? The Role of NAFTA in Mexico-U.S. Migration," *Annals of the American Academy of Political and Social Science* 610, no. 1 (March 2007): 108, https://doi.org/10.1177%2F000271620 6297449; Ted Robbins, "Wave of Illegal Immigrants Gains Speed after NAFTA," NPR, December 26, 2013, https://www.npr.org/2013/12/26/257255787/wave-of-illegal-immigrants-gains-speed-after-nafta.
92. James Bennet, "Candidate's Speech Is Called Code for Controversy," *New York Times,* February 25, 1996, https://www.nytimes.com/1996/02/25/us/politics-patr ick-j-buchanan-candidate-s-speech-is-called-code-for-controversy.html. Curtis Wilkie, "A 'Grand Bargain' That Secured the South for the GOP," *Washington Post,* August 16, 2019, https://www.washingtonpost.com/outlook/a-grand-bargain-that-secured-the-south-for-the-gop/2019/08/16/64166948-976a-11e9-830a-21b9b36 b64ad_story.html.
93. Pitcavage, "Camouflage and Conspiracy," 958.
94. Greg Grandin, *The End of the Myth: From the Frontier to the Border Wall in the Mind of America* (New York: Metropolitan Books, 2019), 209.
95. Sam Jackson, "Conspiracy Theories in the Patriot/Militia Movement," George Washington University Program on Extremism (May 2017), 3, https://extremism.

gwu.edu/sites/g/files/zaxdzs2191/f/downloads/Jackson%2C%20Conspiracy%20T
heories%20Final.pdf.

96. Pitcavage, "Camouflage and Conspiracy," 970–971.

97. Jackson, "Conspiracy Theories in the Patriot/Militia Movement," 15.

98. See Belew, *Bring the War Home*, 159, for several conspiracy theories associated
with ZOG.

99. John M. Cotter, "Sounds of Hate: White Power Rock and Roll and the Neo-Nazi
Skinhead Subculture," *Terrorism and Political Violence* 11, no. 2 (Summer 1999): 126,
https://doi.org/10.1080/09546559908427509.

100. Phone interview with Michael German, January 5, 2021.

101. FBI, "Oklahoma City Bombing," no date, https://www.fbi.gov/history/famous-
cases/oklahoma-city-bombing.

102. Dale Russakoff and Serge F. Kovaleski, "An Ordinary Boy's Extraordinary Rage,"
Washington Post, July 2, 1995, https://www.washingtonpost.com/wp-srv/national/
longterm/oklahoma/bg/mcveigh.htm.

103. Berger, "PATCON," 14; Sam Howe Verhovek, "Branch Davidians Shed No Tears for
McVeigh," *New York Times*, June 13, 2001, https://www.nytimes.com/2001/06/13/
us/branch-davidians-shed-no-tears-for-mcveigh.html.

104. Kaplan, " 'Leaderless Resistance,' " 91; Lou Michel and Dan Herbeck, "Live from
Death Row," *Newsweek*, April 8, 2001, https://www.newsweek.com/live-death-row-
150199.

105. As quoted in Kaplan, " 'Leaderless Resistance,' " 91.

106. "Crimes of the Century: Oklahoma City Bombing," CNN, August 11, 2013;
"Testimony of Oklahoma State Trooper Charles J. Hanger Concerning His Arrest
of Timothy McVeigh on April 19, 1995" (November 5, 1997), in "Timothy McVeigh
Trial: Documents Relating to McVeigh's Arrest and the Search of His Vehicle,"
University of Missouri–Kansas City School of Law, http://law2.umkc.edu/faculty/
projects/ftrials/mcveigh/mcveigharrest.html#TESTIMONY.

107. Perliger, *American Zealots*, 70.

108. Lou Michel and Dan Herbeck, *American Terrorist: Timothy McVeigh and the
Oklahoma City Bombing* (New York: BookBaby, 2015).

109. Berger, "PATCON," 19–20.

110. Blythe, "The Guru of White Hate."

111. Jo Thomas and Ronald Smothers, "Oklahoma City Building Was Target of Plot as
Early as '83, Official Says," *New York Times*, May 20, 1995, https://www.nytimes.
com/1995/05/20/us/oklahoma-city-building-was-target-of-plot-as-early-as-83-
official-says.html. For documents on CSA, see FBI, "The Covenant, The Sword, The
Arm of the Lord." For trial transcripts, see "OKC Bombing Trial Transcript—04/
24/1997 11:39 CDT/CST," *Oklahoman* (Oklahoma City), April 24, 1997, https://
oklahoman.com/article/1074825/okc-bombing-trial-transcript-04241997-1139-
cdtcst; "The Trial of Timothy McVeigh: Selected Excerpts from the Trial Transcript,"
University of Missouri–Kansas City School of Law, no date, https://www.famous-tri
als.com/oklacity/737-excerpts.

112. Belew, *Bring the War Home*, 210–226.

113. Blythe, "The Guru of White Hate."

114. See the remarks of Kathleen Belew, "The Terrorist," NPR, October 30, 2019, https://www.npr.org/transcripts/774437718.

115. Belew, *Bring the War Home*, 229.

116. John K. Wiley, "Jury: Aryans to Pay $6.3M in Suit," *Washington Post*, September 8, 2000, https://www.washingtonpost.com/wp-srv/aponline/20000908/aponline045 946_000.htm; Southern Poverty Law Center, "Keenan v. Aryan Nations," no date, https://www.splcenter.org/seeking-justice/case-docket/keenan-v-aryan-nations.

117. Southern Poverty Law Center, "Berhanu v. Metzger," no date, https://www.splcenter.org/seeking-justice/case-docket/berhanu-v-metzger.

118. Drabble, "From White Supremacy to White Power," 57.

119. Blythe, "The Guru of White Hate"; Mark Potok, "Shipwreck: Ten Years after the Death of Its Founder, the Once-Dominant National Alliance Has Become the Joke of the Neo-Nazi Movement," Southern Poverty Law Center, July 23, 2012, https://www.splcenter.org/hatewatch/2012/07/23/shipwreck-ten-years-after-death-its-founder-once-dominant-national-alliance-has-become-joke.

120. Danny Lewis, "Twenty Years Ago Today, the Montana Freemen Started Its 81-Day Standoff," *Smithsonian*, March 25, 2016, https://www.smithsonianmag.com/smart-news/twenty-years-ago-today-the-montana-freeman-started-its-81-day-standoff-180958568/.

121. Berger, "PATCON."

122. Paul Richter, "Some Republicans Showing Sympathy for Militias' Views," *Los Angeles Times*, May 15, 1995, https://www.latimes.com/archives/la-xpm-1995-05-15-mn-886-story.html; Steven A. Holmes, "Congressman Calls Raid near Waco a Clinton Plot," *New York Times*, May 13, 1995, https://www.nytimes.com/1995/05/13/us/terror-in-oklahoma-in-congress-congressman-calls-raid-near-waco-a-clinton-plot.html.

123. See New American Foundation data, https://www.newamerica.org/in-depth/terror ism-in-america/what-threat-united-states-today/.

Chapter 3

1. Bruce Hoffman, *Right-Wing Terrorism in Europe* (RAND: Santa Monica, CA, March 1982), v; Jakob Aasland Ravndal, "Thugs or Terrorists? A Typology of Right-Wing Terrorism in Western Europe," *Journal for Deradicalization*, no. 3 (Summer 2015), pp. 1-38.

2. Matthew Worley and Nigel Copsey, "White Youth: The Far Right, Punk, and British Youth Culture, 1977–87," *Journalism, Media, and Culture Journal* 9 (2016): 11.

3. Enoch Powell, *Freedom and Reality* (Kingswood, South Gloucestershire: Elliot Right Way Books, 1969).

4. Dyck, "The History of White-Power Music in Britain," 14.

5. Futrell et al., "Understanding Music in Movements," 281.

6. Timothy Scott Brown, "Subcultures, Pop Music and Politics: Skinheads and 'Nazi Rock' in England and Germany," *Journal of Social History* 38, no. 1 (2004): 157; John M. Cotter, "Sounds of Hate: White Power Rock and Roll and the Neo-Nazi Skinhead Subculture," *Terrorism and Political Violence* 11, no. 2 (1999): 116.

7. Dyck, "The History of White-Power Music in Britain," 14.

8. Dave Morris, "A Cultural History of Neo-Nazi Rock," *Globe and Mail*, August 7, 2012.

9. Brown, "Subcultures, Pop Music and Politics," 162–163.

10. Ugo Corte and Bob Edwards, "White Power Music and the Mobilization of Racist Social Movements," *Music and Arts in Action* 1, no. 1 (June 2008), https://www.resea rchgate.net/publication/26620885_White_Power_Music_and_Mobilization_of_ Racist_Social_Movements.

11. Cotter, "Sounds of Hate," 118–119; Dyck, "The History of White-Power Music in Britain," 5.

12. Brown, "Subcultures, Pop Music and Politics," 164.

13. Dyck, "The History of White-Power Music in Britain," 15.

14. Cotter, "Sounds of Hate," 124–125.

15. Cotter, "Sounds of Hate," 129.

16. Brown, "Subcultures, Pop Music and Politics," 164–165; Dyck, "The History of White-Power Music in Britain," 19.

17. Tim Kelsey and Adrian Bridge, "Five Britons Charged after Man Is Stabbed," *Independent*, October 21, 1991.

18. "Thugs Attack Funeral for Mozambican Man in Dresden," Associated Press, April 12, 1991; "Paris: Hommage à Brahim Bouarram, Tué en 1995 Par des Militants d'Extrême Droite," *Le Monde*, May 1, 2018, https://www.lemonde.fr/politique/article/2018/05/ 01/paris-hidalgo-et-griveaux-rendent-hommage-a-brahim-bouarram-tue-en-1995- par-des-militants-d-extreme-droite_5292935_823448.html.

19. Cotter, "Sounds of Hate," 119; Dyck, "The History of White-Power Music in Britain," 19–20; Linda Joffe, "Headbanging Hard to a Nazi Beat," *Independent*, November 11, 1992.

20. Dyck, "The History of White-Power Music in Britain," 21–26; James Hall, "How Britain's Nazi Punk Bands Became a Gateway Drug for US White Supremacy," *Telegraph*, August 23, 2017.

21. Anti-Defamation League, "Hate beyond Borders: The Internationalization of White Supremacy" (n.d.), https://www.adl.org/resources/reports/hate-beyond-borders- the-internationalization-of-white-supremacy.

22. Cotter, "Sounds of Hate," 131.

23. Pollard, "Skinhead Culture," 408.

24. Pollard, "Skinhead Culture," 409.

25. Pollard, "Skinhead Culture, 398–419. The quote on the Italian branch is on 407, and the Combat 18 manifesto is on 408.

26. Brown, "Subcultures, Pop Music and Politics," 159.

27. Dyck, "The History of White-Power Music in Britain," 16.

28. Corte and Edwards, "White Power Music and the Mobilization of Racist Social Movements"; Brown, "Subcultures, Pop Music and Politics," 164.

29. Hall, "How Britain's Nazi Punk Bands Became a Gateway Drug for US White Supremacy."

30. "Neo-Nazis Held for Oslo 'Racist' Murder," *BBC News*, January 29, 2001, http://news.bbc.co.uk/2/hi/europe/1142780.stm; Southern Poverty Law Center, "White Power Music Festival Hammerfest 2000 Draws International Fans to Atlanta," August 29, 2001, https://www.splcenter.org/fighting-hate/intelligence-report/2001/white-power-music-festival-hammerfest-2000-draws-international-fans-atlanta.

31. Futrell et al., "Understanding Music in Movements," 283.

32. Joffe, "Headbanging Hard to a Nazi Beat."

33. Futrell et al., "Understanding Music in Movements," 286–293. The quotes are from 292 and 293, with the spelling in the original.

34. Brown, "Subcultures, Pop Music and Politics," 162.

35. Dyck, "The History of White-Power Music in Britain," 18.

36. Hall, "How Britain's Nazi Punk Bands Became a Gateway Drug for US White Supremacy."

37. As quoted in Brown, "Subcultures, Pop Music and Politics," 168.

38. Microsoft Teams interview with analysts at the Community Security Trust, February 12, 2021.

39. Southern Poverty Law Center, "White Power Music Festival Hammerfest 2000 Draws International Fans to Atlanta."

40. Corte and Edwards, "White Power Music and the Mobilization of Racist Social Movements."

41. Lyrics given in Futrell et al., "Understanding Music in Movements," 298–299.

42. Pollard, "Skinhead Culture," 414.

43. Dyck, "The History of White-Power Music in Britain," 29.

44. Corte and Edwards, "White Power Music and the Mobilization of Racist Social Movements."

45. Southern Poverty Law Center, "White Power Music Festival Hammerfest 2000 Draws International Fans to Atlanta."

46. Futrell et al., "Understanding Music in Movements," 283.

47. Southern Poverty Law Center, "White Power Music Festival Hammerfest 2000 Draws International Fans to Atlanta."

48. Southern Poverty Law Center, "White Power Music Festival Hammerfest 2000 Draws International Fans to Atlanta."

49. Ministry of the Interior of the Czech Republic, *Information on the Issue of Extremism in the Czech Republic in 2007* (Prague: Security Policy Department, 2008), 13.

50. Anti-Defamation League, *The Skinhead International: A Worldwide Survey of Neo-Nazi Skinheads* (New York: Anti-Defamation League, 1995).

51. Futrell et al., "Understanding Music in Movements," 282; Anti-Defamation League, *Sounds of Hate: Neo-Nazi Rock Music from Germany* (1992), https://www.ojp.gov/ncjrs/virtual-library/abstracts/sounds-hate-neo-nazi-rock-music-germany.

52. Futrell et al., "Understanding Music in Movements," 283.

53. Anti-Defamation League, *The Skinhead International*.

54. Southern Poverty Law Center, "White Power Music Festival Hammerfest 2000 Draws International Fans to Atlanta."

55. Anti-Defamation League, *Army of Hate: The Resurgence of Racist Skinheads in America* (2006).

56. Hall, "How Britain's Nazi Punk Bands Became a Gateway Drug for US White Supremacy."

57. Futrell et al., "Understanding Music in Movements," 282–285.

58. Jeff Horwich, "Top 'White Power' Music Label Prospers from Twin Cities Home Base," Minnesota Public Radio, May 13, 2004, http://news.minnesota.publicradio.org/features/2004/05/13_horwichj_panzerfaust/.

59. Hall, "How Britain's Nazi Punk Bands Became a Gateway Drug for US White Supremacy."

60. Zoom interview with Heidi Beirich, January 15, 2021.

61. Futrell et al., "Understanding Music in Movements," 287.

62. Dyck, "The History of White-Power Music in Britain," 20.

63. Corte and Edwards, "White Power Music and the Mobilization of Racist Social Movements."

64. Corte and Edwards, "White Power Music and the Mobilization of Racist Social Movements."

65. Michael Hughes, "The Rise and Fall of Pamyat?," *Religion, State and Society* 20, no. 2 (1992): 214.

66. "Russia Neo-Nazis Jailed for Life over 27 Race Murders," *BBC News*, July 12, 2011, https://www.bbc.com/news/world-europe-14122320.

67. Steven Eke, "Russia Gang Faces Murder Charge," *BBC News*, June 30, 2008, http://news.bbc.co.uk/2/hi/europe/7482125.stm.

68. Mara Bierbach and Karsten Kaminski, "Germany's Confusing Rules on Swastikas and Nazi Symbols," DW Akademie, August 14, 2018, https://www.dw.com/en/germanys-confusing-rules-on-swastikas-and-nazi-symbols/a-45063547.

69. Barbara Manthe, "The Anti-Semitic Murder Germany Forgot," Center for Analysis of the Radical Right, February 1, 2019, https://www.radicalrightanalysis.com/2019/02/01/the-anti-semitic-murder-germany-forgot/; Bruce Hoffman, *Right Wing Terrorism in Europe* (Santa Monica: Rand Corporation, 1982); Tony Paterson, "Oktoberfest Bomb Inquiry: Severed Hand May Prove 1980 Attack Was Carried Out by Neo-Nazis and Not a Lone Wolf," *Independent,* February 4, 2015, https://www.independent.co.uk/news/world/europe/oktoberfest-bomb-inquiry-severed-hand-may-prove-1980-attack-was-carried-out-neo-nazis-and-not-lone-wolf-10024250.html.

70. DW Akademie, "Germany: 1980 Oktoberfest Bombing a 'Far-Right Attack,'" July 8, 2020, https://www.dw.com/en/germany-1980-oktoberfest-bombing-a-far-right-attack/a-54085190.

71. Anti-Defamation League, *The Skinhead International.*

72. Katrin Bennhold, "Germany's Far Right Unified, Too, Making It Much Stronger," *New York Times*, October 3, 2020, https://www.nytimes.com/2020/10/03/world/europe/germany-reunification-far-right.html?referringSource=articleShare.

73. Anti-Defamation League, *The Skinhead International.*

74. Rand C. Lewis, *The Neo-Nazis and German Unification* (Westport, CT: Greenwood, 1996), 6–11.

75. Wesley D. Chapin, "The Turkish Diaspora in Germany," *Diaspora: A Journal of Transnational Studies* 5, no. 2 (Fall 1996): 275–289.

76. Gideon Botsch, "From Skinhead-Subculture to Radical Right Movement: The Development of a 'National Opposition' in East Germany," *Contemporary European History* 21, no. 4 (November 2012): 562–563.

77. Brown, "Subcultures, Pop Music and Politics," 167.

78. Heinz Fassmann and Rainer Munz, "Patterns and Trends of International Migration in Western Europe," *Population and Development Review* 18, no. 3 (1992): 457–480.

79. Thomas Saalfeld, "Up and Down with the Extreme Right in Germany, 1949–1996," *Politics* 17, no. 1 (1997): 1–8.

80. Kenneth R. Langford, "An Analysis of Left and Right Wing Terrorism in Italy" (MS thesis, Defense Intelligence College, July 1985), III-5, https://apps.dtic.mil/dtic/tr/fulltext/u2/a161823.pdf.

81. Jacob Aasland Ravndal, "Right-Wing Terrorism and Militancy in the Nordic Countries: A Comparative Case Study," *Terrorism and Political Violence* 30, no. 5 (2018): 772–792.

82. Counter Extremism Project, "European Ethno-nationalist and White Supremacy Groups," no date, https://www.counterextremism.com/european-white-supremacy-groups.

83. Mark Wilding, "The Rise and Demise of the EDL," *Vice*, March 12, 2018, https://www.vice.com/en_uk/article/qve8wm/the-rise-and-demise-of-the-edl.

84. Sven Felix Kellerhoff, "Seit 1945 Töteten Rechtsextremisten Fast 200 Menschen," *Welt*, June 18, 2019, https://www.welt.de/geschichte/article195455449/Walter-Luebcke-Seit-1945-toeteten-Rechtsextremisten-fast-200-Menschen.html; Peter Hille, "Right-Wing Terror in Germany: A Timeline," DW Akademie, February 20, 2020, https://www.dw.com/en/right-wing-terror-in-germany-a-timeline/a-52451976.

85. Mark Fritz, "Man Accused in Turk Death Slashes Wrists; Skinhead Rock Banned," Associated Press, December 2, 1992, https://apnews.com/article/d0e176a2c4568179694c0ea1a52c479f.

86. Daniel Koehler, "Right-Wing Extremism and Terrorism in Europe," *Prism* 2, no. 6 (July 2016), https://cco.ndu.edu/Portals/96/Documents/prism/prism_6-2/Koehler.pdf?ver=2016-07-05-104619-213.

87. Zoom interview with Daniel Koehler, January 13, 2021.

88. Anti-Defamation League, *The Skinhead International*.

89. Stephen Kinzer, "Germans Sentence Anti-foreign Rioter to 2½ Years," *New York Times*, March 4, 1993, https://www.nytimes.com/1993/03/04/world/germans-sentence-anti-foreign-rioter-to-2-1-2-years.html.

90. Associated Press, "A Brief History of German Neo-Nazi Group NSU," July 10, 2018, https://apnews.com/c9c1d082c8f4464fb0bf7372167fc93d/A-brief-history-of-German-neo-Nazi-group-NSU.

91. Maik Baumgartner, "The Many Shortcomings of Germany's Neo-Nazi Terror Trial," *Der Spiegel*, July 16, 2018, https://www.spiegel.de/international/germany/neo-nazi-terror-trial-fails-to-answer-all-questions-a-1218727.html.

92. Der Spiegel Staff, "A Disturbing New Dimension of Far-Right Terror," *Der Spiegel*, November 14, 2011, https://www.spiegel.de/international/germany/the-brown-army-faction-a-disturbing-new-dimension-of-far-right-terror-a-797569.html; Thomas Meany and Saskia Schäfer, "The Neo-Nazi Murder Trial Revealing Germany's Darkest Secrets," *Guardian*, December 15, 2016, https://www.theguard ian.com/world/2016/dec/15/neo-nazi-murders-revealing-germanys-darkest-secr ets.

93. Meany and Schäfer, "The Neo-Nazi Murder Trial Revealing Germany's Darkest Secrets."

94. Lee McGowan, "Right Wing Violence in Germany: Assessing the Objectives, Personalities, and Terror Trail of the National Socialist Underground and the State's Response to It," *German Politics* 23, no. 3 (2014): 196; Associated Press, "A Brief History of German Neo-Nazi Group NSU."

95. Antonia von der Behrens, "Lessons from Germany's NSU Case," *Race & Class* 59, no. 4 (2018): 87.

96. Steven Greenhouse, "Immigrant Hostel Bombed in France," *New York Times*, December 20, 1988, https://www.nytimes.com/1988/12/20/world/immigrant-hos tel-bombed-in-france.html; Philippe Bernard, "Des Militants du FN Sont Impliqués dans la Mort d'Ibrahim Ali, 17 Ans," *Le Monde*, February 24, 1995, https://www.lemonde.fr/archives/article/1995/02/24/des-militants-du-fn-sont-impliques-dans-la-mort-d-ibrahim-ali-17-ans_3840992_1819218.html.

97. Anti-Defamation League, *The Skinhead International*.

98. Anti-Defamation League, Sounds of Hate.

99. Anti-Defamation League, Army of Hate.

100. Zoom interview with Daniel Koehler, January 13, 2021.

101. "Five Guilty of Moscow Race Attack," *BBC News*, November 20, 2002, http://news.bbc.co.uk/2/hi/europe/2495961.stm; "Russia Neo-Nazis Jailed for Life over 27 Race Murders."

102. Nikolai Kovalev, "Jury Trials for Violent Hate Crimes in Russia: Is Russian Justice Only for Ethnic Russians?," *Chicago-Kent Law Review* 86, no. 2 (April 2011), https://scholarship.kentlaw.iit.edu/cgi/viewcontent.cgi?article=3798&context=cklawrev iew. Johannes Due Enstad, "Right-Wing Terrorism and Violence in Putin's Russia," *Perspectives on Terrorism* 12, no. 6 (2018): 89–103. Among other sources, Enstad draws on SOVA Center data. SOVA reports can be accessed at https://www.sova-center.ru/en/xenophobia/reports-analyses/

103. Jacob Aasland Ravndal, "Right-Wing Terrorism and Violence May Actually Have Declined," *Washington Post*, April 2, 2019, https://www.washingtonpost.com/polit ics/2019/04/02/is-right-wing-terrorism-violence-rise/.

104. Anti-Defamation League, *New Hate and Old: The Changing Face of American White Supremacy*, no date, https://www.adl.org/new-hate-and-old#in-the-sha

dow-of-the-alt-right-the-other-white-supremacists; ZoomZoom interview with Peter Simi, January 6, 2021.

105. Zoom interview with Heidi Beirich, January 15, 2021.

106. Zoom interview with Daniel Koehler, January 13, 2021.

107. Anti-Defamation League, Army of Hate.

108. Kathleen Belew, *Bring the War Home* (Cambridge, MA: Harvard University Press, 2018), 139.

109. Michael Reynolds, "Hammerskin Nation Emerges from Small Dallas Group," Southern Poverty Law Center Intelligence Report, December 15, 1999, https://www.splcenter.org/fighting-hate/intelligence-report/1999/hammerskin-nation-emerges-small-dallas-group.

110. Lisa Rab, "Fall of the Fourth Reich," *Cleveland Scene*, February 15, 2006, https://www.clevescene.com/cleveland/fall-of-the-fourth-reich/Content?oid=1493827; Anti-Defamation League, *Army of Hate*.

111. Reynolds, "Hammerskin Nation Emerges from Small Dallas Group."

Chapter 4

1. Indictment of Anders Behring Breivik, Oslo Public Prosecutors, March 5, 2012, https://upload.wikimedia.org/wikipedia/commons/2/2b/Indictment%2C_Anders_Behring_Breivik.pdf; 22 of July Commission, "Report of the 22 of July Commission—Preliminary English Version of Selected Chapters," August 13, 2012, https://www.regjeringen.no/contentassets/bb3dc76229c64735b4f6eb4dbfcdbfe8/en-gb/pdfs/nou2012_14_eng.pdf; Public Prosecutors of Oslo, "Indictment," Complaint No. 11762579, 10094/11-115/SHO017, March 5, 2012, https://upload.wikimedia.org/wikipedia/commons/2/2b/Indictment%2C_Anders_Behring_Breivik.pdf.

2. Zoom interview with Åsne Seierstad, February 18, 2021.

3. 22 of July Commission, "Report of the 22 of July Commission."

4. Petter Nesser, "Individual Jihadist Operations in Europe: Patterns and Challenges," *CTC Sentinel* 5, no. 1 (January 2012): 18, https://www.ctc.usma.edu/wp-content/uploads/2012/01/Vol5-Iss13.pdf.

5. Jacob Aasland Ravndal, "Anders Behring Breivik's Use of the Internet and Social Media," *Journal EXIT-Deutschland* 2 (2013): 172–185, https://journals.sfu.ca/jed/index.php/jex/article/view/28/45.

6. Zoom interview with Åsne Seierstad, February 18, 2021.

7. Cato Hemmingby and Tore Bjørgo, "Terrorist Target Selection: The Case of Anders Behring Breivik," *Perspectives on Terrorism* 12, no. 6 (December 2018): 164–176, https://www.universiteitleiden.nl/binaries/content/assets/customsites/perspectives-on-terrorism/2018/issue-6/a11-hemmingby-bjorgo.pdf.

8. Ravndal, "Anders Behring Breivik's Use of the Internet and Social Media."

9. Anders Behring Breivik, "2083: A European Declaration of Independence," *Washington Post*, July 24, 2011, 18, https://www.washingtonpost.com/r/2010-2019/ WashingtonPost/2011/07/24/National-Politics/Graphics/2083+-+A+European+ Declaration+of+Independence.pdf.

10. Marianne Angvik, "Security and Rights: The Development of Norwegian Counter-terrorism Measures post 9/11 and Their Impact on the Private Sphere," University of Oslo Faculty of Law (2017), https://www.duo.uio.no/bitstream/handle/10852/57343/ HUMR5200_8010.pdf?sequence=1&isAllowed=y.

11. Åsne Seierstad, "The Anatomy of White Terror," *New York Times*, March 18, 2019, https://www.nytimes.com/2019/03/18/opinion/new-zealand-tarrant-white-supr emacist-terror.html.

12. Zoom interview with Åsne Seierstad, February 18, 2021.

13. Hemmingby and Bjørgo, "Terrorist Target Selection."

14. Tore Bjørgo, Beatrice de Graaf, Liesbeth van der Heide, Cato Hemmingby, and Daan Weggemans, "Performing Justice, Coping with Trauma: The Trial of Anders Breivik, 2012," in *Terrorists on Trial: A Performative Perspective*, ed. Beatrice de Graaf and Alex Schmid (Leiden: Leiden University Press, 2016), 457.

15. Karl Ove Knausgaard, "The Inexplicable: Inside the Mind of a Mass Killer," *New Yorker*, May 25, 2015, http://www.newyorker.com/magazine/2015/05/25/the-inexplicable/.

16. Knausgaard, "The Inexplicable."

17. Weiyi Cai and Simone Landon, "Attacks by White Extremists Are Growing. So Are Their Connections," *New York Times*, April 3, 2019, https://www.nytimes.com/inte ractive/2019/04/03/world/white-extremist-terrorism-christchurch.html; Beatrice de Graaf, Liesbeth van der Heide, Sabine Wanmaker, and Daan Weggemans, "The Anders Behring Breivik Trial: Performing Justice, Defending Democracy," ICCT Research Paper, International Centre for Counter-Terrorism–The Hague (June 2013), https://www.icct.nl/download/file/ICCT-De-Graaf-et-al-The-Anders-Behring-Brei vik-Trial-August-2013.pdf.

18. Emily Turner-Graham, "'Breivik Is My Hero': The Dystopian World of Extreme Right Youth on the Internet," *Australian Journal of Politics & History* 60, no. 3 (2014): 417.

19. Seierstad, "The Anatomy of White Terror"; Zoom interview with Åsne Seierstad, February 18, 2021.

20. Luis Ramiro and Raul Gomez, "Radical-Left Populism during the Great Recession: *Podemos* and Its Competition with the Established Radical Left," *Political Studies* 65 (2017): 108–126, https://journals.sagepub.com/doi/pdf/10.1177/00323 21716647400.

21. Antonis Klapsis, "Economic Crisis and Political Extremism in Europe: From the 1930s to the Present," *European View* 13, no. 2 (2014), https://journals.sagepub.com/ doi/full/10.1007/s12290-014-0315-5#.

22. Bat Ye'Or, *EurAbia: The Euro-Arab Axis* (Madison, NJ: Fairleigh Dickinson University Press, 2005).

23. Zoom interview with Jean-Yves Camus, February 24, 2021.

24. Kirsten Dyck, *Reichsrock: The International Web of White-Power and Neo-Nazi Hate Music* (New Brunswick, NJ: Rutgers University Press, 2016), 32.

25. Zoom interview with Rafal Pankowski, Never Again Foundation, February 9, 2021.

26. Counter Extremism Project, "European Ethno-nationalist and White Supremacy Groups," no date, 9, https://www.counterextremism.com/content/european-ethno-nationalist-and-white-supremacy-groups.

27. See data compiled by Jacob Ware, "The Fifth Wave: The Rise of Homegrown Terrorism" (MA thesis, Georgetown University, 2019).

28. Zoom interview with Jean-Yves Camus, February 24, 2021.

29. Zoom interview with Jacob Aasland Ravndal, January 27, 2021; Daniel Koehler, *Violence and Terrorism from the Far-Right: Policy Options to Counter an Elusive Threat* (The Hague: International Center for Counter-Terrorism, 2019), 5–6.

30. Daniel Koehler, "Recent Trends in German Right-Wing Violence and Terrorism: What Are the Contextual Factors behind 'Hive Terrorism'?" *Perspectives on Terrorism* 12, no. 6 (December 2018): 72–88.

31. Zoom interview with Jacob Aasland Ravndal, January 27, 2021.

32. Simon Cottee, "What Right-Wing Violent Extremists and Jihadists Have in Common," *National Post* (Canada), April 5, 2019.

33. Zoom interview with Daniel Koehler, January 13, 2021.

34. Zoom interview with Rafal Pankowski, Never Again Foundation, February 9, 2021.

35. Daniel Koehler, "The Halle, Germany, Synagogue Attack and the Evolution of the Far-Right Terror Threat," *CTC Sentinel* 12, no. 11 (December 2019): 14–20, https://ctc.usma.edu/halle-germany-synagogue-attack-evolution-far-right-terror-threat/.

36. Jakob Aasland Ravndal, "Thugs or Terrorists? A Typology of Right-Wing Terrorism in Western Europe," Journal for Deradicalization 3 (2015); Koehler, "The Halle, Germany, Synagogue Attack and the Evolution of the Far-Right Terror Threat."

37. Koehler, "Recent Trends in German Right-Wing Violence and Terrorism."

38. J. J. MacNab, U.S. Congress, House, Subcommittee on Intelligence and Counterterrorism of the Committee on Homeland Security, "Assessing the Threat from Accelerationists and Militia Extremists," 116th Congress, 2nd Session, July 16, 2020, https://homeland.house.gov/activities/hearings/assessing-the-threat-from-accelerationists-and-militia-extremists.

39. Zoom interview with Jean-Yves Camus, February 24, 2021.

40. Counter Extremism Project, "European Ethno-nationalist and White Supremacy Groups."

41. Julia Ebner, "Who Are Europe's Far-Right Identitarians?," *Politico Europe*, April 4, 2019, https://www.politico.eu/article/who-are-europe-far-right-identitarians-austria-generation-identity-martin-sellner/.

42. Cristina Maza, "White Supremacists Now Have Their Own Anti-Islam Military Camps," *Newsweek*, November 9, 2017, https://www.newsweek.com/far-right-white-supremacists-islam-military-camps-europe-training-706578.

43. Counter Extremism Project, "Generation Identity," no date, https://www.counterextremism.com/supremacy/generation-identity; "French Far-Right Activists Handed Jail Time for Alpine Anti-migrant Operation," *France24*, August 29, 2019,

https://www.france24.com/en/20190829-france-far-right-activists-generation-ident
ity-prison-sentence-alps-anti-migrant-operation.

44. Deutsche Welle Staff, "Austrian Far-Right Activist Martin Sellner's YouTube Account 'Terminated,'" *Deutsche Welle*, July 14, 2020, https://www.dw.com/en/austrian-far-right-activist-martin-sellners-youtube-account-terminated/a-54172798.

45. Ebner, "Who Are Europe's Far-Right Identitarians?"; "Royal Commission of Inquiry into the Terrorist Attack on Christchurch Mosques on 15 March 2019," pt. 4.7, https://christchurchattack.royalcommission.nz/the-report .

46. "France Bans Far-Right Anti-migrant Group Generation Identity," *France 24*, March 23, 2021, https://www.france24.com/en/france/20210303-france-bans-far-right-anti-migrant-group-generation-identity.

47. Zoom interview with Jonathan Leman of Expo (Sweden), February 12, 2021; Anti-Defamation League, "Hate beyond Borders: The Internationalization of White Supremacy" (n.d.), https://www.adl.org/resources/reports/hate-beyond-borders-the-internationalization-of-white-supremacy.

48. Anna Schecter and Rich Schapiro, "Influential Neo-Nazi Eats at Soup Kitchens, Lives in Government Housing," *NBC News*, November 26, 2019, https://www.nbcnews.com/news/us-news/influential-neo-nazi-eats-soup-kitchens-lives-government-housing-n1091681; Counter Extremism Project, "James Mason's *Siege*: Ties to Extremists," no date, https://www.counterextremism.com/sites/default/files/james-mason-siege-ties-to-extremists.pdf, found 21 "global extremist individuals" and 12 organizations linked to *Siege* (p. 1). Of the 21 people, "nine have been involved in acts of violence, four have been involved in specific murders, and four have been involved in threats or acts of terrorism" (p. 4). Organizations linked to *Siege* include: American Nazi Party, Atomwaffen Division, The Base, Feuerkrieg Division, "The Mansonite Menace" (a podcast), National Socialist Liberation Front, Northern Order, Radio Wehrwolf, Order of Nine Angles, Sonnenkrieg Division, System Resistance Network, and Universal Order.

49. Jacob Aasland Ravndal, "Right-Wing Terrorism and Militancy in the Nordic Countries: A Comparative Case Study," *Terrorism and Political Violence* 30, no. 5 (2018): 772–792.

50. Counter Extremism Project, "European Ethno-nationalist and White Supremacy Groups."

51. Kacper Rekawek, "Career Break or New Career? Extremist Foreign Fighters in Ukraine," Counter Extremism Project (April 2020), https://www.counterextremism.com/sites/default/files/CEP%20Report_Career%20Break%20or%20a%20New%20Career_Extremist%20Foreign%20Fighters%20in%20Ukraine_April%202020.pdf.

52. Maxim Tucker, "Ukraine Arrests Frenchman Smuggling Weapons for Euro 2016 Atrocities," *Times*, June 6, 2016, https://www.thetimes.co.uk/article/ukraine-arrests-frenchman-smuggling-weapons-for-euro-2016-atrocities-xp93z0l68; Anna Nemtsova, "Ukraine's Out-of-Control Arms Bazaar in Europe's Backyard," *Daily Beast*, July 9, 2016, https://www.thedailybeast.com/ukraines-out-of-control-arms-bazaar-in-europes-backyard.

53. Royal Commission of Inquiry, sec. 4.3.

54. Yassin Musharbash, "The Globalization of Far-Right Extremism: An Investigative Report, *CTC Sentinel,* July/August 2021, 43.

55. Yleisradio Oy, "Neo-Nazi Training, Employment Discrimination, Fighting Swans," *Yle.fi,* June 10, 2020, https://yle.fi/uutiset/osasto/news/wednesdays_papers_neo-nazi_training_employment_discrimination_fighting_swans/11393801.

56. Rick Noack, "The European Parties Accused of Being Influenced by Russia," *Washington Post,* November 17, 2017, https://www.washingtonpost.com/news/worldviews/wp/2017/11/17/the-european-parties-accused-of-being-influenced-by-russia/.

57. Elizabeth Grimm Arsenault and Joseph Stabile, "Confronting Russia's Role in Transnational White Supremacist Extremism," *Just Security,* February 6, 2020, https://www.justsecurity.org/68420/confronting-russias-role-in-transnational-white-supremacist-extremism/.

58. Off-the-record Zoom interview, March 16, 2021, and March 14, 2021. For more on my own thoughts and those of a colleague on the Russia question, see Shelby Butt and Daniel Byman, "Right Wing Extremism: The Russian Connection," *Global Politics and Strategy* 62, no. 2 (March 2020), https://doi.org/10.1080/00396338.2020.1739960.

59. Zoom interview with Jonathan Leman of Expo (Sweden), February 12, 2021.

60. Microsoft Teams interview with analysts at the Community Security Trust, February 12, 2021.

61. Zoom interview with Jean-Yves Camus, February 24, 2021.

62. Zoom interview with Jacob Aasland Ravndal, January 27, 2021; Ravndal, "Right-Wing Terrorism and Militancy in the Nordic Countries"; Jacob Aasland Ravndal, "Explaining Right-Wing Terrorism and Violence in Western Europe: Grievances, Opportunities, and Polarisation," *European Journal of Political Research* 57 (2018): 845–866; Jacob Aasland Ravndal, "Right-Wing Terrorism and Violence May Actually Have Declined," *Washington Post,* April 2, 2019, https://www.washingtonpost.com/politics/2019/04/02/is-right-wing-terrorism-violence-rise/.

63. Counter Extremism Project, "European Ethno-nationalist and White Supremacy Groups."

64. Zoom interview with Jonathan Leman of Expo (Sweden), February 12, 2021.

65. Koehler, "Recent Trends in German Right-Wing Violence and Terrorism."

66. Alternative für Deutschland, "Manifesto for Germany," April 12, 2017, https://www.afd.de/wp-content/uploads/sites/111/2017/04/2017-04-12_afd-grundsatzprogramm-englisch_web.pdf.

67. Alternative für Deutschland, "Manifesto for Germany"; Counter Extremism Project, "European Ethno-nationalist and White Supremacy Groups."

68. Cynthia Miller-Idriss, *Hate in the Homeland: The New Global Far Right* (Princeton: Princeton University Press, 2020), 11.

69. Zoom interview with Daniel Koehler, January 13, 2021.

70. Counter Extremism Project, "European Ethno-nationalist and White Supremacy Groups."

71. Zoom interview with Jonathan Leman of Expo (Sweden), February 12, 2021.

72. Counter Extremism Project, "European Ethno-nationalist and White Supremacy Groups."

73. Daniel Trilling, "Golden Dawn: The Rise and Fall of Greece's Neo-Nazis," *Guardian,* March 3, 2020, https://www.theguardian.com/news/2020/mar/03/golden-dawn-the-rise-and-fall-of-greece-neo-nazi-trial.

74. Zoom interview with Jonathan Leman of Expo (Sweden), February 12, 2021.

75. Counter Extremism Project, "Golden Dawn," (no date) Accessed August 4, 2020, https://www.counterextremism.com/threat/golden-dawn#history.

76. Souad Mekhennet and Rick Noack, "Austria's Political Crisis Refocuses Attention of the Far Right's Ties to Russia," *Washington Post,* May 21, 2019, https://www.washingtonpost.com/world/national-security/austrias-political-crisis-refocuses-attention-on-the-far-rights-ties-to-russia/2019/05/21/5e34de0a-71af-11e9-8be0-ca575670e91c_story.html .

77. Counter Extremism Project, "European Ethno-nationalist and White Supremacy Groups."

78. "Executive Summary," in *From the Nordic Resistance Movement to the Alternative Right: A Study of the Swedish Radical Nationalist Milieu,* ed. Magnus Ranstorp and Filip Ahlin, Centrum för Asymmetriska Hot-Och Terrorismstudier and Försvarshögskolan (2020), https://www.fhs.se/download/18.23f6da6b173f8bed598498cc/1598877052261/Summary%20-%20From%20the%20Nordic%20Resistance%20Movement%20to%20the%20Alternative%20Right%20%E2%80%93%20a%20Study%20of%20Radical%20Nationalistic%20Environments%20in%20Sweden.pdf.

79. Mark Wilding, "The Rise and Demise of the EDL," *Vice,* March 12, 2018, https://www.vice.com/en_uk/article/qve8wm/the-rise-and-demise-of-the-edl.

80. Wilding, "The Rise and Demise of the EDL."

81. Madeline Roache, "Why Is the Violent Far Right Still Able to Organise Online?," *Al Jazeera,* July 22, 2019, https://www.aljazeera.com/indepth/features/violent-organise-online-190721185447179.html; Kjetil Malkenes Hovland, "Norway Forms Antiterror Unit after Two Crises," *Wall Street Journal,* February 18, 2013, https://www.wsj.com/articles/SB10001424127887324449104578311920902230876.

82. John M. Cotter, "Sounds of Hate: White Power Rock and Roll and the Neo-Nazi Skinhead Subculture," *Terrorism and Political Violence* 11, no. 2 (1999): 135.

83. Jacob Aasland Ravndal and Tore Bjørgo, "Investigating Terrorism from the Extreme Right: A Review of Past and Present Research," *Perspectives on Terrorism* 12, no. 6 (January 2018): 5–22, https://www.universiteitleiden.nl/binaries/content/assets/customsites/perspectives-on-terrorism/2018/issue-6/a1-ravndal-and-bjorgo.pdf.

84. United Nations Security Council Counter-Terrorism Committee Executive Directorate, "Member States Concerned by the Growing and Increasingly Transnational Threat of Extreme Right-Wing Terrorism" (April 2020), 3, https://www.un.org/sc/ctc/wp-content/uploads/2020/04/CTED_Trends_Alert_Extreme_Right-Wing_Terrorism.pdf.

85. Amnesty International, "Impunity, Excessive Force and Links to Extremist Golden Dawn Blight Greek Police," April 3, 2014, https://www.amnesty.org/en/latest/news/

2014/04/impunity-excessive-force-and-links-extremist-golden-dawn-blight-greek-police/.

86. Zoom interview with Daniel Koehler, January 13, 2021.

87. Zoom interview with Daniel Koehler, January 13, 2021.

88. Amnesty International, "Impunity, Excessive Force and Links to Extremist Golden Dawn Blight Greek Police."

89. Zoom interview with Daniel Koehler, January 13, 2021.

90. Katrin Bennhold, "She Called the Police over a Neo-Nazi Threat. But the Neo-Nazis Were inside the Police," *New York Times,* December 21, 2020, https://www.nytimes.com/2020/12/21/world/europe/germany-far-right-neo-nazis-police.html?referrin gSource=articleShare; Katrin Bennhold, "Germany Disbands Special Forces Group Tainted by Far-Right Extremists," *New York Times,* July 1, 2020, https://www.nyti mes.com/2020/07/01/world/europe/german-special-forces-far-right.html;   Katrin Bennhold, "As Neo-Nazis Seed Military Ranks, Germany Confronts 'an Enemy Within,'" *New York Times,* July 3, 2020, https://www.nytimes.com/2020/07/03/world/europe/germany-military-neo-nazis-ksk.html.

91. Melissa Eddy, "German Court Suspends Right to Surveil Far-Right AfD Party," *New York Times,* March 5, 2021, https://www.nytimes.com/2021/03/05/world/eur ope/afd-germany-extremism.html.

Chapter 5

1. Steve Hendrix and Michael E. Miller, "'Let's Get This Party Started': New Zealand Shooting Suspect Narrated His Chilling Rampage," *Washington Post*, March 15, 2019, https://www.washingtonpost.com/local/lets-get-this-party-started-new-zealand-gunman-narrated-his-chilling-rampage/2019/03/15/fb3db352-4748-11e9-90f0-0cc feec87a61_story.html. The definitive account of Tarrant and the New Zealand government response is the Royal Commission of Inquiry into the Terrorist Attack on Christchurch Mosques on 15 March 2019, https://christchurchattack.royalcommiss ion.nz/the-report.

2. Megan Specia, "The New Zealand Shooting Victims Spanned Generations and Nationalities," *New York Times*, March 19, 2019, https://www.nytimes.com/2019/03/19/world/asia/new-zealand-shooting-victims-names.html.

3. Sean Flynn, "The Harrowing Hours and Defiant Aftermath of the New Zealand Mosque Shootings," *GQ*, October 10, 2019, https://www.gq.com/story/new-zealand-mosque-shooting-christchurch; Statement of Christian Picciolini, U.S. Congress, House, Committee on Foreign Affairs and Committee on Homeland Security, Hearing, "Meeting the Challenge of White Nationalist Terrorism at Home and Abroad," 116th Congress, 1st Session, September 18, 2019 (Washington, DC: Government Publishing Office, 2019), https://www.govinfo.gov/content/pkg/CHRG-116hhrg37706/pdf/CHRG-116hhrg37706.pdf.

4. Royal Commission of Inquiry, pt. 5.3.

5. "'Hello, Brother'—ChCh Victim Haji-Daoud Nabi Laid to Rest," RNZ, March 21, 2019, https://www.youtube.com/watch?v=ncJr1FOp9NY.

6. Flynn, "The Harrowing Hours and Defiant Aftermath of the New Zealand Mosque Shootings."

7. Flynn, "The Harrowing Hours and Defiant Aftermath of the New Zealand Mosque Shootings."

8. Damien Cave and Amanda Saxton, "New Zealand Gives Christchurch Killer a Record Sentence," *New York Times*, August 26, 2020, https://www.nytimes.com/2020/08/26/world/asia/christchurch-brenton-tarrant-sentenced.html?referringSource=artic leShare.

9. Royal Commission of Inquiry, pt. 4, chap. 7, para. 4.

10. Royal Commission of Inquiry, particularly pt. 4 but also 6.6.

11. Royal Commission of Inquiry, pts. 5.1 and 6.5.

12. Charles Levinson, "With Super PAC, QAnon's Con Chases Mainstream—and Money," *Protocol*, March 3, 2020, https://www.protocol.com/qanon-conspir acy-new-super-pac.

13. Tech Against Terrorism, "Analysis: New Zealand Attack and the Terrorist Use of the Internet," March 26, 2019, https://www.techagainstterrorism.org/2019/03/26/analy sis-new-zealand-attack-and-the-terrorist-use-of-the-internet/.

14. Grace Dobush, "Facebook Faces an Ad Boycott after Livestream of the New Zealand Mosque Shooting," *Fortune*, March 18, 2019, https://fortune.com/2019/03/18/faceb ook-new-zealand-shooting-ad-boycott/; Niharika Mandhana and Rhiannon Hoyle, "Facebook Left Up Video of New Zealand Shootings for an Hour," *Wall Street Journal*, March 21, 2019, https://www.wsj.com/articles/facebook-our-ai-tools-failed-to-catch-new-zealand-attack-video-11553156141.

15. U.S. Congress, House, Committee on Homeland Security, Hearing, "Artificial Intelligence and Counterterrorism: Possibilities and Limitations," 116th Congress, 1st Session, June 25, 2019 (Washington, DC: Government Publishing Office, 2020), https://www.govinfo.gov/content/pkg/CHRG-116hhrg38781/pdf/CHRG-116hh rg38781.pdf.

16. Kate Klonick, "Inside the Team at Facebook That Dealt with the Christchurch Shooting," *New Yorker*, April 25, 2019, https://www.newyorker.com/news/news-desk/inside-the-team-at-facebook-that-dealt-with-the-christchurch-shooting.

17. Dobush, "Facebook Faces an Ad Boycott after Livestream of the New Zealand Mosque Shooting."

18. Guy Rosen, "A Further Update on New Zealand Terrorist Attack," *About Facebook*, March 20, 2019, https://about.fb.com/news/2019/03/technical-update-on-new-zealand/.

19. Rosen, "A Further Update on New Zealand Terrorist Attack."

20. Tech Against Terrorism, "Analysis: New Zealand Attack and the Terrorist Use of the Internet."

21. Maura Conway, Ryan Scrivens, and Logan Macnair, "Right-Wing Extremists' Persistent Online Presence: History and Contemporary Trends," *International Centre*

for Counter-Terrorism–The Hague (October 2019), 8, https://icct.nl/wp-content/uplo ads/2019/11/Right-Wing-Extremists-Persistent-Online-Presence.pdf.

22. Zoom interview with Kate Klonick, February 19, 2021.
23. Yoree Koh, "Why Video of New Zealand Massacre Can't Be Stamped Out," *Wall Street Journal,* March 17, 2019, https://www.wsj.com/articles/why-video-of-new-zealand-massacre-cant-be-stamped-out-11552863615.
24. Rosen, "A Further Update on New Zealand Terrorist Attack."
25. Tech Against Terrorism, "Analysis: New Zealand Attack and the Terrorist Use of the Internet."
26. Royal Commission of Inquiry, chap. 17, para. 17.
27. Kevin Roose, "The Making of a YouTube Radical," *New York Times,* June 8, 2019, https://www.nytimes.com/interactive/2019/06/08/technology/youtube-radical.html; Zoom interview with Rafal Pankowski, Never Again Foundation, February 9, 2021.
28. Cynthia Miller-Idriss, *Hate in the Homeland: The New Global Far Right* (Princeton, NJ: Princeton University Press, 2020), 66.
29. Paul Gil, "50 Famous Internet Memes and Viral Videos," *LiveAbout,* February 13, 2020, https://www.liveabout.com/internet-memes-that-have-won-our-hearts-3573553.
30. "Columbine Memes," Tumblr, accessed July 29, 2020, https://www.tumblr.com/sea rch/columbine%20memes; Malcolm Gladwell, "Thresholds of Violence," *New Yorker,* October 12, 2015, https://www.newyorker.com/magazine/2015/10/19/thresholds-of-violence.
31. Zoom interview with Jonathan Leman of Expo (Sweden), February 12, 2021.
32. As quoted in Miller-Idriss, *Hate in the Homeland,* 154.
33. Chris Schiano, "Charlottesville's Violence Planned over Discord Servers," *Unicorn Riot,* September 5, 2017, https://unicornriot.ninja/2017/charlottesville-violence-plan ned-discord-servers-unicorn-riot-reports/.
34. Royal Commission of Inquiry, pt. 4.6, no. 34.
35. Jacob Ware, "Testament to Murder: The Violent Far-Right's Increasing Use of Terrorist Manifestos," International Centre for Counter-Terrorism–The Hague (March 2020), https://icct.nl/wp-content/uploads/2020/03/Jaocb-Ware-Terrorist-Manifestos2.pdf.
36. Royal Commission of Inquiry, sec. 3.2.
37. Weiyi Cai and Simon Landon, "Attacks by White Extremists Are Growing. So Are Their Connections," *New York Times,* April 3, 2019, https://www.nytimes.com/interactive/2019/04/03/world/white-extremist-terrorism-christchurch.html; Flynn, "The Harrowing Hours and Defiant Aftermath of the New Zealand Mosque Shootings"; Sasha Polakow-Suransky and Sarah Wildman, "The Inspiration for Terrorism in New Zealand Came from France," *Foreign Policy,* March 16, 2019, https://foreignpolicy.com/2019/03/16/the-inspiration-for-terrorism-in-new-zeal and-came-from-france-christchurch-brenton-tarrant-renaud-camus-jean-raspail-identitarians-white-nationalism/.
38. Lizzie Dearden, "Revered as a Saint by Online Extremists, How Christchurch Shooter Inspired Copycat Terrorists around the World," *Independent,* August 24, 2019,

https://www.independent.co.uk/news/world/australasia/brenton-tarrant-christchu rch-shooter-attack-el-paso-norway-poway-a9076926.html.

39. "The Russians and Ukrainians Translating the Christchurch Shooter's Manifesto," *Bellingcat*, August 14, 2019, https://www.bellingcat.com/news/uk-and-europe/ 2019/08/14/the-russians-and-ukrainians-translating-the-christchurch-shooters- manifesto/.

40. Lizzie Dearden, "Man Who Stormed Mosque 'Armed with Shotguns' Was Inspired by Christchurch and El Paso Attackers, Messaging Board Post Suggests," *Independent*, August 11, 2019, https://www.independent.co.uk/news/world/europe/norway-mos que-shooting-attack-suspect-philip-manshaus-christchurch-el-paso-4chan-a9052 106.html.

41. Daniel Koehler, "The Halle, Germany, Synagogue Attack and the Evolution of the Far-Right Terror Threat," *CTC Sentinel*, December 2019, 14–20, https://ctc.usma.edu/ halle-germany-synagogue-attack-evolution-far-right-terror-threat/.

42. J. J. MacNab, U.S. Congress, House, Subcommittee on Intelligence and Counterterrorism of the Committee on Homeland Security, "Assessing the Threat from Accelerationists and Militia Extremists," 116th Congress, 2nd Session, July 16, 2020, https://homeland.house.gov/activities/hearings/assessing-the-threat-from- accelerationists-and-militia-extremists.

43. Zoom interview with J. M. Berger, February 5, 2021.

44. Kathleen Belew, *Bring the War Home: The White Power Movement and Paramilitary America* (Cambridge, MA: Harvard University Press, 2018), 120.

45. Pitcavage, "Camouflage and Conspiracy," 961.

46. Zoom interview with J. M. Berger, February 5, 2021.

47. Southern Poverty Law Center, "Stormfront," accessed July 29, 2020, https:// www.splcenter.org/fighting-hate/extremist-files/group/stormfront; Stephanie L. Hartzell, "Whiteness Feels Good Here: Interrogating White Nationalist Rhetoric on Stormfront," *Communication and Critical/Cultural Studies* 17, no. 2 (March 26, 2020): 129–148, https://doi.org/10.1080/14791420.2020.1745858.

48. Hartzell, "Whiteness Feels Good Here."

49. Val Burris, Emery Smith, and Ann Strahm, "White Supremacist Networks on the Internet," *Sociological Focus* 33, no. 2 (May 2000): 216, https://www.jstor.org/stable/ 20832076.

50. Conway et al., "Right-Wing Extremists' Persistent Online Presence," 3–5.

51. Burris et al.,., "White Supremacist Networks on the Internet."

52. Burris et al.,., "White Supremacist Networks on the Internet."

53. MacNab, "Assessing the Threat from Accelerationists and Militia Extremists."

54. Google Meet interview with Beth Goldberg, January 19, 2021.

55. Counter Extremism Project, "James Mason's Siege: Ties to Extremists," 1, https:// www.counterextremism.com/sites/default/files/james-mason-siege-ties-to-extremi sts.pdf.

56. Levinson, "With Super PAC, QAnon's Con Chases Mainstream—and Money"; Mike Wendling, "QAnon: What Is It and Where Did It Come From?," *BBC News*, July 22, 2020, https://www.bbc.com/news/53498434.

57. Colin Drury, "Commander of Feuerkrieg Far-Right Terror Group Unmasked by Police as Estonian Boy, 13," *Independent,* April 11, 2020. https://www.independent.co.uk/news/world/europe/far-right-terror-group-commander-teenage-boy-fire-war-division-estonia-a9460526.html.

58. Roose, "The Making of a YouTube Radical."

59. Amanda Perelli, "The World's Top-Earning YouTube Star Is an 8-Year-Old Boy Who Made $22 Million in a Single Year Reviewing Toys," *Business Insider,* October 20, 2019, https://www.businessinsider.com/8-year-old-youtube-star-ryan-toysreview-made-22-million-2019-10; Frances Solá-Santiago, "Meet Yuya, the 25-Year-Old Vlogger Who Makes $100,000 a Month," *Remezcla,* August 31, 2018, https://remezcla.com/lists/culture/meet-yuya-25-year-old-blogger-makes-100000-month/.

60. Megan Squire, "Alt-Tech & The Radical Right, Part 2: Inside the Radical Right's Video Addiction," Centre for Analysis of the Radical Right, September 24, 2019, https://www.radicalrightanalysis.com/2019/09/24/alt-tech-the-radical-right-part-2-inside-the-radical-rights-video-addiction/.

61. Brent Renaud, "Black Lives Matter in a Haven for White Supremacists," *Boston Globe,* June 19, 2020, https://www.bostonglobe.com/2020/06/19/opinion/black-lives-matter-haven-white-supremacists/.

62. Nicholas Kristof, "When Antifa Hysteria Sweeps America," *New York Times,* June 17, 2020, https://www.nytimes.com/2020/06/17/opinion/antifa-protests.html.

63. Robert Farley, "Was Driver Acting in Self-Defense?," FactCheck.org, August 21, 2017, https://www.factcheck.org/2017/08/driver-acting-self-defense/.

64. Judd Legum, "Murder Exposes Facebook's Boogaloo Problem," *Popular Information,* June 18, 2020, https://popular.info/p/murder-exposes-facebooks-boogaloo.

65. Anti-Defamation League, "The Boogaloo Movement," www.adl.org/boogaloo.

66. Squire, "Alt-Tech & The Radical Right, Part 2."

67. Off-the-record Zoom interview, February 2, 2021.

68. Yarno Ritzen, "Facebook Used Extensively to Spread Neo-Nazi Music," *Al Jazeera,* July 10, 2020, https://www.aljazeera.com/news/2020/7/10/exclusive-facebook-used-extensively-to-spread-neo-nazi-music.

69. Conway et al., "Right-Wing Extremists' Persistent Online Presence," 8.

70. Megan Squire, Twitter, July 10, 2020, 12:10 PM, https://twitter.com/MeganSquire0/status/1281621930987094017; Megan Squire, "Alt-Tech and the Radical Right, Part 3: Why Do Hate Groups and Terrorists Love Telegram?," Centre for Analysis of the Radical Right, February 23, 2020, https://www.radicalrightanalysis.com/2020/02/23/alt-tech-the-radical-right-part-3-why-do-hate-groups-and-terrorists-love-telegram/.

71. Zoom interview with Megan Squire, January 14, 2021.

72. Mattias Ekman, "Anti-refugee Mobilization in Social Media: The Case of the Soldiers of Odin," *Social Media & Society* 4, no. 1 (2018): 1–11.

73. Laura W. Murphy et al., "Facebook's Civil Rights Audit—Final Report," 57.

74. Center on Extremism, "New Hate and Old: The Changing Face of American White Supremacy," 2018, https://www.adl.org/media/11894/download.

75. United Nations Security Council Counter-Terrorism Committee Executive Directorate, "Member States Concerned by the Growing and Increasingly Transnational Threat of Extreme Right-Wing Terrorism" (April 2020), 7, https://www.un.org/sc/ctc/wp-content/uploads/2020/04/CTED_Trends_Alert_Extreme_Right-Wing_Terrorism.pdf.

76. Zoom interview with Heidi Beirich, January 15, 2021.

77. MacNab, "Assessing the Threat from Accelerationists and Militia Extremists."

78. Squire, Twitter, July 10, 2020.

79. Decca Muldowney, "Info Wars: Inside the Left's Online Efforts to Out White Supremacists," ProPublica, October 30, 2017, https://www.propublica.org/article/inside-the-lefts-online-efforts-to-out-white-supremacists.

80. Conway et al., "Right-Wing Extremists' Persistent Online Presence," 9.

81. Hope Not Hate, "Briefing: National Action," accessed August 7, 2020, https://www.hopenothate.org.uk/research/investigations/briefing-national-action/.

82. Lucina Di Meco and Saskia Brechenmacher, "Tackling Online Abuse and Disinformation Targeting Women in Politics," Carnegie Endowment for International Peace, November 30, 2020, https://carnegieendowment.org/2020/11/30/tackling-online-abuse-and-disinformation-targeting-women-in-politics-pub-83331.

83. "The 'Andrew Anglin' Style Guide," *Vox Popoli*, September 6, 2017, https://voxday.blogspot.com/2017/09/the-andrew-anglin-style-guide.html.

84. Center on Extremism, "New Hate and Old."

85. Conway et al., "Right-Wing Extremists' Persistent Online Presence," 12.

86. Robert Evans, "Shitposting, Inspirational Terrorism, and the Christchurch Mosque Massacre," *Bellingcat*, March 15, 2019, https://www.bellingcat.com/news/rest-of-world/2019/03/15/shitposting-inspirational-terrorism-and-the-christchurch-mosque-massacre/.

87. Robert Evans, "Ignore the Poway Synagogue Shooter's Manifesto: Pay Attention to 8chan's /pol/ Board," *Bellingcat*, April 28, 2019, https://www.bellingcat.com/news/americas/2019/04/28/ignore-the-poway-synagogue-shooters-manifesto-pay-attention-to-8chans-pol-board/.

88. Zoom interview with Heidi Beirich, January 15, 2021.

89. Yannick Veilleux-Lepage and Emil Archambault, "Mapping Transnational Extremist Networks: An Exploratory Study of the Soldiers of Odin's Facebook Network, Using Integrated Social Network Analysis," *Perspectives on Terrorism* 13, no. 2 (April 2019): 26, https://www.jstor.org/stable/26626863.

90. MacNab, "Assessing the Threat from Accelerationists and Militia Extremists."

91. Barbara Perry and Ryan Scrivens, "A Climate for Hate? An Exploration of the Right-Wing Extremist Landscape in Canada," *Critical Criminology* 26 (2018:), https://www.researchgate.net/publication/324714463_A_Climate_for_Hate_An_Exploration_of_the_Right-Wing_Extremist_Landscape_in_Canada.

92. Google Meet interview with Beth Goldberg, January 19, 2021.

93. Skype interview with Heidi Beirich, February 14, 2020.

94. Zoom interview with Cassie Miller, February 5, 2021.

95. Magnus Ranstorp and Filip Ahlin, eds., "Executive Summary: From the Nordic Resistance Movement to the Alternative Right: A study of the Swedish Radical Nationalist Milieu," Centrum För Asymmetriska Hot-Och Terrorismstudier–Försvarshögskolan (2020), https://www.fhs.se/download/18.23f6da6b173f8bed5 98498cc/1598877052261/Summary%20-%20From%20the%20Nordic%20Resista nce%20Movement%20to%20the%20Alternative%20Right%20%E2%80%93%20 a%20Study%20of%20Radical%20Nationalistic%20Environments%20in%20Swe den.pdf.

96. United Nations Security Council Counter-Terrorism Committee Executive Directorate, "Member States Concerned by the Growing and Increasingly Transnational Threat of Extreme Right-Wing Terrorism."

97. Zoom interview with Megan Squire, January 14, 2021.

98. Jeff Horwitz and Deepa Seetharaman, "Facebook Executives Shut Down Efforts to Make the Site Less Divisive," Wall Street Journal, May 26, 2020, https://www.wsj. com/articles/facebook-knows-it-encourages-division-top-executives-nixed-soluti ons-11590507499.

99. Rebecca Hersher, "What Happened When Dylann Roof Asked Google for Information about Race?," NPR, January 10, 2017, https://www.npr.org/sections/ thetwo-way/2017/01/10/508363607/what-happened-when-dylann-roof-asked-google-for-information-about-race.

100. Derek O'Callaghan, Derek Greene, Maura Conway, Joe Carthy, and Pádraig Cunningham, "Down the (White) Rabbit Hole: The Extreme Right and Online Recommender Systems," Social Science Computer Review 33, no. 4 (October 16, 2014):: 459, https://doi.org/10.1177/0894439314555329.

101. Alistair Reed, Joe Whittaker, Fabio Votta, and Seán Looney, "Radical Filter Bubbles, Social Media Personalisation Algorithms and Extreme Content," Global Research Network on Terrorism and Technology (2019), https://gnet-research.org/2020/01/ 07/radical-filter-bubbles/.

102. Roose, "The Making of a YouTube Radical."

103. Off-the-record Zoom interview, March 16, 2021.

104. "Statement by Nick Pickles" and "Statement by Derek Slater," U.S. Congress, House, Committee on Homeland Security, "Examining Social Media Companies' Efforts to Counter Online Terror Content and Misinformation," 116th Congress, 1st Session, June 26, 2019 (Washington, DC: Government Publishing Office, 2020), https://www. govinfo.gov/content/pkg/CHRG-116hhrg38783/pdf/CHRG-116hhrg38783.pdf.

105. Zoom interview with Kate Klonick, February 19, 2021.

106. Off-the-record Zoom interview with technology company official, February 2, 2021.

107. Conway et al., "Right-Wing Extremists' Persistent Online Presence"; "Statement by Nick Pickles"; Conway et al., "Right-Wing Extremists' Persistent Online Presence," 6.

108. Counter Extremism Project, "White Supremacy Groups in Europe," 17.

109. Roose, "The Making of a YouTube Radical."

110. Murphy et al., "Facebook's Civil Rights Audit—Final Report," 7–42, 56.

111. "Statement by Nick Pickles."

112. Southern Poverty Law Center, "The Year in Hate: Rage against Change," February 20, 2019, https://www.splcenter.org/fighting-hate/intelligence-report/2019/year-hate-rage-against-change.

113. Nitasha Tiku, "Tech Platforms Treat White Nationalism Different from Islamic Terrorism," *Wired*, March 20, 2019, https://www.wired.com/story/why-tech-platfo rms-dont-treat-all-terrorism-same/.

114. Julia Alexander, "YouTube Tries to Become More Transparent with In-Depth Guide to Monetization," *Verge*, June 8, 2020, https://www.theverge.com/2020/6/8/21283 843/youtube-advertising-guidelines-monetization-content-rules-hateful-content-sensitive-subjects-pranks.

115. Off-the-record Zoom interview with technology company official, February 2, 2021.

116. Zoom interview with Maura Conway, February 2, 2020.

117. Zoom interview with Maura Conway, February 2, 2020.

118. Zoom interview with J. M. Berger, February 5, 2021.

119. Squire, Twitter, July 10, 2020.

120. Adi Robertson, "Two Months Ago, the Internet Tried to Banish Nazis. No One Knows If It Worked," *Verge*, October 9, 2017, https://www.theverge.com/2017/10/9/16446920/internet-ban-nazis-white-supremacist-hosting-providers-charlottesville.

121. Will Bedingfield, "Deplatforming Works, But It's Not Enough to Fix Facebook and Twitter," *Wired,* January 15, 2021, https://www.wired.co.uk/article/deplatforming-parler-bans-qanon.

122. Virtual interview with technology company executive, January 2021.

123. "How Trust & Safety Addresses Violent Extremism on Discord," *Discord Blog,* May 25, 2021, https://blog.discord.com/how-trust-safety-addresses-violent-extremism-on-discord-c15613dae03a

124. Kate Klonick and Benjamin Wittes, "In Lieu of Fun, Episode 85)," *In Lieu of Fun*, June 19, 2020, https://www.youtube.com/watch?v=Ud0juduEvEc.

125. MacNab, "Assessing the Threat from Accelerationists and Militia Extremists."

126. Kevin Roose, "On Gab, an Extremist-Friendly Site, Pittsburgh Shooting Suspect Aired His Hatred in Full," *New York Times*, October 28, 2018, https://www.nytimes.com/2018/10/28/us/gab-robert-bowers-pittsburgh-synagogue-shootings.html.

127. Steven Johnson, "Why Cloudfare Let an Extremist Stronghold Burn," *Wired*, January 16, 2018, https://www.wired.com/story/free-speech-issue-cloudflare/.

128. William J. Broad, "Putin's Long War against American Science," *New York Times*, April 13, 2020, https://www.nytimes.com/2020/04/13/science/putin-russia-dis information-health-coronavirus.html?action=click&module=Spotlight&pgtype= Homepage.

129. Johnson, "Why Cloudfare Let an Extremist Stronghold Burn."

130. Murphy et al., "Facebook's Civil Rights Audit—Final Report," 51.

131. Zoom interview with Cassie Miller, February 5, 2021.

132. As quoted in Issie Lapowsky, "Tech Spent Years Fighting Foreign Terrorists. Then Came the Capitol Riot," *Protocol*, March 8, 2021, https://www.protocol.com/policy/big-tech-domestic-extremism#toggle-gdpr.

133. Horwitz and Seetharaman, "Facebook Executives Shut Down Efforts to Make the Site Less Divisive."

134. Mandhana and Hoyle, "Facebook Left Up Video of New Zealand Shootings for an Hour."

135. Jeff Horwitz, "Facebook Knew Calls for Violence Plagued 'Groups,' Now Plans Overhaul," *Wall Street Journal,* January 31, 2021, https://www.wsj.com/articles/faceb ook-knew-calls-for-violence-plagued-groups-now-plans-overhaul-11612131374.

136. Off-the-record interview, January 15, 2021.

137. Off-the-record interview, January 15, 2021.

138. Sarah Kaplan, "Founder of App Used by ISIS Once Said 'We Shouldn't Feel Guilty.' On Wednesday He Banned Their Accounts," *Washington Post*, November 19, 2015, https://www.washingtonpost.com/news/morning-mix/wp/2015/11/19/founder- of-app-used-by-isis-once-said-we-shouldnt-feel-guilty-on-wednesday-he-banned- their-accounts/.

139. Zoom interview with Cassie Miller, February 5, 2021.

140. Megan Squire, "Alt-Tech & the Radical Right, Part 1: Why the Shift? Why Do Hate Groups and Terrorists Love Telegram?," Centre for Analysis of the Radical Right, February 23, 2020, https://www.radicalrightanalysis.com/2020/02/23/alt-tech-the- radical-right-part-3-why-do-hate-groups-and-terrorists-love-telegram/.

141. Off-the-record interview, January 15, 2021.

142. Soufan Center, "White Supremacy Extremism: The Transnational Rise of the Violent White Supremacist Movement," September 2019, 52, https://thesoufancen ter.org/research/white-supremacy-extremism-the-transnational-rise-of-the-viol ent-white-supremacist-movement/.

143. Natasha Lomas, "Facebook's AI Couldn't Spot Mass Murder," *TechCrunch*, March 21, 2019, https://social.techcrunch.com/2019/03/21/facebooks-ai-couldnt-spot- mass-murder/.

144. Koh, "Why Video of New Zealand Massacre Can't Be Stamped Out."

145. Murphy et al., "Facebook's Civil Rights Audit—Final Report," 51–56.

146. Olivia B. Waxman, "Here's the Real Reason We Associate 420 with Weed," *Time*, April 13, 2018, https://time.com/4292844/420-april-20-marijuana-pot-holiday- history/.

147. Off-the-record interview, January 15, 2021.

148. Murphy et al., "Facebook's Civil Rights Audit—Final Report," 51.

149. Zoom interview with Rafal Pankowski, Never Again Foundation, February 9, 2021.

150. Casey Newton, "The Trauma Floor," *Verge*, February 25, 2019, https://www.theve rge.com/2019/2/25/18229714/cognizant-facebook-content-moderator-interviews- trauma-working-conditions-arizona.

151. Tiku, "Tech Platforms Treat White Nationalism Different from Islamic Terrorism."

152. Off-the-record interview, January 15, 2021.

153. Matthew Prince, "Terminating Service for 8Chan," *Cloudflare Blog*, August 4, 2019, https://blog.cloudflare.com/terminating-service-for-8chan/.

154. As quoted in Conway et al., "Right-Wing Extremists' Persistent Online Presence," 9.

155. Roose, "On Gab, an Extremist-Friendly Site, Pittsburgh Shooting Suspect Aired His Hatred in Full."

156. Conway et al., "Right-Wing Extremists' Persistent Online Presence," 10.

157. Koehler, "The Halle, Germany, Synagogue Attack and the Evolution of the Far-Right Terror Threat," 14–20.

158. Evans, "Ignore the Poway Synagogue Shooter's Manifesto."

159. Southern Poverty Law Center, "SPLC Report: Nearly 100 Murdered by Stormfront Users," April 17, 2014, https://www.splcenter.org/hatewatch/2014/04/17/splc-rep ort-nearly-100-murdered-stormfront-users.

160. Squire, Twitter, July 10, 2020; Zoom interview with Megan Squire, January 14, 2021.

161. Will Bedingfield, "Deplatforming Works, But It's Not Enough to Fix Facebook and Twitter."

162. Manoel Horta Ribeiro et al., "Does Platform Migration Compromise Content Moderation? Evidence from r/The_Donald and r/Incels," *24th ACM Conference on Computer-Supported Cooperative Work and Social Computing* (October 2020), https://arxiv.org/abs/2010.10397.

163. Off-the-record interview, January 15, 2021.

164. Micah Loewinger and Hampton Stall, "Revealed: Walkie-Talking App Zello Hosted Far-Right Groups Who Stormed Capitol," *Guardian,* January 13, 2021, https://www. theguardian.com/us-news/2021/jan/13/zello-app-us-capitol-attack-far-right.

165. Zoom interview with Megan Squire, January 14, 2021.

166. Zoom interview with Daniel Koehler, January 13, 2021.

167. James L. Walker, "Brandenburg v. Ohio (1969)," in *The First Amendment Encyclopedia* (Murfreesboro: Middle Tennessee State University, 2009), https://www.mtsu.edu/ first-amendment/article/189/brandenburg-v-ohio.

168. Tarleton Gillespie, "Regulation of and by Platforms," in *SAGE Handbook of Social Media* eds. Jean Burgess, Thomas Poell, and Alice Marwick (2017), https://www. microsoft.com/en-us/research/wp-content/uploads/2016/12/Gillespie-Regulation-ofby-Platforms-PREPRINT.pdf.).

169. Mary Wood, "At Cutting Edge of Free Speech, Citron Advocates for Reform," February 15, 2021, https://www.law.virginia.edu/news/202102/cutting-edge-free-speech-citron-advocates-reform.

170. Zoom interview with Kate Klonick, February 19, 2021.

171. Horwitz and Seetharaman, "Facebook Executives Shut Down Efforts to Make the Site Less Divisive."

172. Zoom interview with Rafal Pankowski, Never Again Foundation, February 9, 2021.

173. Tiku, "Tech Platforms Treat White Nationalism Different from Islamic Terrorism."

174. Off-the-record Zoom interview with technology company officer, February 2, 2021.

175. Joseph Cox and Jason Koebler, "Why Won't Twitter Treat White Supremacy Like ISIS? Because It Would Mean Banning Some Republican Politicians Too," *Vice,* April 25, 2019, https://www.vice.com/en_us/article/a3xgq5/why-wont-twitter-treat-white-supremacy-like-isis-because-it-would-mean-banning-some-republican-poli ticians-too.

176. Murphy et al., "Facebook's Civil Rights Audit—Final Report," 40.

177. Em Steck and Andrew Kaczynski, "In Reference to Facebook Posts Made by Marjorie Taylor Greene," *CNN*, January 26, 2021, https://www.cnn.com/2021/01/26/politics/marjorie-taylor-greene-democrats-violence/index.html.

178. "Arrested Klansman Tells of Plot to Kill Rights Lawyer," *Los Angeles Times*, February 10, 1985, https://www.latimes.com/archives/la-xpm-1985-02-10-mn-3361-story.html.

179. Jason Wilson, "Google Giving Far-Right Users' Data to Law Enforcement, Documents Reveal," *Guardian*, August 17, 2020, https://www.theguardian.com/technology/2020/aug/17/google-giving-user-data-authorities-documents-reveal.

180. Maik Baumgartner, Julia Juttner, Roman Lehberger, Sven Robel, Fidelius Schmid, and Wolf Wiedmann-Schmidt, "Teutonico and Its Terror Cell."

181. Seth G. Jones, "The Rise of Far-Right Extremism in the United States," Center for Strategic and International Studies (November 2018), 1–9, https://www.csis.org/analysis/rise-far-right-extremism-united-states.

182. Zoom interview with Megan Squire, January 14, 2021.

183. Drew Harwell and Craig Timberg, "How America's Surveillance Networks Helped the FBI Catch the Capitol Mob," *Washington Post*, April 2, 2021, https://www.washingtonpost.com/technology/2021/04/02/capitol-siege-arrests-technology-fbi-privacy/.

184. Off-the-record Zoom interview, March 16, 2021.

185. Off-the-record Zoom interview with technology company official, February 2, 2021.

186. Zoom interview with J. M. Berger, February 5, 2021.

Chapter 6

1. Patrick Crusius, "The Inconvenient Truth," Internet Archive, https://archive.org/details/patrickcrusiusmanifesto.

2. Peter Baker and Michael D. Shear, "El Paso Shooting Suspect's Manifesto Echoes Trump's Language," *New York Times*, August 4, 2019, https://www.nytimes.com/2019/08/04/us/politics/trump-mass-shootings.html.

3. Arie Perliger, *American Zealots: Inside Right-Wing Domestic Terrorism* (New York: Columbia University Press, 2020), 90–91.

4. Perliger, *American Zealots*, 92–106.

5. Gideon Rachman, "Iran, David Duke and Me," *Financial Times*, December 12, 2006, https://web.archive.org/web/20061213212318/http://blogs.ft.com/rachmanblog/2006/12/iran_david_duke.html#more.

6. Stephen Vertigans, "Beyond the Fringe? Radicalisation within the American Far-Right," *Totalitarian Movements and Political Religions* 8, no. 3–4 (2007): 646–650.

7. Kathleen Belew, *Bring the War Home: The White Power Movement and Paramilitary America* (Cambridge, MA: Harvard University Press, 2018), 44.

8. Nikki Ramirez, "A Racist Conspiracy Theory Called the 'Great Replacement' Has Made Its Way from the Far-Right Media to the GOP," *Business Insider*, September 7, 2020, https://www.businessinsider.com/racist-great-replacement-conspiracy-far-alt-right-gop-mainstream-2020-9; Southern Poverty Law Center, "The Year in

Hate and Extremism 2019," March 18, 2020, https://www.splcenter.org/news/2020/03/18/year-hate-and-extremism-2019; Southern Poverty Law Center, "The Year in Hate: Rage against Change," February 20, 2019, https://www.splcenter.org/fighting-hate/intelligence-report/2019/year-hate-rage-against-change.

9. Zoom interview with Peter Simi, January 6, 2021.

10. Vanessa Williamson and Isabella Gelfand, "Trump and Racism: What Do the Data Say?," Brookings, August 14, 2019, https://www.brookings.edu/blog/fixgov/2019/08/14/trump-and-racism-what-do-the-data-say/.

11. Southern Poverty Law Center, "The Year in Hate."

12. Perliger, *American Zealots*, 90–92.

13. Zoom interview with Rafal Pankowski, Never Again Foundation, February 9, 2021.

14. Zoom interview with Cassie Miller, February 5, 2021.

15. Belew, *Bring the War Home*, 4.

16. James Mason, *Siege*, 3rd ed., September 5, 2017, ironmarch.org, 39. *Siege* has been taken down from many websites, and the citations are taken from the author's private copy, which came from the above source.

17. Mason, *Siege*, 43.

18. FBI, "State of the Domestic White Nationalist Extremist Movement in the United States," December 13, 2006,https://archive.org/details/foia_FBI_Monograph-State_of_Domestic_White_Nationalist_Extremist_Movement_in_the_U.S., 5.

19. As quoted in Betty A. Dobratz and Stephanie L. Shanks-Meile, "The Strategy of White Separatism," *Journal of Political and Military Sociology* 34, no. 1 (Summer 2006): 54; capitalization as in the original.

20. Steven Hahn, "'Extravagant Expectations' of Freedom: Rumour, Political Struggle, and the Christmas Insurrection Scare of 1865 in the American South," *Past & Present* 157, no. 1 (November 1997): 122–158, https://doi.org/10.1093/past/157.1.122.

21. Belew, *Bring the War Home*, 40, 108.

22. Anti-Defamation League, "Feuerkrieg Division," accessed June 18, 2020, https://www.adl.org/resources/backgrounders/feuerkrieg-division-fkd.

23. Alexander Mallin and Luke Barr, "Inside the Neo-Nazi Hate Group 'the Base,' Which Is the Center of an FBI Investigation," *ABC News*, January 23, 2020, https://abcnews.go.com/US/inside-neo-nazi-hate-group-base-center-fbi/story?id=68459758.

24. Original Beam video was available at https://www.youtube.com/watch?v=yV14nQIzMjU. Since removed by YouTube.

25. Mason, *Siege*, 12, 51, quote on 304.

26. Leaked chats available at https://twitter.com/UR_Ninja/status/1173768129068990464?s=20.

27. Leaked chats available at https://twitter.com/UR_Ninja/status/1173768129068990464?s=20.

28. United States v. Allen et al., 6:16-cr-10141-EFM, "Sealed Criminal Complaint," October 14, 2016, https://www.courtlistener.com/recap/gov.uscourts.ksd.114048/gov.uscourts.ksd.114048.1.0.pdf; United States v. Allen et al., 6:16-cr-10141-EFM,

"Government's Sentencing Memorandum, And, in the Alternative, Motion for Upward Departure and/or Variance," October 29, 2018.

29. Andy Beckett, "Accelerationism: How a Fringe Philosophy Predicted the World We Live In," *Guardian*, May 11, 2017, https://www.theguardian.com/world/2017/may/11/accelerationism-how-a-fringe-philosophy-predicted-the-future-we-live-in.

30. Mason, *Siege*, 61.

31. Leaked chats available at https://twitter.com/UR_Ninja/status/1173768129068990464?s=20.

32. J. J. MacNab, U.S. Congress, House, Subcommittee on Intelligence and Counterterrorism of the Committee on Homeland Security, "Assessing the Threat from Accelerationists and Militia Extremists," 116th Congress, 2nd Session, July 16, 2020, 6, https://docs.house.gov/meetings/HM/HM05/20200716/110911/HMTG-116-HM05-Wstate-MacNabJ-20200716.pdf.

33. Jamestown Foundation, "Belgium and the Netherlands Ring in the New Year under the Shadow of Terrorism," January 15, 2008, https://jamestown.org/program/belgium-and-the-netherlands-ring-in-the-new-year-under-the-shadow-of-terrorism/.

34. Khaled Diab, "Neo-Nazism Is Europe's Hidden Terrorist Menace," *Guardian*, July 11, 2010, https://www.theguardian.com/commentisfree/2010/jul/11/islam-white-racist-terror-attack.

35. "German Far-Right Group 'Planned Attacks on Mosques,'" *BBC News*, February 17, 2020, https://www.bbc.com/news/world-europe-51526357.

36. "Anatomy of a Movement," *World Press Review*, December 1980, 39, as quoted in Bruce Hoffman, "Right-Wing Terrorism in Europe," RAND Corporation, N-1856-AF (March 1982), https://apps.dtic.mil/dtic/tr/fulltext/u2/a114129.pdf, 2.

37. Tobias Hof, "From Extremism to Terrorism: The Radicalisation of the Far Right in Italy and West Germany," *Contemporary European History* 27, no. 3 (August 2018): 412–431, https://doi.org/10.1017/S096077731800019X.

38. For Pew Research polling, see Pew Research, "Partisan Antipathy: More Real, More Intense," October 9, 2019, https://www.pewresearch.org/politics/2019/10/10/partisan-antipathy-more-intense-more-personal/; Pew Research, "Voters' Attitudes about Race and Gender Are Even More Divided Than in 2016," September 10, 2020, https://www.pewresearch.org/politics/2020/09/10/voters-attitudes-about-race-and-gender-are-even-more-divided-than-in-2016/.

39. MacNab, "Assessing the Threat from Accelerationists and Militia Extremists," 5.

40. Mason, *Siege*, 49, and with the quote, 304.

41. Leaked chats available at https://twitter.com/UR_Ninja/status/1173768129068990464?s=20.

42. Mason, *Siege*, 129, 305.

43. Mason, *Siege*, 129, 305.

44. Belew, Bring the War Home, 143.

45. Josephine Huetlin, "Vigilante 'Justice' Targets Europe's Migrants," *Daily Beast*, May 22, 2017, https://www.thedailybeast.com/germanys-lynch-mob-vigilantes-they-hunt-immigrants.

46. Bridge Initiative, Georgetown University, "Factsheet: Soldiers of Odin," March 9, 2019, https://bridge.georgetown.edu/research/factsheet-soldiers-of-odin/.

47. Paul Jackson, "Transnational Neo-Nazism in the USA, United Kingdom and Australia" *The George Washington University Program on Extremism*, February 2020, 5.

48. Daniel Trilling, "Golden Dawn: The Rise and Fall of Greece's Neo-Nazis," *Guardian*, March 3, 2020, https://www.theguardian.com/news/2020/mar/03/golden-dawn-the-rise-and-fall-of-greece-neo-nazi-trial.

49. Southern Poverty Law Center, "The Year in Hate."

50. Belew, Bring the War Home, 161.

51. Joseph Stabile, "Pursuit of an Ethnostate: Political Culture and Violence in the Pacific Northwest," *Georgetown Security Studies Review* 7, no. 2 (August 2019), https://georgetownsecuritystudiesreview.org/wp-content/uploads/2019/09/Download-File.pdf.

52. As quoted in Betty A. Dobratz and Stephanie L. Shanks-Meile, "The Strategy of White Separatism," *Journal of Political and Military Sociology* 34, no. 1 (Summer 2006): 63.

53. Pierce and Berry, as quoted in Dobratz and Shanks-Meile, "The Strategy of White Separatism," 62, 70.

54. Jeffrey Kaplan, "'Leaderless Resistance,'" *Terrorism and Political Violence* 9, no. 3 (1997): 87–88, https://doi.org/10.1080/09546559708427417.

55. Belew, Bring the War Home, 133.

56. Louis Beam, "Leaderless Resistance," *Seditionist*, February 1992, http://www.louisbeam.com/leaderless.htm.

57. Belew, *Bring the War Home*, 108.

58. Beam, "Leaderless Resistance."

59. J. M. Berger, "The Strategy of Violent White Supremacy Is Evolving," *Atlantic*, August 7, 2019, https://www.theatlantic.com/ideas/archive/2019/08/the-new-strategy-of-violent-white-supremacy/595648/.

60. 22 of July Commission, "Report of the 22 of July Commission—Preliminary English Version of Selected Chapters," August 13, 2012, https://www.regjeringen.no/contentassets/bb3dc76229c64735b4f6eb4dbfcdbfe8/en-gb/pdfs/nou2012_14_eng.pdf.

61. Mark Pitcavage, "Cerberus Unleashed: The Three Faces of the Lone Wolf Terrorist," *American Behavioral Scientist* 59, no. 13 (2015): 8, https://journals.sagepub.com/doi/pdf/10.1177/0002764215588817.

62. Anti-Defamation League, "Hate beyond Borders: The Internationalization of White Supremacy" (2019), https://www.adl.org/media/13538/download; "Executive Summary," in "From the Nordic Resistance Movement to the Alternative Right: A Study of the Swedish Radical Nationalist Milieu," ed. Magnus Ranstorp and Filip Ahlin, Centrum För Asymmetriska Hot-Och Terrorismstudier (CATS) (2020), https://www.fhs.se/download/18.23f6da6b173f8bed598498cc/1598877052261/Summary%20-%20From%20the%20Nordic%20Resistance%20Movement%20to%20the%20Alternative%20Right%20%E2%80%93%20a%20Study%20of%20Radical%20Nationalistic%20Environments%20in%20Sweden.pdf.

63. Jake Hanrahan, Twitter, December 10, 2019, 8:38 AM, https://twitter.com/Jake_Hanrahan/status/1204395058608381952.

64. United States Senate Youth Program, "Director Rasmussen Opening Remarks," March 9, 2017, https://www.dni.gov/files/NCTC/documents/news_documents/NJR _Senate-Youth-Program-Final.pdf.

65. Berger, "The Strategy of Violent White Supremacy Is Evolving."

66. Bart Schuurman, Lasse Lindekilde, Stefan Malthaner, Francis O'Connor, Paul Gill, and Noémie Bouhana, "End of the Lone Wolf: The Typology That Should Not Have Been," *Studies in Conflict & Terrorism* 42, no. 8 (2019): 771–778, https://doi.org/10.1080/1057610X.2017.1419554.

67. "The Secret History of White Power," *New York Times*, May 19, 2018, https://www.nytimes.com/2018/05/19/us/the-secret-history-of-white-power.html.

68. Souad Mekhennet and Rachel Weiner, "As Trump Vows Crackdown on 'Antifa,' Growth of Right-Wing Extremism Frustrates Europeans," *Washington Post,* June 5, 2020, https://www.washingtonpost.com/national-security/as-trump-vows-crackdown-on-antifa-growth-of-right-wing-extremism-frustrates-europeans/2020/06/05/7006eb40-9b94-11ea-ad09-8da7ec214672_story.html.

69. Eric Hollyoak (pseudonym for Steven Barry), "The Fallacy of Leaderless Resistance," *Resistance Magazine* 10 (Winter 2000): 14–18.

70. Leaked chats available at https://twitter.com/UR_Ninja/status/1173768129068990464?s=20.

71. Mason, *Siege*, 111.

72. Leaked chats available at: https://twitter.com/UR_Ninja/status/1173768129068990464?s=20.

73. Perliger, *American Zealots*, 11.

74. Phillip W. Gray, "Leaderless Resistance, Networked Organization, and Ideological Hegemony," *Terrorism and Political Violence* 25, no. 5 (2013): 655–671, https://doi.org/10.1080/09546553.2012.674077.

75. Berger, "The Strategy of Violent White Supremacy Is Evolving."

76. Leaked chats available at https://twitter.com/UR_Ninja/status/1173768129068990464?s=20.

77. As quoted in Pitcavage, "Cerberus Unleashed," 10. See also 11 for white supremacists' critiques of the leaderless resistance concept.

78. Perliger, *American Zealots*, 83.

79. FBI and Department of Homeland Security, "Strategic Intelligence Assessment and Data on Domestic Terrorism" (May 2021), 8, https://www.fbi.gov/file-repository/fbi-dhs-domestic-terrorism-strategic-report.pdf/view.

Chapter 7

1. "Domestic Violence Extremism Poses Heightened Threat in 2021," *Office of the Director of National Intelligence*, March 1, 2021, https://www.dni.gov/files/ODNI/documents/assessments/UnclassSummaryofDVEAssessment-17MAR21.pdf.

2. Arie Perliger, *American Zealots: Inside Right-Wing Domestic Terrorism* (New York: Columbia University Press, 2020), 83, 119.

3. See the Anti-Defamation League heat map at adl.org, with terms selected for white supremacists and by year.

4. Weiyi Cai and Simone Landon, "Attacks by White Extremists Are Growing. So Are Their Connections," *New York Times*, April 3, 2019, https://www.nytimes.com/interactive/2019/04/03/world/white-extremist-terrorism-christchurch.html; Jeff Asher, "Why There's Not Much Data on Anti-Asian Violence," *Lawfare*, March 23, 2021.

5. Perliger, *American Zealots*, 74–81, 110.

6. U.S. Congress, House, Hate Crime Statistics Act, HR 1048, 101st Cong., 1st sess., introduced in House, February 22, 1989, https://www.govtrack.us/congress/bills/101/hr1048/text.

7. FBI, "2019 Hate Crime Statistics," 2019 https://ucr.fbi.gov/hate-crime/2019.

8. Robert O'Harrow, Jr., Andra Ba Tran, and Derek Hawkins, "The Rise of Domestic Extremism in America," *Washington Post*, April 12, 2021, https://www.washingtonpost.com/investigations/interactive/2021/domestic-terrorism-data/.

9. Seth G. Jones, Catrina Doxsee, and Nicholas Harrington, "The Tactics and Targets of Domestic Terrorists," Center for Strategic and International Studies, July 30, 2020, 1, https://csis-website-prod.s3.amazonaws.com/s3fs-public/publication/200729_Jones_TacticsandTargets_v4_FINAL.pdf.

10. Jones et al., "The Tactics and Targets of Domestic Terrorists," 4.

11. Audrey Carlsen and Sahil Chinoy, "How to Buy a Gun in 16 Countries," *New York Times*, August 6, 2019, https://www.nytimes.com/interactive/2018/03/02/world/international-gun-laws.html; Jonathan Masters, "How Do U.S. Gun Laws Compare to Other Countries?," *PBS NewsHour*, June 13, 2016, https://www.pbs.org/newshour/nation/how-do-u-s-gun-laws-compare-to-other-countries.

12. Jacob Aasland Ravndal, Sofia Lygren, Anders Ravik Jupskås, and Tore Bjørgo, "RTV Trend Report 2020: Right-Wing Terrorism and Violence in Western Europe, 1990–2019," University of Ohio: C-Rex—Center for Research on Extremism (2020), https://www.sv.uio.no/c-rex/english/topics/online-resources/rtv-dataset/rtv_trend_report_2020.pdf.

13. Hannah Allam, "Vehicle Attacks Rise as Extremists Target Protesters," *NPR*, June 21, 2020, https://www.npr.org/2020/06/21/880963592/vehicle-attacks-rise-as-extremists-target-protesters; Neena Satija, Emily Davies, and Dalton Bennett, "Amid Massive Demonstrations, Vehicles Striking Protesters Raise Disturbing Echoes of 2017 Charlottesville Attack," *Washington Post*, June 15, 2020, https://www.washingtonpost.com/investigations/2020/06/15/cars-ramming-protests/.

14. Daniel Koehler, "The Halle, Germany, Synagogue Attack and the Evolution of the Far-Right Terror Threat," *CTC Sentinel* 12, no. 11 (December 2019): 14–20, https://ctc.usma.edu/halle-germany-synagogue-attack-evolution-far-right-terror-threat/.

15. Stephen Vertigans, "Beyond the Fringe? Radicalisation within the American Far-Right," *Totalitarian Movements and Political Religions* 8, no. 3–4 (2007): 641–659, https://doi.org/10.1080/14690760701571254.

16. Perliger, *American Zealots*, 121–123.

17. Steven M. Chermak, Joshua D. Freilich, William S. Parkin, and James Lynch, "American Terrorism and Extremist Crime Data Sources and Selectivity Bias: An Investigation Focusing on Homicide Events Committed by Far-Right Extremists," *Journal of Quantitative Criminology* 28, no. 1 (2012): 191–218, https://link.springer.com/article/10.1007/s10940-011-9156-4.

18. Europol, "European Union Terrorism Situation and Trend Report" (2020), https://www.europol.europa.eu/activities-services/main-reports/european-union-terrorism-situation-and-trend-report-te-sat-2020; Clare Ellis, Raffaello Pantucci, Jeanine de Roy van Zuijdewijn, Edwin Bakker, Benoît Gomis, Simon Palombi, and Melanie Smith, "Lone-Actor Terrorism Analysis Paper," Royal United Services Institute for Defence and Security Studies 4 (2016), 21, http://icct.nl/wp-content/uploads/2016/02/CLAT-Series-4-Analysis-Paper.pdf.

19. YLE Staff, "Most Members of Far-Right PVL and Soldiers of Odin Have Criminal Records," *YLE News*, December 3, 2018, https://yle.fi/uutiset/osasto/news/most_members_of_far-right_pvl_and_soldiers_of_odin_have_criminal_records/10537622.

20. Pete Simi, "Unpacking the Links between Ideas and Violent Extremism," George Washington University Program on Extremism, August 2020, 9, https://extremism.gwu.edu/sites/g/files/zaxdzs2191/f/Simi%20-%20Ideas%20and%20Violence%20final.pdf.

21. Simi, "Unpacking the Links between Ideas and Violent Extremism," 11.

22. Zoom interview with Peter Simi, January 6, 2021.

23. "Domestic Violence Extremism Poses Heightened Threat in 2021."

24. On membership, see Joshua D. Freilich, Steven M. Chermak, and David Caspi, "Critical Events in the Life Trajectories of Domestic Extremist White Supremacist Groups: A Case Study Analysis of Four Violent Organizations," *Criminology & Public Policy* 8, no. 3 (August 2009): 497–530, https://doi.org/10.1111/j.1745-9133.2009.00572.x.

25. Miller-Idriss, *Hate in the Homeland*, 20.

26. Perliger, *American Zealots*, 83, 119.

27. Soufan Center, "The Atomwaffen Division: The Evolution of the White Supremacy Threat" (August 2020), https://thesoufancenter.org/research/the-atomwaffen-division-the-evolution-of-the-white-supremacy-threat/; Alexander Mallin and Luke Barr, "Inside the Neo-Nazi Hate Group 'the Base,' Which Is the Center of an FBI Investigation," *ABC News*, January 23, 2020, https://abcnews.go.com/US/inside-neo-nazi-hate-group-base-center-fbi/story?id=68459758.

28. Anti-Defamation League, "Murder and Extremism in the United States in 2020" (2021), https://www.adl.org/media/15825/download.

29. Dave Morris, "A Cultural History of Neo-Nazi Rock," *Globe and Mail*, August 7, 2012, https://www.theglobeandmail.com/arts/music/a-cultural-history-of-neo-nazi-rock/article4468118/.

30. Perliger, *American Zealots*, 10.

31. Jonathan Krohn, "How a Gay Teen, an Internet Nazi, and a Late-Night Rendezvous Turned to Tragedy," *Mother Jones*, March/April 2019, https://www.motherjones.com/

crime-justice/2019/03/how-a-gay-teen-an-internet-nazi-and-a-late-night-rendezv
ous-turned-to-tragedy/.

32. Soufan Center, "The Atomwaffen Division"; Mallin and Barr, "Inside the Neo-Nazi Hate Group 'the Base'"; United States v. Lemley, Jr. et al., 8:20-cr-00033-TDC, "Motion for Detention Pending Trial," January 21, 2020, https://www.courtlistener.com/recap/gov.uscourts.mdd.474939/gov.uscourts.mdd.474939.33.0.pdf; Zoom interview with Cassie Miller, February 5, 2021.

33. Miller-Idriss, *Hate in the Homeland*, 18.

34. Zoom interview with J. M. Berger, February 5, 2021.

35. See the statement by the Anti-Defamation League in U.S. Congress, House, Committee on Homeland Security, Hearing, "World-Wide Threats: Keeping America Secure in the New Age of Terror," 115th Congress, 1st Session, November 30, 2017 (Washington, DC: Government Printing Office, 2018), https://www.govinfo.gov/content/pkg/CHRG-115hhrg29474/pdf/CHRG-115hhrg29474.pdf.

36. Southern Poverty Law Center, "Hate Groups Reach Record High," February 19, 2019, https://www.splcenter.org/news/2019/02/19/hate-groups-reach-record-high.

37. Mallin and Barr, "Inside the Neo-Nazi Hate Group 'the Base.'"

38. Google Meet interview with Beth Goldberg, January 19, 2021.

39. Microsoft Teams interview with analysts at the Community Security Trust, February 12, 2021.

40. Katrin Bennhold and Michael Schwirtz, "Capitol Riots Puts Spotlight on 'Apocalyptically Minded' Global Far Right," *New York Times*, January 24, 2021, https://www.nytimes.com/2021/01/24/world/europe/capitol-far-right-global.html.

41. Associated Press, "Police Fail to Consistently Report Hate Crime Numbers to FBI, AP Investigation Finds," June 3, 2016, https://www.oregonlive.com/data/2016/06/no_full_accounting_of_hate_cri.html.

42. Zoom interview with Jacob Aasland Ravndal, January 27, 2021.

43. Zoom interview with Rafal Pankowski, Never Again Foundation, February 9, 2021.

44. FBI, "2019 Hate Crime Statistics."

45. Asher, "Why There's Not Much Data on Anti-Asian Violence."

46. Ryan Katzfor, "Hate Crime Law Results in Few Convictions and Lots of Disappointment," ProPublica, April 10, 2017, https://www.propublica.org/article/hate-crime-law-results-in-few-convictions-and-lots-of-disappointment; phone interview with Michael German, January 5, 2021.

47. Zoom interview with [anonymous], January 26, 2021.

48. Asher, "Why There's Not Much Data on Anti-Asian Violence."

49. Katzfor, "Hate Crime Law Results in Few Convictions and Lots of Disappointment."

50. Phone interview with Michael German, January 5, 2021.

51. Zoom interview with Seamus Hughes, January 19, 2021.

52. Zoom interview with [anonymous], January 26, 2021.

53. See statistics available at the Bureau of Justice Statistics, https://www.bjs.gov/index.cfm?ty=tp&tid=37.

54. As quoted in German Lopez, "Is There a Rise in Hate Crimes in America? The Unsettling Truth: We Have No Idea," *Vox*, November 15, 2016, https://www.vox.com/identities/2016/11/15/13628200/trump-hate-crimes-racism.

55. Simone Weichselbaum, Joseph Neff, and Beth Schwartzapfel, "Why Is It So Hard to Prosecute White Extremists?," Marshall Project, April 1, 2021, https://www.themars hallproject.org/2021/04/01/why-is-it-so-hard-to-prosecute-white-extremists.

56. William Luther Pierce, "The New Protocols," November 1999, https://archive. org/stream/PierceWilliamL.FREESPEECHESSAYS19952002/Pierce%2C%20 William%20L.%20-%20FREE%20SPEECH%20ESSAYS%201995-2002_djvu.txt.)

57. Sam Jackson, "Conspiracy Theories in the Patriot/Militia Movement," George Washington University Program on Extremism, May 2017, 6–8, https://extremism. gwu.edu/sites/g/files/zaxdzs2191/f/downloads/Jackson%2C%20Conspiracy%20T heories%20Final.pdf.

58. Jackson, "Conspiracy Theories in the Patriot/Militia Movement," 9–10.

59. Mark Pitcavage, "Camouflage and Conspiracy," *American Behavioral Scientist* 44, no. 6 (February 2001): 962–965, https://doi.org/10.1177/00027640121956610.

60. "Hate beyond Borders: The Internationalization of White Supremacy," Anti-Defamation League (n.d.), https://www.adl.org/resources/reports/hate-beyond-bord ers-the-internationalization-of-white-supremacy.

61. Cipher Brief, "White Supremacists and the Weaponization of the Coronavirus (COVID-19)" (n.d.), https://www.thecipherbrief.com/column_article/white-supre macists-and-the-weaponization-of-the-coronavirus-covid-19.

62. Joel Achenbach, "A Conspiracy Theory about George Soros and a Migrant Caravan Inspired Horror," *Washington Post*, October 28, 2018, https://www.washingtonpost. com/national/a-conspiracy-theory-about-george-soros-and-a-migrant-caravan-inspired-horror/2018/10/28/52df587e-dae6-11e8-b732-3c72cbf131f2_story.html.

63. Andrew Brown, "The Myth of Eurabia: How a Far-Right Conspiracy Theory Went Mainstream," *Guardian*, August 16, 2019, https://www.theguardian.com/world/ 2019/aug/16/the-myth-of-eurabia-how-a-far-right-conspiracy-theory-went-mai nstream.

64. "How Conspiracy Theorists Have Tapped into Race and Racism to Further Their Message," *PBS Frontline*, July 28, 2020, https://www.pbs.org/wgbh/frontline/article/ how-conspiracy-theorists-have-tapped-into-race-and-racism-to-further-their-message/.

65. David Nakamura, John Hudson, and Isaac Stanley-Becker, "'Dangerous and Poisoned': Critics Blast Trump for Endorsing White-Nationalist Conspiracy Theory on South Africa," *Washington Post*, August 23, 2018, https://www.washingtonpost. com/politics/dangerous-and-poisoned-critics-blast-trump-for-endorsing-white-nationalist-conspiracy-theory-on-south-africa/2018/08/23/6c3b160e-a6df-11e8-a656-943eefab5daf_story.html.

66. Emma Grey Ellis, "That Racist Kamala Harris Birther Conspiracy Is Nothing New," *Wired*, August 19, 2020, https://www.wired.com/story/kamala-harris-racist-conspir acy-theories/.

67. Zoom interview with Peter Simi, January 6, 2021.

68. Issie Lapowsky, "Tech Spent Years Fighting Foreign Extremists. Then Came the Capitol Riot," *Protocol*, March 8, 2021, https://www.protocol.com/policy/big-tech-domestic-extremism#toggle-gdpr.

69. Kelly Weill, "Satanism Drama Is Tearing Apart the Murderous Neo-Nazi Group Atomwaffen," *Daily Beast*, March 21, 2018, https://www.thedailybeast.com/satanism-drama-is-tearing-apart-the-murderous-neo-nazi-group-atomwaffen.

70. Anti-Defamation League, "Hate beyond Borders."

71. Pitcavage, "Camouflage and Conspiracy," 969.

72. FBI, "Anti-government, Identity-based, and Fringe Political Conspiracy Theories Very Likely Motivate Some Domestic Extremists to Commit Criminal, Sometimes Violent Activity," May 30, 2019, https://www.justsecurity.org/wp-content/uploads/2019/08/420379775-fbi-conspiracy-theories-domestic-extremism.pdf.

73. Kathleen Belew, *Bring the War Home: The White Power Movement and Paramilitary America* (Cambridge, MA: Harvard University Press, 2018), 164.

74. Barbara Perry and Ryan Scrivens, "A Climate for Hate? An Exploration of the Right-Wing Extremist Landscape in Canada," *Critical Criminology* 26 (April 2018): 169–187, https://doi.org/10.1007/S10612-018-9394-Y.

75. Rachel Weiner, "Prosecutors Say an Alleged Member of a White-Supremacist Group Was Involved with Illegal Guns, Drugs," *Washington Post*, September 20, 2019, https://www.washingtonpost.com/local/public-safety/psychedelic-nazis-prosecut ors-say-member-of-white-supremacist-group-involved-with-illegal-guns-drugs/2019/09/20/8a41c880-dbbf-11e9-a688-303693fb4b0b_story.html.

76. Jeffrey Kaplan, "'Leaderless Resistance,'" *Terrorism and Political Violence* 9, no. 3 (1997): 81.

77. Freilich et al., "Critical Events in the Life Trajectories of Domestic Extremist White Supremacist Groups," 506.

78. As quoted in Will Blythe, "The Guru of White Hate," *Rolling Stone*, June 8, 2000, https://www.rollingstone.com/culture/culture-features/guru-white-hate-william-pie rce-timothy-mcveigh-831091/.

79. Freilich et al., "Critical Events in the Life Trajectories of Domestic Extremist White Supremacist Groups," 504.

80. Craig R. Whitney, "Germans Begin to Recognize Danger in Neo-Nazis' Surge," *New York Times*, October 21, 1993, https://www.nytimes.com/1993/10/21/world/sha dow-germany-special-report-germans-begin-recognize-danger-neo-nazis-surge. html; Pete Simi and Steven Windisch, "Why Radicalization Fails: Barriers to Mass Casualty Terrorism," *Terrorism and Political Violence* 32, no. 4 (2020): 840.

81. United States of America v. Brian Mark Lemley, Jr. et al., United States District Court for the District of Maryland, January 21, 2020, https://www.courtlistener.com/recap/gov.uscourts.mdd.474939/gov.uscourts.mdd.474939.33.0.pdf; A. C. Thompson, Ali Winston, and Jake Hanrahan, "Inside Atomwaffen As It Celebrates a Member for Allegedly Killing a Gay Jewish College Student," ProPublica, February 23, 2018, https://www.propublica.org/article/atomwaffen-division-inside-white-hate-group.

82. Ben Makuch and Mack Lamoureux, "Neo-Nazis Are Organizing Secretive Paramilitary Training across America," *VICE News*, November 20, 2018, https://www.vice.com/en_us/article/a3mexp/neo-nazis-are-organizing-secretive-paramilit ary-training-across-america.

83. Zoom interview with Megan Squire, January 14, 2021.

84. Soufan Center, "The Atomwaffen Division: The Evolution of the White Supremacy Threat," August 12, 2020, https://thesoufancenter.org/research/the-atomwaffen-division-the-evolution-of-the-white-supremacy-threat/; FBI, "State of the Domestic White Nationalist Extremist Movement in the United States," December 13, 2006, https://archive.org/details/foia_FBI_Monograph-State_of_Domestic_White_Nationalist_Extremist_Movement_in_the_U.S., 7.

85. Christopher F. Schuetze and Katrin Bennhold, "Far-Right Extremism Taints German Security Services in Hundreds of Cases," New York Times, October 6, 2020, https://www.nytimes.com/2020/10/06/world/europe/germany-police-far-right-report.html; Katrin Bennhold, "Body Bags and Enemy Lists: How Far-Right Police Officers and Ex-soldiers Planned for 'Day X,'" New York Times, August 1, 2020, https://www.nytimes.com/2020/08/01/world/europe/germany-nazi-infiltration.html.

86. Bill Simmons, "Key Prosecution Witness Admits to Prophecies, Visions," Associated Press, February 24, 1988.

87. Belew, Bring the War Home, 139.

88. Belew, Bring the War Home, 118–122.

89. Anna Schecter and Rich Schapiro, "Influential Neo-Nazi Eats at Soup Kitchens, Lives in Government Housing," NBC News, November 26, 2019, https://www.nbcnews.com/news/us-news/influential-neo-nazi-eats-soup-kitchens-lives-government-housing-n1091681.

90. Simi and Windisch, "Why Radicalization Fails," 841.

91. Andrew Mines and Devorah Margolin, "Cryptocurrency and the Dismantling of Terrorism Financing Campaigns," Lawfare, August 26, 2020, https://www.lawfareblog.com/cryptocurrency-and-dismantling-terrorism-financing-campaigns.

92. Freilich et al., "Critical Events in the Life Trajectories of Domestic Extremist White Supremacist Groups," 497–530.

93. Nick Ryan, "Combat 18: Memoirs of a Street-Fighting Man," Independent, February 1, 1998, https://www.independent.co.uk/arts-entertainment/combat-18-memoirs-street-fighting-man-1142204.html.

94. Clare Ellis, Raffaello Pantucci, Jeanine de Roy van Zuijdewijn, Edwin Bakker, Benoît Gomis, Simon Palombi, and Melanie Smith, "Lone-Actor Terrorism Analysis Paper," Royal United Services Institute for Defence and Security Studies, 2016, http://icct.nl/app/uploads/2016/04/201604_CLAT_Final-Report.pdf; U.S. Attorney's Office, Eastern District of Texas, "Drug-Dealing, White Supremacist Stripper Sentenced for Obstruction of Justice," August 13, 2020, https://www.justice.gov/usao-edtx/pr/drug-dealing-white-supremacist-stripper-sentenced-obstruction-justice; Christian Terry and Stephanie Frazier, "Male Stripper Accused of Drug Trafficking, Threatening to Shank Guards in Jail, Convicted on Obstruction of Justice Charges," ABC 7 KLTV, March 9, 2020, https://www.kltv.com/2020/03/09/male-stripper-accused-drug-trafficking-threatening-shank-guards-jail-convicted-obstruction-justice-charges/; Michael Gold, "Man with White Supremacist Material and Weapons Is Arrested, Police Say," New York Times, September 12, 2019, https://www.nytimes.com/2019/09/12/nyregion/white-supremacist-sussex-county.html.

95. Belew, Bring the War Home, 124.

96. Jacob Aasland Ravndal, "Right-Wing Terrorism and Militancy in the Nordic Countries: A Comparative Case Study," *Terrorism and Political Violence* 30, no. 5 (2018): 772–792, https://doi.org/10.1080/09546553.2018.1445888.

97. Perliger, *American Zealots*, 83, 119.

98. Perliger, *American Zealots*, 126.

99. Perliger, *American Zealots*, 79.

100. Anti-Defamation League, "Vanguard America," https://www.adl.org/resources/backgrounders/vanguard-america; Southern Poverty Law Center, "Patriot Front," https://www.splcenter.org/fighting-hate/extremist-files/group/patriot-front.

101. Freilich et al., "Critical Events in the Life Trajectories of Domestic Extremist White Supremacist Groups," 497–530.

102. Brett Barrouquere and Rachel Janik, "TWP Chief Matthew Heimbach Arrested for Battery after Affair with Top Spokesman's Wife," Southern Poverty Law Center, March 13, 2018, https://www.splcenter.org/hatewatch/2018/03/13/twp-chief-matthew-heimbach-arrested-battery-after-affair-top-spokesmans-wife; Halley Freger, "The Right Divided: Inside the Far-Right's Year of Turmoil after Charlottesville," *ABC News*, August 12, 2018, https://abcnews.go.com/Politics/divided-inside-rights-year-turmoil-charlottesville/story?id=57144902.

103. Zoom interview with Jacob Aasland Ravndal, January 27, 2021.

104. Makuch and Lamoureux, "Neo-Nazis Are Organizing Secretive Paramilitary Training across America."

105. Mack Lamoureux and Ben Makuch, "An American Neo-Nazi Group Has Dark Plans for Canada," *VICE Canada*, July 10, 2018, https://www.vice.com/en/article/ev847a/an-american-neo-nazi-group-has-dark-plans-for-canada; Soufan Center, "The Atomwaffen Division."

106. Perliger, *American Zealots*, 107–108.

107. Bradden Weaver, "Violence as Memory and Desire: Neo-Nazism in Contemporary Germany," in David E. Apter, ed., *The Legitimation of Violence* (London: Palgrave Macmillan, 1997), 137–138.

108. Simi and Windisch, "Why Radicalization Fails," 837–838.

109. Vegas Tenold, *Everything You Love Will Burn: Inside the Rebirth of White Nationalism in America* (New York: Nation Books, 2018), 130.

110. Zoom interview with Heidi Beirich, January 15, 2021; Tyler Bridges, "How David Duke's (Very Live) Ghost Haunts Donald Trump," *Politico*, March 12, 2016, https://www.politico.com/magazine/story/2016/03/how-david-dukes-very-live-ghost-haunts-donald-trump-213720.

111. Brian A. Jackson, "Organizational Decisionmaking by Terrorist Groups," in Paul K. Davis and Kim Cragin, eds., *Social Science for Counterterrorism: Putting the Pieces Together* (Santa Monica, CA: RAND Corporation, 2009), 213.

112. Thomas Hegghammer and Petter Nesser, "Losing the Plot: The Limits of Attack Data in Terrorism Research" (forthcoming).

113. Peter Bergen and David Sterman, "Terrorism in America after 9/11," *New America*, https://www.newamerica.org/international-security/reports/terrorism-in-america/.

114. "Hate by the Numbers," *Jigsaw* (n.d.), https://jigsaw.google.com/the-current/white-supremacy/data-visualization/.

115. Devlin Barrett, "Arrests in Domestic Terror Probes Outpace Those Inspired by Islamic Extremists," *Washington Post,* March 9, 2018, washingtonpost.com/world/national-security/arrests-in-domestic-terror-probes-outpace-those-inspired-by-islamic-extremists/2019/03/08/0bf329b6-392f-11e9-a2cd-307b06d0257b_story.html.

116. Matt Zapotopsky, "Wray Says FBI Has Recorded about 100 Domestic Terrorism Arrests in Fiscal 2019 and Many Investigations Involve White Supremacy," *Washington Post,* July 23, 2019, https://www.washingtonpost.com/national-secur ity/wray-says-fbi-has-recorded-about-100-domestic-terrorism-arrests-in-fiscal-2019-and-most-investigations-involve-white-supremacy/2019/07/23/600d49a6-aca1-11e9-bc5c-e73b603e7f38_story.html.

117. Jacob Aasland Ravndal, "Right-Wing Terrorism and Violence May Actually Have Declined," *Washington Post,* April 2, 2019, https://www.washingtonpost.com/polit ics/2019/04/02/is-right-wing-terrorism-violence-rise/.

118. Hegghammer and Nesser, "Losing the Plot."

119. Barrett, "Arrests in Domestic Terror Probes Outpace Those Inspired by Islamic Extremists."

120. As quoted in Bruce Hoffman, *Inside Terrorism* (New York: Columbia University Press, 2006), 239.

121. Dhrumil Mehta, "Americans Are More Worried about White Nationalism after El Paso," *FiveThirtyEight,* August 16, 2019, https://fivethirtyeight.com/features/americ ans-are-more-worried-about-white-nationalism-after-el-paso/.

122. Ian Shapira, "Inside Jason Kessler's Hate-Fueled Rise," *Washington Post,* August 11, 2018, https://www.washingtonpost.com/local/inside-jason-kesslers-hate-fueled-rise/2018/08/11/335eaf42-999e-11e8-b60b-1c897f17e185_story.html.

123. Beth Reingold, Kerry Haynie, and Kirsten Widner, "Women of Color Won Congressional Seats in Record Numbers. How Will They Legislate?," *Washington Post,* November 24, 2020, https://www.washingtonpost.com/politics/2020/11/24/women-color-won-congressional-seats-record-numbers-how-will-they-legislate/; Jennifer E. Manning, "Membership of the 116th Congress: A Profile," Congressional Research Service Report R45583, October 2, 2020, https://fas.org/sgp/crs/misc/R45 583.pdf.

124. See rates from the Kaiser Family Foundation at this source: Kaiser Family Foundation, "Voting and Voter Registration as a Share of the Voter Population, by Race/Ethnicity," November 2018, https://www.kff.org/other/state-indicator/voting-and-voter-registration-as-a-share-of-the-voter- population-by-raceethnicity/?currentTimeframe=0&sortModel=%7B%22colId%22:%22Location%22,%22sort%22:%22asc%22%7D.

125. For writings on the legacy of racism, see Ta-Nehisi Coates, "The Case for Reparations," *Atlantic,* June 2014, https://www.theatlantic.com/magazine/archive/2014/06/the-case-for-reparations/361631/.

126. Naa Oyo A. Kwate and Melody S. Goodman, "Cross-sectional and Longitudinal Effects of Racism on Mental Health among Residents of Black Neighborhoods in New York City," *American Journal of Public Health* 105, no. 4 (April 2015): 711–718, https://dx.doi.org/10.2105%2FAJPH.2014.302243.

127. Zoom interview with Rafal Pankowski, Never Again Foundation, February 9, 2021.

128. Southern Poverty Law Center, "The Year in Hate and Extremism 2019," March 18, 2020, https://www.splcenter.org/news/2020/03/18/year-hate-and-extrem ism-2019.

129. Claire Brockway and Carroll Doherty, "Growing Share of Republicans Say U.S. Risks Losing Its Identity If It Is Too Open to Foreigners," Pew Research Center, July 17, 2019, https://www.pewresearch.org/fact-tank/2019/07/17/growing-share-of-repu blicans-say-u-s-risks-losing-its-identity-if-it-is-too-open-to-foreigners/; Juliana Menasce Horowitz and Ruth Igielnik, "A Century after Women Gained the Right to Vote, Majority of Americans See Work to Do on Gender Equality," Pew Research Center, July 7, 2020, https://www.pewsocialtrends.org/2020/07/07/a-century-after-women-gained-the-right-to-vote-majority-of-americans-see-work-to-do-on-gen der-equality/?LSLSL; Anti-Defamation League, "Antisemitic Attitudes in the U.S.: A Guide to ADL's Latest Poll," January 29, 2020, https://www.adl.org/survey-of-ameri can-attitudes-toward-jews.

130. Angie Drobnic Holan, "In Context: Donald Trump's 'Very Fine People on Both Sides' Remarks (Transcript)," *PolitiFact*, April 26, 2019, https://www.politifact.com/article/2019/apr/26/context-trumps-very-fine-people-both-sides-remarks/.

131. Matt Stevens, "Half of Voters Believe President Trump Is Racist, Poll Shows," *New York Times*, July 30, 2019, https://www.nytimes.com/2019/07/30/us/politics/is-trump-racist.html.

132. Christina Wilkie and Kevin Brueninger, "Trump Officials Altered Intel to Downplay Threats from Russia, White Supremacists, DHS Whistleblower Says," CNBC, September 10, 2020, https://www.cnbc.com/2020/09/09/trump-intel-threats-rus sia-white-supremacists-dhs-whistleblower.html.

133. Alison Durkee, "More Than Half of Republicans Believe Voter Fraud Claims and Most Still Support Trump, Poll Finds," *Forbes*, April 5, 2021, https://www.forbes.com/sites/alisondurkee/2021/04/05/more-than-half-of-republicans-believe-voter-fraud-claims-and-most-still-support-trump-poll-finds/?sh=51edfb9b1b3f.

Chapter 8

1. U.S. Attorney's Office, District of Nevada, "Las Vegas Resident Who Discussed Setting Fire to a Synagogue with a White Supremacist Extremist Group Sentenced for Possession of Bomb-Making Components," November 13, 2020, https://www.justice.gov/usao-nv/pr/las-vegas-resident-who-discussed-setting-fire-synagogue-white-supremacist-extremist-group; Ken Ritter and Michael Kunzelman, "White Supremacist Sentenced to 2 Years in Bomb Plot Case," *Las Vegas Sun*, November 13,

2020, https://lasvegassun.com/news/2020/nov/13/white-supremacist-sentenced-to-2-years-in-bomb-plo/.

2. Zoom interview with Daniel Benjamin, March 4, 2021.

3. Zoom interview with Maura Conway, February 2, 2020. Italics added to reflect tone of voice in interview.

4. S. Chermak, J. Freilich, and J. Simone, "Surveying American State Police Agencies about Lone Wolves, Far-Right Criminality, and Far Right and Islamic Jihadist Criminal Collaboration," *Studies in Conflict & Terrorism* 33, no. 1 (2010): 1019–1041; Arun Kundnani, "Blind Spot? Security Narratives and Far-Right Violence in Europe," International Centre for Counter-Terrorism–The Hague, 3, no. 5 (2012); Peter Lehr, "Still Blind in the Right Eye? A Comparison of German Responses to Political Violence from the Extreme Left and the Extreme Right," in *Extreme Right Wing Political Violence and Terrorism*, eds. Max Taylor, P.M. Currie, and Donald Holbrook (London: Bloomsbury, 2013), 187–214; Barbara Perry and Ryan Scrivens, "A Climate for Hate? An Exploration of the Right-Wing Extremist Landscape in Canada," *Critical Criminology* 26 (2018): 169–187.

5. Perry and Scrivens, "A Climate for Hate."

6. Zoom interview with former senior counterterrorism official, April 21, 2021; Betty Woodruff Swan, "They Tried to Get Trump to Care about Right-Wing Terrorism. He Ignored Them," *Politico*, August 26, 2020, https://www.politico.com/news/2020/08/26/trump-domestic-extemism-homeland-security-401926.

7. Michael German, "Hidden in Plain Sight: Racism, White Supremacy, and Far-Right Militancy in Law Enforcement," Brennan Center for Justice, August 27, 2020, https://www.brennancenter.org/our-work/research-reports/hidden-plain-sight-racism-white-supremacy-and-far-right-militancy-law.

8. Michael German and Emmanuel Mauleón, "Fighting Far-Right Violence and Hate Crimes," Brennan Center for Justice, July 1, 2019, https://www.brennancenter.org/our-work/research-reports/fighting-far-right-violence-and-hate-crimes.

9. Sean Flynn, "The Harrowing Hours and Defiant Aftermath of the New Zealand Mosque Shootings," *GQ*, October 10, 2019, https://www.gq.com/story/new-zeal and-mosque-shooting-christchurch.

10. German Lopez, "The Portland Stabbing Is the Latest in a Wave of Racist Attacks across America," *Vox*, May 30, 2017, https://www.vox.com/identities/2017/5/30/15711640/portland-stabbing-hate-crime.

11. Phone interview with Michael German, January 5, 2021.

12. Drew Desilver, Michael Lipka, and Dalia Fahmy, "10 Things We Know about Race and Policing in the U.S.," Pew Research Center, June 3, 2020, https://www.pewresea rch.org/fact-tank/2020/06/03/10-things-we-know-about-race-and-policing-in-the-u-s/; "Royal Commission of Inquiry into the Terrorist Attack on Christchurch Mosques on 15 March 2019," https://christchurchattack.royalcommission.nz/the-report.

13. Katerina Papatheodorou, "Preventing, Not Just Countering, Violence Extremism," *Lawfare*, April 29, 2018; Vikram Dodd and Jamie Grierson, "Fastest-Growing UK Terrorist Threat Is from Far Right, Say Police," *Guardian*, September 19, 2019,

https://www.theguardian.com/uk-news/2019/sep/19/fastest-growing-uk-terrorist-threat-is-from-far-right-say-police.

14. Zoom interview with Maura Conway, February 2, 2020; off-the-record interview, January 19, 2021.

15. Zoom interview with Daniel Koehler, January 13, 2021.

16. Southern Poverty Law Center, "The Year in Hate and Extremism 2019," March 18, 2020, https://www.splcenter.org/news/2020/03/18/year-hate-and-extremism-2019.

17. Zoom interview with Daniel Koehler, January 13, 2021.

18. Zoom interview with Seamus Hughes, January 19, 2021.

19. German and Mauleón, "Fighting Far-Right Violence and Hate Crimes."

20. James Mason, Siege, September 5, 2017, 95–96, ironmarch.org.

21. Weichselbaum et al., "Why Is It So Hard to Prosecute White Extremists?" The Marshall Project, April 1, 2021, https://www.themarshallproject.org/2021/04/01/why-is-it-so-hard-to-prosecute-white-extremists.

22. Daniel Koehler, "Recent Trends in German Right-Wing Violence and Terrorism: What are the Contextul Factors behind 'Hive Terrorism'?" Perspectives on Terrorism 12, no. 6 (December 2018), https://www.jstor.org/stable/26544644.

23. Interview with Benjamin Wittes, February 6, 2021.

24. Anti-Defamation League, "Hutaree Militia Verdict Shows Sedition Charges Risky," March 30, 2012, https://www.adl.org/blog/hutaree-militia-verdict-shows-sedition-charges-risky.

25. Jon Lewis, Seamus Hughes, Oren Segal, and Ryan Greer, "White Supremacist Terror: Modernizing Our Approach to Today's Threat," George Washington University Program on Extremism, Anti-Defamation League (April 2020), https://extremism.gwu.edu/sites/g/files/zaxdzs2191/f/White%20Supremacist%20Terror%20final.pdf.

26. Philip Zelikow, "The Domestic Terrorism Danger: Focus on Unauthorized Private Military Groups," Lawfare, August 15, 2017, https://www.lawfareblog.com/domestic-terrorism-danger-focus-unauthorized-private-military-groups.

27. Souad Mekhennet and Rachel Weiner, "As Trump Vows Crackdown on 'Antifa,' Growth of Right-Wing Extremism Frustrates Europeans," Washington Post, June 5, 2020, https://www.washingtonpost.com/national-security/as-trump-vows-crackdown-on-antifa-growth-of-right-wing-extremism-frustrates-europeans/2020/06/05/7006eb40-9b94-11ea-ad09-8da7ec214672_story.html.

28. Interview with Benjamin Wittes, February 6, 2021.

29. United States v. Lemley, Jr. et al., Case 8:20-cr-00033-TDC, "Government's Sentencing Memo," U.S. District Court of Maryland.

30. Radio Sweden Staff, "Trial Begins for Neo-Nazi Accused of Targeting Journalists," Radio Sweden, August 23, 2018, https://sverigesradio.se/sida/artikel.aspx?programid=2054&artikel=7025697.

31. Zoom interview with Jonathan Leman of Expo (Sweden), February 12, 2021.

32. Interview with Benjamin Wittes, February 6, 2021.

33. Michel Martin, "Are Citizen Militias Legal?," NPR, August 30, 2020.

34. Erik Bleich and Francesca Lambert, "Why Are Racist Associations Free in Some States and Banned in Others? Evidence from 10 Liberal Democracies," West European

Politics 36, no. 1 (2013): 122–149; Paul Jackson, "Transnational Neo-Nazism in the USA, United Kingdom and Australia," George Washington University Program on Extremism (February 2020), https://extremism.gwu.edu/sites/g/files/zaxdzs2191/f/Jackson%20-%20Transnational%20neo%20Nazism%20in%20the%20USA%2C%20United%20Kingdom%20and%20Australia.pdf, 5.

35. Thomas Saalfeld, "Up and Down with the Extreme Right in Germany, 1949–1996," *Politics* 17, no. 1 (1997): 7.

36. Daniel Trilling, "Golden Dawn: The Rise and Fall of Greece's Neo-Nazis," *Guardian*, March 3, 2020, https://www.theguardian.com/news/2020/mar/03/golden-dawn-the-rise-and-fall-of-greece-neo-nazi-trial.

37. Stephen Vertigans, "Beyond the Fringe? Radicalisation within the American Far-Right," *Totalitarian Movements and Political Religions* 8, no. 3–4 (2007): 653; Mark Pitcavage, "Camouflage and Conspiracy: The Militia Movement from Ruby Ridge to Y2K," *American Behavioral Scientist* 44, no. 6 (February 2001): 971.

38. Phone interview with Michael German, January 5, 2021.

39. Skype interview with Heidi Beirich, February 14, 2020.

40. Alexander Gillespie, "A Year from the Christchurch Terror Attacks, NZ Intelligence Records a Surge in Reports," *Conversation*, February 26, 2020, https://theconversation.com/a-year-from-the-christchurch-terror-attacks-nz-intelligence-records-a-surge-in-reports-131895.

41. David Neiwert, "Domestic Terror in the Age of Trump," *Type Investigations*, July 9, 2020, https://www.typeinvestigations.org/investigation/2020/07/09/domestic-terror-in-the-age-of-trump/.

42. Kathleen Belew, *Bring the War Home* (Cambridge, MA: Harvard University Press, 2018), 134–137.

43. Robert Jimison, "How the FBI Smashed White Supremacist Group The Order," *East Idaho News*, October 20, 2017, https://www.eastidahonews.com/2017/10/fbi-smashed-white-supremacist-group-order/.

44. Dina Temple-Raston, "How the FBI Got inside the Hutaree Militia," NPR, April 12, 2010, https://www.npr.org/templates/story/story.php?storyId=125856761.

45. Zoom interview with J. M. Berger, February 5, 2021.

46. Mason, *Siege*, 107.

47. Counter Extremism Project, "Extremist Content Online: Telegram Continues Providing an Open Channel for Extremists to Spread Violent Propaganda, Hate Speech," May 18, 2020, https://www.counterextremism.com/press/extremist-content-online-telegram-continues-providing-open-channel-extremists-spread-violent.

48. Zoom interview with former senior counterterrorism official, April 21, 2021.

49. Weichselbaum et al., "Why Is It So Hard to Prosecute White Extremists?"

50. Zoom interview with Seamus Hughes, January 19, 2021.

51. Jackson, "Transnational Neo-Nazism in the USA, United Kingdom, and Australia," 26; "Jack Renshaw, Neo-Nazi Pedophile, Jailed for Life over Plot to Murder Labour MP," *Jewish Chronicle*, May 17, 2019, https://www.thejc.com/news/uk-news/jack-renshaw-neo-nazi-paedophile-jailed-for20-years-over-plot-to-murder-labour-mp-1.484337.

52. Microsoft Teams interview with analysts at the Community Security Trust, February 12, 2021.

53. Joshua D. Freilich, Steven M. Chermak, and David Caspi, "Critical Events in the Life Trajectories of Domestic Extremist White Supremacist Groups: A Case Study of Four Violent Organizations," *Criminology & Public Policy* 8, no. 3 (September 25, 2009):: 497–530.

54. BBC Staff, "Ethan Stables Sentenced over Gay Pride Attack Plot," *BBC News*, May 30, 2018, https://www.bbc.com/news/uk-england-cumbria-44299561.

55. Alexander Mallin and Luke Barr, "Inside the Neo-Nazi Hate Group 'the Base,'" *ABC News*, January 23, 2020, https://abcnews.go.com/US/inside-neo-nazi-hate-group-base-center-fbi/story?id=68459758.

56. Zoom interview with J. M. Berger, February 5, 2021.

57. J. M. Berger, "PATCON: The FBI's Secret War against the 'Patriot' Movement, and How Infiltration Tactics Relate to Radicalizing Influences," New America Foundation (May 2012), 4.

58. Zoom interview with J. M. Berger, February 5, 2021.

59. Interview with Benjamin Wittes, February 6, 2021.

60. Zoom interview with Daniel Benjamin, March 4, 2021.

61. J. M. Berger, "Does the F.B.I. Have an Informant Problem?," *Foreign Policy,* September 7, 2012, https://foreignpolicy.com/2012/09/07/does-the-f-b-i-have-an-informant-problem/.

62. Ben Makuch, "Audio Recording Claims Neo-Nazi Terror Group Is Disbanding," *VICE*, March 15, 2020.

63. Vikram Dodd and Jamie Grierson, "Fastest-Growing UK Terrorist Threat Is from Far Right, Say Police," *Guardian,* September 19, 2019, https://www.theguardian.com/uk-news/2019/sep/19/fastest-growing-uk-terrorist-threat-is-from-far-right-say-police.

64. Ben Makuch, "Neo-Nazi Terror Group Atomwaffen Division Re-emerges under New Name," *Vice.com*, August 5, 2020, https://www.vice.com/en_us/article/wxq7jy/neo-nazi-terror-group-atomwaffen-division-re-emerges-under-new-name.

65. United States v. Lemley, Jr. et al., Case: 8:20-cr-00033-TDC, "Motion for Detention Pending Trial," U.S. District Court of Maryland, 14.

66. Zoom interview with Seamus Hughes, January 19, 2021.

67. Zoom interview with Jacob Aasland Ravndal, January 27, 2021.

68. Zolan Kanno-Youngs, "62 Border Agents Belonged to Offensive Facebook Group, Investigation Finds," *New York Times,* July 15, 2019, https://www.nytimes.com/2019/07/15/us/politics/border-patrol-facebook-group.html; Zoom interview with J. M. Berger, February 5, 2021.

69. Franklin Foer, "How Trump Radicalized ICE," *Atlantic* (September 2018), https://www.theatlantic.com/magazine/archive/2018/09/trump-ice/565772/.

70. German, "Hidden in Plain Sight"; FBI Counterterrorism Division, "Counterterrorism Policy Directive and Policy Guide," April 1, 2015, https://www.documentcloud.org/documents/3423189-CT-Excerpt.html; "This Group Compiled Police Officers' Offensive Facebook Posts. Now Departments Are Taking Action," WRCB, June 20,

2019, https://www.wrcbtv.com/story/40686665/this-group-compiled-police-offic ers-offensive-facebook-posts-now-departments-are-taking-action.

71. German, "Hidden in Plain Sight"; J. J. MacNab, U.S. Congress, House, Subcommittee on Intelligence and Counterterrorism of the Committee on Homeland Security, "Assessing the Threat from Accelerationists and Militia Extremists," 116th Congress, 2nd Session, July 16, 2020, https://docs.house.gov/meetings/HM/HM05/20200716/ 110911/HMTG-116-HM05-Wstate-MacNabJ-20200716.pdf.

72. Phone interview with Michael German, January 5, 2021.

73. German, "Hidden in Plain Sight."

74. Will Carless and Michael Corey, "To Protect and Slur," Center for Investigative Reporting, June 14, 2019, https://www.revealnews.org/article/inside-hate-groups-on-facebook-police-officers-trade-racist-memes-conspiracy-theories-and-islam ophobia/; German, "Hidden in Plain Sight."

75. Phone interview with Michael German, January 5, 2021.

76. Associated Press, "Italian Police Breakup Neo-Fascist Plot," December 22, 2014, https://apnews.com/13709c85234a4ad6a595230deb1ba182.

77. Zoom interview with Heidi Beirich, January 15, 2021.

78. Daniel Byman, "The Intelligence War on Terrorism," *Intelligence and National Security* 29, no. 6 (2014): 837–863.

79. Zoom interview with Daniel Benjamin, March 4, 2021.

80. Zoom interview with Eric Rosand, January 21, 2021.

81. Zoom interview with Daniel Benjamin, March 4, 2021.

82. Souad Mekhennet and Rachel Weiner, "As Trump Vows Crackdown on 'Antifa,' Growth of Right-Wing Extremism Frustrates Europeans," *Washington Post,* June 5, 2020, https://www.washingtonpost.com/national-security/as-trump-vows-crackd own-on-antifa-growth-of-right-wing-extremism-frustrates-europeans/2020/06/05/ 7006eb40-9b94-11ea-ad09-8da7ec214672_story.html.

83. Zoom interview with Eric Rosand, January 21, 2021.

84. Jacob Aasland Ravndal, "Right-Wing Terrorism and Militancy in the Nordic Countries: A Comparative Case Study," *Terrorism and Political Violence* 30, no. 5 (2018): 786.

85. Tyler Bridges, "How David Duke's (Very Live) Ghost Haunts Donald Trump," *Politico,* March 12, 2016, https://www.politico.com/magazine/story/2016/03/how-david-dukes-very-live-ghost-haunts-donald-trump-213720.

86. Jesse Newell, "British Paper Says 3 Men Responsible for Trump Pushing Voter Fraud. Kobach Is One," *Kansas City Star,* October 27, 2020, https://www.kansascity.com/ news/politics-government/article246745826.html.

87. Zoom interview with Peter Simi, January 6, 2021.

88. Zoom interview with Heidi Beirich, January 15, 2021.

89. Phone interview with Kathleen Blee, March 18, 2021.

90. Off-the-record Zoom interview, March 16, 2021.

91. U.S. Congress, House, Committee on Homeland Security Hearing, "The Rise of Radicalization: Is the U.S. Government Failing to Counter International and Domestic Terrorism?," 114th Congress, 1st Session, July 15, 2015 (Washington,

DC: Government Printing Office, 2016), https://www.govinfo.gov/content/pkg/CHRG-114hhrg97916/pdf/CHRG-114hhrg97916.pdf.

92. Nitasha Tiku, "Tech Platforms Treat White Nationalism Different from Islamic Terrorism," *Wired*, March 20, 2019, https://www.wired.com/story/why-tech-platforms-dont-treat-all-terrorism-same/; Alex Thompson, "Why the Right Wing Has a Massive Advantage on Facebook," *Politico*, September 26, 2020, https://www.politico.com/news/2020/09/26/facebook-conservatives-2020-421146.

Index

For the benefit of digital users, indexed terms that span two pages (e.g., 52–53) may, on occasion, appear on only one of those pages.

Page numbers followed by *f* indicate figures.